Helping Kids
with
Special Needs

*Resources for Parenting and Teaching
Children with
Emotional and Neurological Disorders*

Compiled by

Julie Nekola

Published by:

Nekola Books
1161 Wayzata Blvd. E., #221
Wayzata, MN 55391-1935

First Printing, April, 2001

Helping Kids with Special Needs
ISBN 0-9706791-0-6
Copyright © 2001 by Julie Nekola
All rights reserved.

DSM IV excerpts from:
American Psychiatric Association: *Diagnostic and Statistical Manual of Mental Disorders, Fourth Edition, Text Revision.*
Washington, DC, American Psychiatric Association, 2000.

Printed in the United States of America

To my blessing, Ben, who opened my eyes to those with special needs.

To our blessed savior, Jesus Christ. Through Him all things are possible.

-   JN

Then He took a little child and set him in the midst of them.

And when He had taken him in His arms, He said to them,

"Whoever receives one of these little children in My name

receives Me.

And whoever receives Me, receives not Me,

but Him who has sent Me."

- Mark 9:36

--- *Thanks Go To...*

- Donna Thomas and Sara Camfield, my good friends, who were the initial drivers for this project and who were supportive through it all.

- My mother, Rita Fasching, and mother-in-law, Margaret Nekola, who in every phone call and letter, asked me how the book was coming and reaffirmed the need for it -- and never once doubted that I could complete this project.

- My brother, Chris Fasching and my daughter, Abbey Nekola, whose written work was published before mine and thus unknowingly gave me an incentive to catch up with them.

- My husband, Mark Nekola, who dutifully hauled books between the library and home, fixed the printer when it was broken, upgraded my computer when it proved inadequate to finish the project, and only fussed once in four years about me being up at all hours of the night reading and writing.

- My frequent "research assistants", my children, Abbey Nekola and Ben Nekola, who can use a library's computerized catalogs with the best of them.

- The librarians at the Wayzata, MN branch of Hennepin County Library who frequently gave me my own shelf for reserved books, never balked when I walked out with 20 books at a time, nor raised their eyebrows when at one point I had $100 in overdue fines.

- My managers at my job who took a chance and moved me into a writing job that provided valuable experience that gave me the confidence to complete this project.

- All those people who, when hearing about this project, wisely did NOT tell me that I couldn't do it because I didn't have the medical background.

- My pastor, Mac Hammond of Living Word Christian Center, who speaks continuously of the importance of living out God's plan for our lives -- and twice in sermons referred to "finishing that book that God wants you to write" while looking directly at me.

- Sue Venn, who in the final hours, stood shining to help me with "whatever you need." And she did! What a loyal friend.

---Table of Contents

---- A Message to Caregivers

Consider that in America:

- Mental disorders have become the leading disability among young people, age 10-18, outnumbering all other chronic physical and medical conditions.

- An estimated 2,000 teenagers per year commit suicide in the U.S., typically the result of depression. Suicide is the leading cause of death after accidents and homicide.

- Ten percent of boys have ADD / ADHD. Over half of these also have learning disorders and a third suffer from depression.

- At least half of the children with Tourette's syndrome have obsessive compulsive symptoms. About half have ADD disorders. About one third exhibit aggressive behavior.

- Eating disorders, such as anorexia (self-induced starvation), are affecting young children -- before they're even out of elementary school.

- Five to ten percent of school-age children have a form of learning disorder.

Emotional, mental health and neurological disorders in children are not uncommon, but in spite of the frequency with which we see them in our population as a whole, the only thing that matters to us as parents, teachers and caregivers is this: Why is my child struggling with school and at home with bad behavior, depression, impulse control, food, drugs, etc., and how can we help to make things better?

For we must make things better -- it's our role as caregivers. The literature and news are filled with examples of children whose situations were allowed to go undiagnosed and untreated too long because their caregivers, people who can make the greatest positive impact in the life of a child, lacked the information or resources to help their child.

Helping your child takes several elements in addition to seeking appropriate professional advice:

- *Observation* -- You must be in tune with the child for whom you're caring and know him or her well. Without this, it's difficult to paint a meaningful picture to share with people who can offer valuable assistance.

- ***Commitment*** -- You must be committed to obtaining the proper assistance for a challenged child. You have to continually search and ask for information and assistance. A good piece of advice that someone at a service agency gave me: "Don't let anyone you talk with off the hook. If they can't provide any assistance, have them give you at least two referrals to other people, organizations or information sources." Armed with information, you must then be willing to modify the environment, teaching style, medication, expectations, schedule and other elements in a child's life as needed.

- ***Information*** -- You must seek information and be committed to using it to help your child. With free public libraries, the Internet and thousands of helpful organizations that dispense free or low-cost information, lack of information is no longer an acceptable excuse for not providing assistance to a challenged child. Information will not replace proper medical counsel and treatment; but the caregiver who seeks will find, the one who knocks will find doors of assistance opening. But no one will come to you with information --- you must seek it yourself.

That's where this book can be of assistance. My goal in writing *Helping Kids with Special Needs* is to give you information and resources so you can further your information search and so that you can share information with other caregivers for your child. As loving as a caregiver may be, he or she may be lazy when it comes to getting information. I'll never forget an elementary teacher's response to my offer to loan him a book on classroom management for my son, Ben, who has Tourette's syndrome, ADHD and mild OCD. This low-keyed teacher said, "Well, I have a fish tank in my classroom. Ben will enjoy looking at the fish. Besides, we used to have a neighbor with Tourette's. This shouldn't be a problem." (In fairness to the teacher, Ben *did* have a good year -- the teacher had a watchful eye and headed off problems before they occurred. Ben also was working with the special ed. resource staff. None the less, as a parent I was surprised at the teacher's lack of interest in getting information and was holding my breath wondering when things would fall apart for Ben.)

You *Can* Do This

As a parent, teacher or caregiver of a challenged child, remember this:

- *You* haven't directly or knowingly caused your child's problem, nor has the child himself. While knowing the root cause of a child's challenge may be helpful, what's more important is what you're doing right now to help the child.
- You don't have to become an expert on a child's disorder nor should you ever diagnose a child without proper professional assistance. But you do have an obligation to help the child grow and be successful. God placed this special needs child under your care and He's given you the resources to care for the child. Becoming knowledgeable about the child's disorder and his or her needs is a most important first step.

Can you become knowledgeable? Yes. I'm not in the medical or teaching profession. I'm a writer and editor -- but I have a child and husband with special needs. I've walked down some of your paths. I've found the information I've needed and you can, too. Being knowledgeable will make visits to the physician more productive, it will assist you when developing IEPs at school, it will help you to thoughtfully deflect thoughtless comments from others, it will increase your advocacy skills and it will help you to better understand and love the child who's in your care.

What's In, What's Out

I took some liberties regarding the topics included in *Helping Kids with Special Needs*; some technically shouldn't be included given the title of the book. However, I kept imagining readers being disappointed in not finding a topic for which they're searching for information, so I took the liberty of including more rather than fewer conditions. What's here is half of what I have; Volume II is being assembled while Volume I rolls off the presses.

While I was liberal on topics, I put more restrictions around the informational sources noted (all of which are U.S.-based):

- I did not include Internet references to:
    - Generic medical sites. Many are excellent, but you often have to wade through a good deal of unrelated information to find the "gold nuggets" which are also available on more subject-specific sites anyway.
    - Online forums and chat lines. Talking with other parents and caregivers can be good for the heart. But I opted to focus on web sites that were more information-filled.
    - Sites that need extensive maintenance or don't have a clearly established owner or credentials.
    - Sites that convey a strong political bias or that include an overdose of unrelated material.

- No regional organizations are noted due to space constraints. Check your yellow pages, schools and other social organizations such as the United Way for referrals.

- Little is included on behavior modification for children in general.

- Very few resources with scientific or research bents are included. These resources tend to be challenging to read and less likely to focus on advice that parents and teachers can use day to day.

Some of the recommended reading is focused on challenged adults rather than challenged children. As a parent, I think about what life may be like for my son as an adult. As I talk with friends with grown children, I realize that even if a child has grown up and left the nest, their lives are still intertwined with those of their parents and information is still valuable.

A word about DSM IV Diagnostic Criteria: Each disorder has DSM IV diagnostic criteria noted. It's important that you have this information because it's the criteria by which medical professionals make their diagnoses.

When Contacting Organizations for Information

Please enclose a legal-sized, self-addressed stamped envelope with extra postage and consider making a contribution. Non-profit organizations operate on a shoestring and provide great services. We need to support them and not expect something for nothing. Consider offering additional "seed money" for another family that doesn't have the resources to make a contribution but whose child desperately needs assistance.

Credits

The information in this reference manual is a distillation of the tremendous amount of information that's found in the many references in these pages. Each book, each web site, each organization, each video, each vendor site offered a thought or some information to include. To include a bibliography of all the works that are already listed in this manual is redundant. I wish that I could do justice to the wonderful organizations and people that are referenced in these pages; they all have much more to offer than what you'll find mentioned here. To make this reference usable, however, I had to pare things done to a few words about each one. Please investigate further; I know that you, too, will be impressed and helped.

I hope that within these pages you find the resources you need to provide your child, grandchild, student, student's family, friends, etc., the help they need and deserve.

Disclaimers

- The information included in this book is for reference for parents, teachers and caregivers of children with special needs. It's not intended to be a diagnostic tool; only qualified medical health professionals can make proper diagnoses. Use the resources here to increase your understanding of your child and as a means to help you communicate more effectively with the professionals who care for your child. This information is not intended to be a substitute for professional care. If you suspect your child may have a health problem, you should consult your health care provider.

- All information included in these pages was believed to be correct at publication time. The information is subject to change, based on new research and development. Internet and mailing addresses change frequently. Don't be discouraged if you can't find something -- just move on to another source of information.

- The purpose of this book is to be a resource of information for parents for teachers. Neither the author nor the publisher accepts liability or responsibility for anyone or any entity with respect to loss, damage, or any other problem caused or alleged to be caused directly or indirectly with information contained in this book.

---- *Anxiety Disorder*

Anxiety is a vague fear that is not directed at anything in particular, but rather at the *anticipation* of danger. Anxiety may be accompanied by panic attacks. During panic, the body responds with many of the same psychological changes that occur during a real emergency, but in exaggerated form. Anxiety can come "out of the blue" and in more severe cases, a spontaneous panic attack may develop. Continual panic attacks may cause one to avoid situations, even to the extent of being unwilling to leave home.

Types

- ✓ Generalized anxiety disorder (GAD)
- ✓ Acute stress
- ✓ Panic
- ✓ Agoraphobia
- ✓ Agoraphobia with or without panic
- ✓ Panic with or without agoraphobia

- ✓ Post traumatic stress
- ✓ Anxiety disorder due to a general medical condition
- ✓ Substance-induced anxiety
- ✓ Phobias
- ✓ Anxiety not otherwise specified.

Frequency

- ▪ 1 in 10 have anxiety disorder, panic attack, phobias or other anxiety disorders.
- ▪ Anxiety is the top mental health problem among American women, second to alcohol and drug abuse.
- ▪ Median age of anxiety onset is 15.
- ▪ Phobias affect 5-12% of Americans.
- ▪ Three million American adults -- at least one in 60 -- experience panic disorder. Most will develop it in their late teens or early to mid twenties.
- ▪ 5% suffer from panic attacks accompanied by agoraphobia.

Symptoms and Possible Effects
Generalized anxiety disorder (GAD)
- ❑ Low-grade, long-lasting (6 months or more) anxiety, tension and worry.
- ❑ Social, academic, occupational areas of one's life are impacted.
- ❑ Difficulty sleeping.
- ❑ Aches and pains (headaches, stomachaches, menstrual cramps, back aches.)
- ❑ Over time, GAD tends to turn into depression.
- ❑ High risk of alcoholism.

Acute stress disorder
❑   Short-lived (1 month or less) anxiety caused by exposure to a traumatic event.   If the anxiety lasts longer than one month, the diagnosis changes to post traumatic stress syndrome.
❑   Numbness, detachment, feelings of unreality.
❑   Avoidance of things that remind one of the traumatic incident.
❑   Difficulty sleeping, irritability, poor concentration, quick to startle, restless.
❑   School, work and relationships are negatively impacted.

Panic
❑   Condition which causes recurring physical "fight or flight" reactions, though there's no apparent reason.
❑   Panic attacks can last 5-30 minutes, but their effects can last longer.   Fear of having another attack can last for hours, weeks or months causing severe anxiety.
❑   Shortness of breath, difficulty breathing, feelings of smothering or choking, chest pain.
❑   Dizziness, light headedness, rapid heart beat.
❑   Shakiness, trembling, sweating, nausea.
❑   Feelings of unreality, perceptual distortions.
❑   Numbness, tingling.
❑   Hot flashes, chills.
❑   Fear of dying or going insane.
❑   Terror, a sense that something terrible is about to occur, but one is powerless to prevent it.
❑   Fear of losing control and doing something embarrassing.
❑   Fear of being in public if a panic attack occurs. Avoidance of specific places or situations, refusal to leave home (agoraphobia.)
❑   Worry over small ailments, others' well being.

Phobias
❑   Fear of things or situations that causes avoidance. The fear may interfere with one's ability to function.
❑   Panic, sweating, rapid heartbeat, difficulty breathing.

<u>What Else Could it Be?</u>
Children with anxiety, panic attacks and phobias cause symptoms that are also seen with other conditions, such as those below. To properly diagnose a problem, these may need to be ruled out as causes.

✓   Angina
✓   Asthma
✓   Allergic rochitis
✓   Caffeinism
✓   Cancer
✓   Cardiovascular disorder
✓   Central nervous system disorder
✓   Colitis
✓   Depression
✓   Drug-related disorder

✓   Ear disorder
✓   Gastrointestinal disorder
✓   Hiatal hernia
✓   Hyperinsulinism
✓   Hypertension
✓   Hyperthyroidism
✓   Hypoglycemia
✓   Infection
✓   Irritable bowel
✓   Kidney disorder

✓   Menopause (in older women)
✓   Metabolic disorder
✓   Mitral valve prolapse
✓   Neurological or muscular Disorder
✓   Obsessional thoughts
✓   PMS
✓   Post concussion syndrome
✓   Postural hypotension
✓   Respiratory disorder
✓   Vertigo

Causes

- Result of a phobia or fear that is so strong that a person avoids it causing anxiety or panic attacks.
- May be the result of stress, feelings of perfectionism, low self esteem, and major transitions. "Fight or flight" situations may trigger anxiety; instead of taking advantage of the body's rapidly increased strength, the individual experiencing panic becomes overwhelmed by the resulting physical symptoms. The more he or she focuses on physical symptoms, the more anxiety results.
- Agoraphobia (reluctance to leave home or to go to certain places) is caused by the fear of panic attacks.
- Some evidence for a genetic predisposition if the sufferer is experiencing high stress.
- Can be a symptom of another psychological or medical problem, such as depression, substance abuse or withdrawal, diabetes, brain tumors, thyroid disease, hyper- and hypothyroidism, pheochronocytoma, hypoglycemia, cardiovascular conditions, metabolic conditions, neurological conditions, vestibular problems, encephalitis. It's estimated that the average patient, newly diagnosed with panic disorder, has seen 10 physicians before obtaining a diagnosis of anxiety.
- People with severe anxiety, especially panic, often have a history of major depression.
- One theory maintains that shallow breathing and hyperventilation are the causes for many of the physical symptoms of panic attacks.

DSM IV Diagnostic Criteria

Reprinted with permission from the *Diagnostic and Statistical Manual of Mental Disorders, Fourth Edition, Text Revision.* Copyright 2000 American Psychiatric Association.

For a panic attack:

A discrete period of intense fear or discomfort, in which four (or more) of the following symptoms developed abruptly and reached a peak within 10 minutes:

    (1) palpitations, pounding heart or accelerated heart rate
    (2) sweating
    (3) trembling or shaking
    (4) sensations of shortness of breath or smothering
    (5) feeling of choking
    (6) chest pain or discomfort
    (7) nausea or abdominal distress
    (8) feeling dizzy, unsteady, lightheaded or faint
    (9) feelings of unreality or being detached from oneself
    (10) fear of losing control or going crazy
    (11) fear of dying
    (12) paresthesias (numbness or tingling sensations)
    (13) chills or hot flushes.

For agoraphobia:

A. Anxiety about being in places or situations from which escape might be difficult (or embarrassing) or in which help may not be available in the event of having an unexpected or situationally predisposed Panic Attack or panic-like symptoms. Agoraphobic fears typically involve characteristic clusters of situations that include being outside the home alone; being in a crowd or standing in a line; being on a bridge; and traveling in a bus, train or automobile.

B. The situations are avoided (e.g., travel is restricted) or else are endured with marked distress or with anxiety about having a Panic Attack or panic-like symptoms, or require the presence of a companion.

C. The anxiety or phobic avoidance is not better accounted for by another mental disorder, such as Social Phobia (e.g., avoidance limited to social situations because of fear of embarrassment), Specific Phobia (e.g., avoidance limited to a single situation like elevators), Obsessive-Compulsive Disorder (e.g., avoidance of dirt in someone with an obsession about contamination), Posttraumatic Stress Disorder (e.g., avoidance of stimuli associated with a severe stressor) or Separation Anxiety Disorder (e.g., avoidance of leaving home or relatives.)

For generalized anxiety disorder:

A. Excessive anxiety and worry (apprehensive expectation), occurring more days than not for at least 6 months, about a number of events or activities (such as work or school performance).

B. The person finds it difficult to control the worry.

C. The anxiety and worry are associated with three (or more) of the following six symptoms (with at least some symptoms present for more days than not for the past 6 months). Note: Only one item is required in children.
    (1) restlessness or feeling keyed up or on edge
    (2) being easily fatigued
    (3) difficulty concentrating or mind going blank
    (4) irritability
    (5) muscle tension
    (6) sleep disturbance (difficulty falling or staying asleep, or restless unsatisfying sleep)

D. The focus of the anxiety and worry is not confined to features of an Axis I disorder, e.g., the anxiety or worry is not about having a Panic Attack (as in Panic Disorder), being embarrassed in public (as in Social Phobia), being contaminated (as in Obsessive-Compulsive Disorder), being away from home or close relatives (as in separation anxiety disorder), gaining weight (as in Anorexia Nervosa), having multiple physical complaints (assign Somatization Disorder) or having a serious illness (as in Hypochondriasis) and the anxiety and worry do not occur exclusively during Posttraumatic Stress Disorder.

E. The anxiety, worry or physical symptoms cause clinically significant distress or impairment in social, occupational or other important areas of functioning.

F. The disturbance is not due to the direct physiological effects of a substance (e.g., a drug of abuse, a medication) or a general medical condition (e.g., hyperthyroidism) and does not occur exclusively during a Mood Disorder, a Psychotic Disorder or a Pervasive Developmental Disorder.

Treatment
Symptoms are treated concurrently: physiological reaction, panic, avoidant behavior, psychological reactions (self talk and worry.)

▪ Anxiety and phobias can be treated with medications.
▪ Therapy to understand the causes, to unlearn reactions and learn new coping skills.
▪ Exposure therapy to desensitize one against the source of anxiety and to teach relaxation skills.
▪ Breathing skills training and monitoring to avoid panic symptoms.
▪ Nutritional and exercise changes.
▪ Assertiveness training.
▪ Long-term monitoring to prevent relapse.

Outcomes

With proper treatment, 70-80% of people with panic disorders significantly improve within two months. Though stressful events may make things worse, people with generalized anxiety are anxious even if everything is going fine.

Who to Contact

Also refer to "Who Else to Contact." Organizations listed below target their work specifically toward anxiety.

Agoraphobics in Action, Inc.
P.O. Box 1662
Antioch, TN 37011-1662
Ph: (615) 316-0036
E-mail: faithline@mindspring.org
Web: http://www.geocities.com/Nashville/2227/
Supports, educates those with or supporting those with agoraphobia.

Agoraphobics Building Independent Lives (ABIL)
3805 Cutshaw Ave., Suite 415, Dept. W
Richmond, VA 23230
Ph: (804) 353-3964
Fax: (804) 353-3687
E-mail: answers@anxietysupport.org
Web: http://www.anxietysupport.org
Information and self-help groups on anxiety and agoraphobia.

Agoraphobics in Motion (AIM)
1719 Crooks
Royal Oak, MI 48067
Ph: (248) 547-0400
E-mail: anny@ameritech.net
Web: http://detroit.freenet.org/~xx892/
Supports anxiety sufferers and their families.

Anxiety Disorders Association of America (ADAA)
11900 Parklawn Dr., Suite 100
Rockville, MD 20852
Ph: (301) 231-9350
Fax: (301) 231-7392
E-mail: AnxDis@adda.org
Web: http://www.adaa.org
Promotes the prevention and cure of anxiety disorders.

Freedom from Fear
308 Seaview Ave.
Staten Island, NY 10305
Ph: (718) 351-1717
Fax: (718) 667-8893
Web: http://www.freedomfromfear.org/programs.asp
Helps individuals who suffer from anxiety and depression.

National Anxiety Foundation
3135 Custer Dr.
Lexington, KY 40517- 4001
Ph: (859) 272-7166
Web: http://lexington-on-line.com/naf.html
Educates the public and professionals.

Recovery, Inc.
802 N. Dearborn St.
Chicago, IL 60610
Ph: (312) 337-5661
Fax: (312) 337-5756
Web: http://www.recovery-inc.com
Self-help methods to regain and maintain mental health.

Trichotillomania Learning Center, Inc.
1215 Mission St.
Santa Cruz, CA 95060
Ph: (831) 457-1004
Fax: (831) 426-4383
E-mail: trichster@aol.com
Web: http://www.trich.org
Builds understanding of compulsive hair pulling.

Recommended Reading

The 12 Steps of Phobics Anonymous
Marilyn Gellis
Institute of Phobic Awareness, 1989

Advances in the Neurobiology of Anxiety Disorders
H. G. M. Westenberg, Dennis Murphy, Johan Den Boer
John Wiley and Sons, Inc., 1996

Anxiety Chronic Disease Book
Great Performance (Ed.)
Great Performance, Inc., 1996

Anxiety & Depression: The Best Resources to Help You Cope
Rich Wemhoff (Ed.)
Resource Pathways, 1999

Anxiety and Depression: A Natural Approach
Shirley Trickett
Ulysses Press, 1997

Anxiety and Phobia Workbook
Edmund Bourne, Ph.D.
New Harbinger Publications, Inc., 1995

Anxiety, Phobias and Panic: A Step-by-Step Program for Regaining Control of Your Life
Reneau Peurifoy, M.A., MFCC
Warner Books, 1995

Anxiety Panic: Anxiety Attacked
John MacArthur
Chariot Victor Books, 1993

Anxiety Disorders in African Americans
Steven Friedman, Ph.D. (Ed.)
Springer Publishing, 1994

Anxiety and Panic Attacks: Their Cause and Cure
Robert Handly
Fawcett Book Group, 1987

Anxiety, Panic Attacks and Agoraphobia – Information for Friends, Family and Caregivers, 2nd ed.
Kenneth Stronh
Oakminster, Publishing, 1997

Anxiety and Its Treatment
John Griest, M.D., James Jefferson, M.D., Isaac Marks, M.D.
Warner Books, 1987

Beyond Fear
Robert Handly, Pauline Neff
Rawson Associates, 1987

Beyond Shyness: How to Conquer Social Anxieties
Jonathan Berent, Amy Lemley
Simon & Schuster, 1994

The Breath Connection: How to Reduce Psychosomatic and Stress-Related Disorders with Easy-to-Do Breathing Exercises
Robert Fried
Plenum Press, 1990

Children, Youth, and Suicide: Developmental Perspectives
Gil Noam, Sophie Borst (Eds.)
Jossey-Bass, Inc. Publishers, 1994

Chronic Anxiety: Generalized Anxiety Disorder and Mixed Anxiety-Depression
Ronald Rapee, Ph.D., David Barlow, Ph.D. (Eds.)
Guilford Publications, 1991

Clergy Response to Suicidal Persons and Their Family Members: An Interfaith Resource Book For Clergy and Congregations
David Clark (Ed.)
Exploration Press, 1993

Client's Manual for the Cognitive-Behavioral Treatment of Anxiety Disorders
Larry Smyth
Red Tar R Publishing, 1994

College Student Suicide
Leighton Whitaker, Richard Slimak (Eds.)
Haworth Press, Inc., 1990

Common Mental Disorders: A Bio-Social Model
David Goldberg, Peter Huxley
Routledge, 1992

Conquering Shyness: The Battle Anyone Can Win
Jonathan Cheek, Bronwen Cheek, Larry Rothstein
G.P. Putman's Son, 1989

Constructing Panic: The Discourse of Agoraphobia
Lisa Capps, Jerome Bruner, Elinor Ochs
Harvard University Press, 1997

Coping with Anxiety: Integrated Approaches to Treatment
W. Walter Menninger, M.D. (Ed.)
Jason Aronson, 1996

Coping with Panic: A Drug Free Approach to Dealing with Anxiety Attacks
George Clum
Brooks/Cole, 1990

Dancing with Fear: Overcoming Anxiety in a World of Stress and Chaos
Paul Foxman
Jason Aronson, Inc., 1996

Don't Panic: Taking Control of Anxiety Attacks
Reid Wilson, Ph.D.
Harper Perennial, 1996

Dying of Embarrassment: Help for Social Anxiety and Phobia
Barbara Markway, Ph.D., Cheryl Carmin, Ph.D.,
C. Alec Pollard, Ph.D., Teresa Flynn, Ph.D.
New Harbinger Publications, Inc., 1992

The Encyclopedia of Phobias, Fears and Anxieties
Ronald Doctor, Ph.D., Ada Kahn
Facts on File, Inc., 1989

An End to Panic: Breakthrough Techniques for Overcoming Panic Disorder
Elke Zuercher-White, Ph.D.
New Harbinger Publications, 1995

The Exercise Prescription for Depression and Anxiety
Keith Johnsgard
Plenum, 1989

The Feeling Good Handbook
David Burns
William Morrow and Co., 1990

Free from Fears: New Help for Anxiety, Panic and Agoraphobia
Ann Seagrave, Faison Covington
Poseidon Press, 1987

Freedom from Fear Forever
Dr. James Durlacher, Roger Callahan, Ph.D.
Van Ness Publishing, 1997

From Anxiety Addict to Serenity Seeker: Interpreting and Working the Twelve Steps of Phobics Anonymous
Marilyn Gellis, Ph.D.
Institute for Phobic Awareness, 1990

From Panic to Peace of Mind: Overcoming Panic and Agoraphobia
C. Scrignar, M.S., M.D.
Bruno Press, 1991

From Panic to Power
Lucinda Bassett
Harper Collins Publishers, 1995

The Good News About Panic, Anxiety and Phobias
Mark Gold, M.D.
Villard Books, 1989

Great Anxiety Escape: A Revolutionary Approach to Escape Anxiety, Insomnia, Depression, and Drug Depression
Max Ricketts, Edin Bien
Matulungin Publishing, 1990

Healing the Anxiety Diseases
Thomas Leaman
Plenum Press, 1992

The Hidden Face of Shyness: Understanding and Overcoming Social Anxiety
Franklin Schneier M.D., Lawrence Welkowitz, Ph.D.
Avon Books, 1996

How to Help Your Loved One Recover From Agoraphobia
Karen Williams
New Horizon Press, 1993

Journey from Anxiety to Freedom: Moving Beyond Panic and Phobia and Learning to Trust Yourself
Mani Feniger
Prima Publishing, 1997

Keys to Parenting Your Anxious Child (Barron's Parenting Keys)
Katharina Manassis
Barron's Educational Series, Inc., 1996

Life Isn't Just a Panic: Stories of Hope by Recovering Agoraphobics
Anita Pace
Baby Steps Press, 1996

Life With the Panic Monster: A Guide for the Terrified
Evelyn Stewart
Routledge, 1996

Learning to Tell Myself the Truth: A 6-Week Guide to Freedom from Anger, Anxiety, Depression, and Perfectionism
William Backus
Bethany House, 1994

Managing Your Anxiety: Regaining Control When You Feel Stressed, Helpless and Alone
Christopher McCullough, Robert Mann
Berkley Publishing, 1994

Master Your Panic and Take Back Your Life, 2nd ed.
Denise Beckfield, Ph.D.
Impact Publishers, 1998

The Panic Attack Recovery Book
Shirley Swede, Seymour Jaffe, M.D.
Mass Market Paperbacks, 1989

Mastering Anxiety: The Nature and Treatment of Anxious Conditions
Ronald Kleinknecht
Plenum Press, 1991

Panic Attacks
Christine Ingham
Thorsons, 1998

Mastering Phobias: Cases, Causes, and Cures
Richard Stern
Viking Penguin, 1995

Panic Attacks: A Natural Approach, 2nd ed.
Shirley Trickett
Ulysses Press, 1999

Math Panic, 2nd ed.
Laurie Buxton
Heinemann, 1991

Panic Buster: Learn to Conquer Panic Attacks and Agoraphobia
Bonnie Crandall
Hatch Creek Publishing, 1995

Meaning of Anxiety, 2nd ed.
Rollo May
W. W. Norton and Co., Inc., 1996

Panic Attack, Anxiety and Phobia Solutions Handbook
Muriel MacFarlane
United Research Publishers, 1995

Overcoming Anxiety: From Short-Time Fixes to Long-Term Recovery
Reneau Peurifoy, M.A., M.P.C.A.
Henry Holt and Company, 1997

Panic Disorder: What You Don't Know May Be Dangerous to Your Health, 2nd Ed.
William Kernodle, M.D.
William Byrd Press, 1993

Overcoming Anxiety: A Primer for Better Life Management
Lynn Fossum
Crisp Publications, 1995

Panic Disorder and Agoraphobia: A Guide, rev. ed.
John Greist, M.D., James Jefferson, M.D.
Dean Foundation, 1998

Overcoming Anxiety at Work
Vincent Miskell, Jane Miskell
McGraw Hill, 1993

Panic Disorder: The Medical Point of View, rev.
William Kernodle, M.D.
William Kernodle, 1995

Overcoming Panic, Anxiety and Phobias: New Strategies to Free Yourself from Worry and Fear
Shirley Babior, Carol Goldman
Pfeifer – Hamilton Publishers, 1996

Panic Free: Eliminate Anxiety-Panic Attacks Without Drugs and Take Control of Your Life
Lynne Freeman, Ph. D.
Healthwise, 1998

Performance Anxiety: Overcoming Your Fear in the Work Place, Social Situations, Interpersonal Communication, and the Performing Arts
Mitchell Robin, Rochelle Balter
Adams Publishing, 1995

Phobics and Other Panic Victims: A Practical Guide for Those Who Help Them
Janice McLean, Sheila Knights
Continuum Publishing Co., 1989

Prisoner of Fear: My Long Road to Freedom from Anxiety Disease, Panic Attacks and Agoraphobia
Richard Maro
Hickory Grove Press, 1991

Psychological Treatment of Panic
David Barlow, Jerome Cerny
Guilford Publications, 1988

Questions Most Asked about Anxiety and Phobias: A Lively, Down to Earth Guide for Overcoming Panic
Jane Miller
Pretext Press, 1998

Sampling Inner Experience in Disturbed Affect
Russell Hurlburt
Plenum Press, 1993

Social Anxiety
Mark Leary, Ph.D., Robin Kowalski, Ph.D.
Guilford Publications, 1995

Social Phobia: A Guide
John Griest, M.D., James Jefferson, M.D., David Katzelnick, M.D.
Dean Foundation Information Centers, 1997

Social Phobia: From Shyness to Stage Fright
John Marshall, M.D.
Basic Books, 1994

Stress, Anxiety, and Depression: The Natural Way of Healing
Diana Ajjan
Dell Publishing Co., Inc., 1995

Stress, Anxiety, and Insomnia: How You Can Benefit from Diet, Vitamins, Minerals, Herbs, Exercise, and Other Natural Methods
Michael Murray
Prima Publishing, 1994

Taking the Anxiety Out of Tests: A Step by Step Guide
Susan Johnson
New Harbinger Publications, 1997

Too Scared to Learn: Overcoming Academic Anxiety
Cara Garcia
Corwin Press, Inc., 1998

Trichotillomania: A Guide, rev. ed.
Jeffrey Anders, M.D., James Jefferson, M.D.
Dean Foundation, 1998

Triumph Over Fear: A Book of Help and Hope for People with Anxiety, Panic Attacks, and Phobias
Jerilyn Ross
Bantam Books, 1995

The Twelve Steps of Phobics Anonymous
Marilyn Gellis, Rosemary Muat
Institute for Phobic Awareness, 1989

When Anxiety Attacks: What the Health Care Community Does Not Know About Anxiety
Stan Looper, Cynthia Scott
Swan Publishers, 1993

When Words Are Not Enough: The Women's Prescription for Depression and Anxiety
Valerie Davis Raskin, M.D.
Broadway Books, 1997

Women and Anxiety: A Step-by-Step Program for Managing Anxiety and Depression
Helen Derosis M. D.
Hatherleigh Press, 1998

Worry: When Life Is More Scary Than It Should Be and What You Can Do About It
Edward Hallowell
Ballantine Books, 1998

Why Women Worry: And How to Stop
Robert Handly, Jane Handly, Paul Neff
Fawcett, 1992

You Are Not Alone: Compulsive Hair Pulling, the Enemy Within
Cheryn Salazar
Cheryn Intl., 1995

Books for Youth

Cat's Got Your Tongue: A Story for Children Afraid to Speak
Charles Schaefer
Gareth Stevens Publishing, 1993

Coping with Anxiety and Panic Attacks
Jordan Lee, Carolyn Simpson
Rosen Group, 1997

The Facts About Fears and Phobias
Renardo Barden
Crestwood House, 1989

How to Survive Unbearable Stress
Steve Burns, M.D.
1990

Straight Talk About Anxiety and Depression
Michael Maloney, Rachel Kranz
Facts on File, 1991

Periodicals / Newsletters

ABIL Newsletter
ABIL Incorporated
3805 Cutshaw Ave., Suite 415, Dept. W
Richmond, VA 23230
Ph: (804) 353-3964
Web: http://www.anxietysupport.org/b001menu.htm

Agoraphobics in Motion Newsletter
1719 Crooks
Royal Oak, MI 48067
Ph: (248) 547-0400
E-mail: anny@ameritech.net
Web: http://detroit.freenet.org/~xx892/news.html

Web Sites
Also see "General Web Sites". Many include sections on anxiety.

David Baldwin's Trauma Information Pages
Web: http://www.trauma-pages.com
Collection of anxiety and PTSD articles.

tAPir
Web: http://www.algy.com/anxiety/
Self-help information.

Vendors

Center for Anxiety and Stress Treatment
4225 Executive Square, Suite 1110
La Jolla, CA 92037
Ph: (619) 542-0536
Fax: (619) 542-0730
E-mail: health@stressrelease.com
Web: http://www.stressrelease.com
Books, tapes.

Center for Help for Anxiety / Agoraphobia through New Growth Experience (CHAANGE)
128 Country Club Dr.
Chula Vista, CA 91911
Ph: (619) 425-3992
Fax: (619) 691 7940
E-mail: info@chaange.com
Web: http://www.chaange.com
Books, tapes.

How to Treat Your Own Panic Disorder: Bert Anderson
P.O. Box 7157
Redlands, CA 92375
Ph: (909) 793-9942
      (888) 243-0228
E-mail: panicdoc@healingpanic.com
Web: http://www.eadd.com/~berta
Books, tapes.

Midwest Center for Stress and Anxiety
106 N. Church St.
P.O.Box 205
Oak Harbor, OH 43449
Ph: (800) 511-6896
      (419) 898-4357
Fax: (419) 898-0669
Web: http://www.stresscenter.com
Self help, home study programs.

Reid Wilson
Web: http://www.anxieties.com
Books, tapes.

---- *Attention Deficit Disorder (ADD)*
With Hyperactivity (ADHD)

A neurological disorder in which a child has a short attention span, is easily distracted, excessively impulsive, restless, and perhaps hyperactive.

Types
- Attention deficit / hyperactivity disorder (ADHD)
  - Inappropriate impulse control and motor activity (hyperactivity) for the child's age.
- Attention deficit disorder without hyperactivity (ADD)
  - Inattention, disorganization, slow processing of information, slow fine motor speed.

Also called:
- Hyperactivity
- Hyperkinesis
- Hyperkinetic reaction/syndrome of childhood
- Minimal brain damage
- Minimal brain dysfunction
- Minimal cerebral dysfunction
- Post-encephalitic disorder.

Frequency
- ADHD: 9% of boys, 3% of girls. In adolescence, this changes to 3% of boys, 1% of girls.
- ADD: 1% of boys, 1% of girls.
- On the average, at least one child in every classroom has ADD or ADHD.   But many above average students, especially those with ADD, may not experience school problems until later childhood.
- Adopted children are 4 times more likely to have ADD/ADHD than other children.
- Age of onset is 2-7 years old.   But 65% show symptoms by age 2 in terms of irregular eating, sleeping, elimination, failure to adjust to a routine. Hyperactive infants are more fussy, take longer to adjust to change and are difficult to hold.

Symptoms and Possible Effects
- ❑ Difficulty paying attention, poor short-term memory, easily distracted.
- ❑ May have difficulty in learning, abstract thinking. Confusion.
- ❑ May have trouble in being still, getting started, staying focused, finishing tasks.

❑ Disorganization, difficulty with losing and finding things, personal space is cluttered.

❑ Impatience.

❑ Poor coordination and motor skills. May have poor eye-hand coordination or appear clumsy and uncoordinated.

❑ Difficulty with toilet training.

❑ Seemingly lacks motivation.

❑ Difficulty with articulation, understanding, finding the right words to use.

❑ Difficulty with perceptual motor skills used in things such as handwriting and coloring.

❑ Inflexible.

❑ Responds too rapidly and inappropriately to tasks, applying little effort in tasks for which one has little interest. Not goal-oriented.

❑ Food cravings, allergies and sensitivities.

❑ Lack of self-control. High activity; may run around without stopping.

❑ Acting without considering the consequences.

❑ Difficulty with turn taking.

❑ More broken bones and bruises than others because of failure to recognize dangerous situations.

❑ High tolerance for pain.

❑ Distorted sense of space, problems with directions (e.g., bumping into others, difficulty reading maps.)

❑ Unaware of body states.

❑ Developmental rates are different from those of others.

❑ Emotional difficulties, such as self-centeredness, impatience, recklessness, extreme emotions, weak conscience, mood swings, low tolerance for frustration.

❑ Answers questions before they're completed, interrupts.

❑ Usually behaves better in structured or new settings or when they are alone with an adult.

❑ May be afraid of the dark.

❑ Some are very dependent on their mother, experience separation anxiety. Immature.

❑ If they have friends, they are usually younger. May prefer toys of younger children.

❑ Poor social graces.

❑ Poor sequencing skills; doesn't understand cause and effect.

❑ Sensitive to noise.

❑ Experience a high numbers of ear infections.

❑ As an infant may dislike cuddling, have irregular sleep patterns. More prone to crying spells unrelated to colic, poor eater.

❑ As a toddler, misbehavior is noticeable, needs instructions repeated, is accident-prone.

❑ As a preschooler, doesn't consider consequences of actions, isn't deterred by punishment; aggressive, taking toys apart.

❑ May become a loner, but not by choice. May start being untrustworthy, potentially engaging in petty theft, not recognizing the consequences. Learning moral values is a challenge.

❑ As an adolescent, sexual urges and acting out are more intense. More likely to drive recklessly, experiment with drugs and alcohol.

❑ Girls with ADHD often display slightly different difficulties: more anxiety, more severe cognitive challenges, less hyperactivity, less physical aggression, less likely to lose their tempers.

❑ Underachievement, depression, low motivation, poor self esteem.

❑ Repeats bad behavior in spite of correction.

❑ Speaks out of turn in class, despite reminders.

❑ Poor sense of the passage of time.

❑ May talk incessantly.

❏ Has difficulty forming and maintaining relationships.
❏ Unable to respect others.
❏ Can't self-control or soothe.
❏ Selfish, dishonest.
❏ Rebellious, depressed.
❏ Thinks freely, at times creatively; at other times chaotically.
❏ Acts unpredictably, not stopping to think about planned actions.
❏ Most are kinesthetic (in-motion) and/or auditory learners.
❏ Irregular patterns of sleeplessness and reawakening, or very deep sleep.
❏ May be meek and not speak in self-defense.
❏ May suffer from self-consciousness and need excessive reassurance. Fear being alone; avoid separation from their parents, even when attending school or other activities.

What Can Be Going On at the Same Time?
- Learning disabilities (25-40%).
- Tourette's syndrome, anxiety, depression, obsessive-compulsive disorder.
- Oppositional defiance disorder.
- Bed wetting and soiling, sleep disorders.
- Auditory and visual distractions -- will respond to sounds or sights that most would ignore.
- ADD children are smaller and thinner than others their age, even bone structure is immature. They grow slower and are behind in development.
- Children with ADHD appear to have a higher number of physical ailments, such as ear infections, allergies, speech, hearing and vision problems, stomachaches and headaches.

Diagnostic Processes
Diagnosing ADD can be difficult due to individual developmental rates, coexisting problems that affect behavior and learning, and the wide range of symptoms possible. ADHD diagnoses normally aren't made before age 5 because preschoolers all seem to have high energy levels. Exceptions are made for those children with seemingly tremendous amounts of energy.

Gathering of historical and current observations of family, teachers, others involved in child's care. Observations are compared to diagnostic criteria for attention-deficit disorder in children.

Diagnosis is based on the assessment of test results, home and social history, behavior, academic record, intelligence level, emotional adjustment, peer relations, child rearing practices, medical history and evaluation, parent and teacher interviews, birth history, habits, development to date, temperament, response to prior treatments.

DSM IV Diagnostic Criteria
Reprinted with permission from the *Diagnostic and Statistical Manual of Mental Disorders, Fourth Edition, Text Revision.* Copyright 2000 American Psychiatric Association.

A. Either (1) or (2):
    (1) six (or more) of the following symptoms of **inattention** have persisted for at least 6 months to a degree that is maladaptive and inconsistent with developmental level:

Inattention
(a) often fails to give close attention to details or makes careless mistakes in schoolwork, work or other activities
(b) often has difficulty sustaining attention in tasks or play activities
(c) often does not seem to listen when spoken to directly
(d) often does not follow through on instructions and fails to finish schoolwork, chores, or duties in the workplace (not due to oppositional behavior or failure to understand instructions)
(e) often has difficulty organizing tasks and activities
(f) often avoids, dislikes, or is reluctant to engage in tasks that require sustained mental effort (such as schoolwork or homework)
(g) often loses things necessary for tasks or activities (e.g., toys, school assignments, pencils, books, or tools)
(h) is often easily distracted by extraneous stimuli
(i) is often forgetful in daily activities

(2) six (or more) of the following symptoms of **hyperactivity-impulsivity** have persisted for at least 6 months to a degree that is maladaptive and inconsistent with developmental level:

Hyperactivity
(a) often fidgets with hands or feet or squirms in seat
(b) often leaves seat in classroom or in other situations in which remaining seated is expected
(c) often runs about or climbs excessively in situations in which it is inappropriate (in adolescents or adults, may be limited to subjective feelings of restlessness)
(d) often has difficulty playing or engaging in leisure activities quietly
(e) is often "on the go" or often acts as if "driven by a motor"
(f) often talks excessively

Impulsivity
(g) often blurts out answers before questions have been completed
(h) often has difficulty awaiting turn
(i) often interrupts or intrudes on others (e.g., butts into conversations or games)

B. Some hyperactive-impulsive or inattentive symptoms that caused impairment were present before age 7 years.

C. Some impairment from the symptoms is present in two or more settings (e.g., at school [or work] and at home).

D. There must be clear evidence of clinically significant impairment in social, academic, or occupational functioning.

E. The symptoms do not occur exclusively during the course of a Pervasive Developmental Disorder, Schizophrenia, or other Psychotic Disorder and are not better accounted for by another mental disorder (e.g., Mood Disorder, Anxiety Disorder, Dissociative Disorder, or a Personality Disorder.)

What Else Could it Be?

Children with ADD and ADHD have symptoms that may mimic those of other conditions, such as those noted below. To properly diagnose a problem, these may need to be ruled out as a cause for the problem.

✓ Allergies, asthma, sensitivities	✓ Hearing or vision problem	✓ Pheochromocytoma
✓ Anxiety disorder	✓ Iron deficiency	✓ Post traumatic stress
✓ Bipolar disorder or mania	✓ Lead poisoning	✓ Seizure disorder
✓ Caffeinism	✓ Learning disability	✓ Sensory impairment
✓ Chronic fatigue	✓ Medication effect	✓ Situational disturbance
✓ Depression	✓ Mental retardation	✓ Substance abuse
✓ Diabetes or hypoglycemia	✓ Mood disorder	✓ Tactile defensiveness
✓ Diet problems	✓ Obsessive compulsive disorder	✓ Tantrums
✓ Food sensitivities	✓ Oppositional behavior	✓ Thyroid dysfunction
✓ Hearing impairment	✓ Personality disorder	✓ Tourette's syndrome
✓ Fetal alcohol syndrome		

Causes

Unknown. Environmental factors, including parenting techniques, diet, and toxins may impact the symptoms, but they do not cause ADHD. Theories include:

- Faulty biochemical interactions related to the brain's neurotransmitters, especially involving the dopamine and serotonin pathways. Norepinephrine may be insufficient. One theory suggests a problem with the candate nucleus (located in the middle of the brain).
- Heredity, though the pattern of inheritance is not clear. Siblings of ADD children are likely to have similar problems.
- Prenatal complications.
- Birth complications, premature birth.
- For some, diet (sensitivity to food additives, dyes, artificial flavors, sugar) and can worsen symptoms.
- Environmental toxins may play a role; one third of children with lead poisoning have symptoms of ADD.
- Fetal injury due to medications, fetal alcohol syndrome, drug abuse by mother, prenatal infection, lack of oxygen in utero, structural abnormalities of the brain, infections involving the brain (e.g., meningitis), brain injury, exposure to cranial radiation.
- Hormone levels.
- Indicators of risk for ADHD in infancy include allergies, colds, asthma, upper respiratory infections, fluid buildup in the middle ear.

What Could Be Going on at the Same Time?

A child may have other disorders that result in attentional disorders:
- Depression, bipolar disorder.
- Tourette's syndrome, neurocutaneous disorders, epilepsy, other neurological disorders.
- Fragile X syndrome or other chromosomal disorders.
- Fetal alcohol syndrome.
- Trauma.
- Disorders of the skin and nervous system such as tuberous scherosis, neurofibromatosis.
- Williams syndrome.

Treatment

- Medication to help the child focus, reduce inner stress.
- Tasks divided into small parts.
- Diet modification.
- Megavitamin therapy.
- Sensory integration therapy.
- Behavior modification involving the entire family.
- Therapy for depression, building self esteem.
- School assistance and appropriate placement. Classroom modification to fit random, kinesthetic learning styles. Curriculum or homework adjustment to ensure focus is on doing what's essential. Study areas, noise levels, lighting adjustments.
- Clearly understood structured environment that the children can understand and tolerate. For example, lists, reminders, daily planning, goal setting.
- Structured environment.
- Relaxation and biofeedback.

Outcomes

- Some symptoms (especially excessive activity level) may lessen in puberty. Inattention and impulsivity often persist. Symptoms may remain throughout life. Conversely, symptoms may disappear before adulthood.
- 80% will repeat at least one grade. Less likely to attend college.
- 1/4 - 1/3 experience at least one episode of major depression during childhood. Some develop low self esteem after continual failures. May brag or lie to compensate for negative feelings.
- More likely to drop out of school, become truant, even become involved in juvenile crime. Disruption of family life is more likely as they get older (staying out late, temper outbursts, threats to parents.)
- Children and teens with ADHD who are aggressive or defiant at a young age are at risk for developing oppositional defiance and/or conduct disorder.
- Girls are more likely to have poor peer relationships, low self esteem, memory and learning impairment, depression, and emotional problems as they approach adolescence than boys, but less likely to show oppositional behavior.

Who to Contact

Also refer to "Who Else to Contact." Organizations listed below target their work specifically toward ADHD and ADD.

ADD Action Group
P.O. Box 1440
Ansonia Station
New York, NY 10023
Ph: (212) 769-2457
Web: http://www.addgroup.org/
Helps people find alternative solutions for attention deficit disorder, learning differences, dyslexia, autism.

Attention Deficit Information Network (AD-IN)
475 Hillside Ave.
Needham, MA 02194
Ph: (781) 455-9895
Fax: (781) 444-5466
E-mail: adin@gis.net
Web: http://addinfonetwork.com
Supports and informs families of children with ADD, adults with ADD, and professionals through a network of local chapters.

Children and Adults with Attention-Deficit Disorders (CH. A.D.D.)
8181 Professional Place, Suite 201
Landover, MD 20785
Ph: (800) 233-4050
       (301) 306-7070
Fax: (301) 306-7090
Web: http://www.chadd.org
Supports and educates those with ADD, caregivers.

National Attention Deficit Disorder Association (ADDA)
1788 Second St., Suite 200
Highland Park, IL 6003
Ph: (847) 432-ADDA
Fax: (847) 432-5874
E-mail: mail@add.org
Web: http://www.add.org
Education, research, and public advocacy on ADD.

Recommended Reading

The ADD/ADHD Checklist: An Easy Reference for Parents and Teachers
Sandra Rief
P T R Prentice Hall, 1998

ADD: Helping Your Children: Untying the Knot of Attention Deficit Disorders
Warren Umansky, Ph.D., Barbara Steinberg Smalley
Warner Books, 1994

ADD Behavior-Change Resource Kit: Ready-to-Use Strategies and Activities for Helping Children with Attention Deficit Disorder
Grad Flick, Ph.D.
Center for Applied Research in Education, 1998

ADD Hyperactivity Handbook for Schools: Effective Strategies for Identifying and Teaching Students with Attention Deficit Disorder in Elementary and Secondary Schools, 2nd ed.
Harvey Parker, Ph.D.
Specialty Press, 1995

The ADD Book: New Understandings, New Approaches to Parenting Your Child
William Sears, M.D., Lynda Thompson, Ph.D.
Little Brown and Company, 1998

The ADD Hyperactivity Workbook for Parents, Teachers and Kids, 3rd ed.
Harvey Parker, Ph.D.
Specialty Press, 1996

ADD Brain: Diagnosis, Treatment and Science of Attention Deficit Disorder
Monroe Gross
Nova Sci Press, 1997

ADD on the Job: Making Your ADD Work for You
Lynn Weiss, Ph.D.
Taylor Publications, 1996

ADD and Creativity: Tapping Your Inner Muse
Lynn Weiss
Taylor Publishing Co., 1997

ADD Kaleidoscope: The Many Facets of Adult Attention Deficit Disorder
Joan Andrews, Denise Davis
Hope Press, 1997

A.D.D. to Excellent without Drugs
Meredith Day
Blue Bird, 1997

ADD -- A Lifetime Challenge: Life Stories of Adults with Attention Deficit Disorder, rev. ed.
Mary Jane Johnson
ADD Resources, 1994

A.D.D. the Natural Approach: Help for Attention Deficit Disorder and Hyperactivity
Nina Anderson, Howard Peiper
Safe Goods, 1996

ADD: A Path to Success: A Revolutionary Theory and New Innovation in Drug-Free Therapy
Lawrence Weathers, Ph.D.
Ponderosa Press, 1998

A.D.D. Quest for Identity: Inside the Mind of Attention Deficit Disorder, 4th ed.
George Green, Ph.D.
Biofeedback Center Press, 1999

ADD Quick Tips – Practical Ways to Manage ADD Successfully
Carla Crutsinger, M.S., Debra Moore
Brainworks, 1997

ADD and Success
Lynn Weiss
Taylor Publishing, 1998

ADD Success Stories
Thom Hartmann
Underwood Books, 1995

ADD in the Workplace: Choices, Changes, and Challenges
Kathleen Nadeau, Ph.D.
Brunner/Mazel, 1997

ADHD/Hyperactivity: A Consumer's Guide for Parents and Teachers
Michael Gordon, Ph.D.
GSI Publications, 1991

ADHD and the Nature of Self-Control
Russell Barkley
Guilford Publications, 1997

The ADHD Parenting Handbook: Practical Advice for Parents from Parents
Colleen Alexander-Roberts
Taylor Publishing, 1994

ADHD: Questions and Answers for Parents
Gregory Greenberg, Wade Horn
Research Press, 1991

ADHD in the Schools: Assessment and Intervention Strategies
George DuPaul, Ph.D., Gary Stoner
Guilford Publications, 1994

ADHD and Teens: A Parent's Guide to Making It Through the Tough Years
Colleen Alexander-Roberts
Taylor Publishing, 1995

Adult ADD -- The Complete Handbook: Everything You Need to Know About How to Cope and Live Well with ADD/ADHD
David Sudderth, Joseph Kandel, M. D.
Prima Publishing, 1996

Adult A.D.D.: A Reader Friendly Guide to Identifying, Understanding, and Treating Adult Attention Deficit Disorder
Thomas Whiteman, Ph.D., Randy Petersen, Michele Novotni
Pinon Press, 1995

Adventures in Fast Forward: Life, Love and Work for the ADD Adults
Kathleen Nadeau
Brunner/Mazel, 1995

All About A. D. D.: Overcoming Attention Deficit Disorder
Mark Selikowitz
Oxford University Press, Inc., 1995

All About ADHD – The Complete Practical Guide for Classroom Teachers
Linda Pfiffner, Ph.D.
Scholastic, 1996

All About Attention Deficit: Symptoms, Diagnosis, and Treatment: Children and Adults
Thomas Phelan, Ph.D.
Child Management Inc., 1996

Answers to Distraction
Edward Hallowell, John Ratey
Pantheon Books, 1994

Attention Deficit Answer Book: The Best Medications and Parenting Strategies for Your Child
Alan Wachtel, M.D., Michael Boyette
Plum, 1998

Attention Deficit Disorder: Helpful, Practical Information: A Guide for Parents and Educators
Elaine McEwain
Harold Shaw, 1995

Attention Deficit Disorder in Adults, 3rd ed.
Lynn Weiss, Ph.D.
Taylor Publishing, 1997

Attention Deficit Disorder in Adults: The Attention Deficit Disorder in Adults Workbook
Lynn Weiss, Ph.D.
Taylor Publishing Co., 1994

Attentional Deficit Disorder in Children and Adolescents
Jack Fadely, Ed.D., Virginia Hosler, M.S.
Charles Thomas, 1992

Attention Deficit Disorder: A Common but Often Overlooked Disorder of Children
Glenn Hunsucker
Forresst, 1993

Attention Deficit Disorder: Diagnosis and Treatment from Infancy to Adulthood
Patricia Quinn, M.D.
Brunner/Mazel, 1996

Attention Deficit Disorder: A Different Perception
Thom Hartmann
Underwood Books, 1993

Attention Deficit Disorder and Hyperactivity, 2nd ed.
Ronald Friedman, Ph.D., Guy Doyal, Ph.D.
Interstate Printers and Publishers, 1987

Attention Deficit Disorder and Learning Disabilities: Realities, Myths, and Controversial Treatments
Barbara Ingersoll, Ph.D., Sam Goldstein, Ph.D.
Doubleday, 1993

Attention Deficit Disorder: Practical Coping Methods
Barbara Fisher, Ross Beckley
CRC Press, Inc., 1998

Attention Deficit Disorders
Lisa Bain
Dell Publishing, 1991

Attention Deficit Disorders: Assessment and Teaching
Janet Lerner, Barbara Lowenthal, Sue Lerner
Brooks/Cole, 1995

Attention Deficit Disorders: Hyperactivity and Associated Disorders: A Handbook for Parents and Professionals, 6th ed.
Wendy Coleman
Calliope, 1993

The Attention Deficit Hyperactive Child in the Classroom
Lucy Martin, Kathleen Nadeau
Chesapeake Psychological Publications, 1991

Attention-Deficit Hyperactivity Disorder in Adults
Paul Wender
Oxford University Press, Inc., 1995

Attention Deficit Hyperactivity Disorder in Adults and Children: The Latest Assessment and Treatment Strategies
Juliet Jett, Ph.D., C. Keith Conners
Compact Clinicals, 1999

Attention-Deficit Hyperactivity Disorder in Children: A Medication Guide
Hugh Johnston, Jay Fruehling, Hugh Johnston, M.D.
Dean Foundation for Health Research and Education, 1997

Attention-Deficit/Hyperactivity Disorder in the Classroom: A Practical Guide for Teachers
Tom Smith, James Patton, Edward Polloway, Carol Dowdy
PRO-ED, 1997

Attention-Deficit Hyperactivity Disorder: A Clinical Workbook, 2nd ed.
Russell Barkley, Kevin Murphy
Guilford Publications, 1998

Attention Deficit/Hyperactivity Disorder: A Practical Guide for Teachers
Paul Cooper, Katherine Ideus
Taylor and Francis, 1996

Attention-Deficit Hyperactivity Disorder: What Every Parent Wants to Know, 2nd ed.
David Wodrich, Ph.D.
Paul H. Brookes, 1999

Attention Deficit Hyperactivity and Learning Disorders: Q&A
J. Gordon Millichap, M.D.
PNB Publishers, 1998

Attention Deficit, Learning Disabilities and Ritalin: A Practical Guide 2nd ed.
Robert Johnston, M.D.
Singular Publishing Group Inc. , 1991

Attention Deficits and Hyperactivity in Children
Stephen Hinshaw
Sage Publications, Inc., 1994

Attention, Please! A Comprehensive Guide for Successfully Parenting Children with Attention Disorders and Hyperactivity
Edna Copeland, Valerie Love
Specialty Press, 1995

Attention Without Tension: A Teacher's Handbook on Attention Disorders
Edna Copeland, Valerie Love
Specialty Press, Inc., 1995

The Attention Zone: A Parent's Guide to Attention Deficit/Hyperactivity Disorder
Michael Cohen
Brunner/Mazel, 1997

Beyond ADD: Hunting for Reasons in the Past and Present
Thom Hartmann
Underwood Books, 1996

Beyond Ritalin
Stephen Garber, Ph.D.
Harper Perennial, 1997

Brain Mechanisms, Attention-Deficit, and Related Mental Disorders: A Clinical and Theoretical Assessment of Attention-Deficit
Jordan Joseph
Charles C. Thomas Pub., 1992

Brainstorms: Understanding and Treating the Emotional Storms of ADHD and Related Disorders
H. Joseph Horacek
Jason Aronson, Inc., 1998

Classroom Success for the LD and ADHD Child
Suzanne Stevens
John F. Blair, 1997

Coping with ADD-ADHD
Jaydene Morrison, M.S.
Hazelden Foundation, 1997

Daredevils and Daydreamers-New Perspectives on Attention-Deficit/Hyperactivity Disorder
Barbara Ingersoll, Ph.D.
Doubleday, 1997

Defiant Children: A Clinician's Manual for Parent Training, 2nd ed.
Russell Barkley
Guilford Publications, 1997

Do You Have Attention Deficit Disorder?
James Thomas, Ph.D.
Dell Publishing Co., Inc., 1996

Dr. Silver's Advice to Parents on Attention-Deficit Hyperactivity Disorder
Larry Silver
American Psychiatric Press, 1993

Dreamers, Discovers, and Dynamos: How to Help the Child Who is Bright, Bored, and Having Trouble in School
Lucy Jo Palladino, Ph.D.
Ballantine Books, 1999

Driven to Distraction: Attention Deficit Disorder in Children and Adults
Edward Hallowell, M.D., John Ratey, M.D.
Pantheon Books, 1994

Fathering the ADHD Child: A Book for Fathers, Mothers, and Professionals
Edward Jacobs
Jason Aronson, Inc., 1997

Focus Your Energy: Hunting for Success in Business with Attention Deficit Disorder
Thom Hartmann
Pocket Books, 1994

Give Your ADD Teen a Chance: A Guide for Parents of Teenagers with Attention Deficit Disorder
Lynn Weiss
Pinon Press, 1996

Grandma's Pet Wildebeest Ate My Homework (and Other Suspect Stories): A Practical Guide for Parenting and Teaching ADHD Kids
Tom Quinn
Dunvegan Publishing, 1998

Handbook of Childhood Impulse Disorders and ADHD: Theory and Practice
Leonard Koziol, Chris Stout, Douglas Ruben
Charles C. Thomas Publisher, 1993

Handbook of Hyperactivity in Children
Johnny Matson
Allyn and Bacon, 1993

Healing ADD: Simple Exercises that Will Change Your Daily Life
Thom Hartmann
Underwood Books, 1998

Help for the Hyperactive Child - A Good Sense Guide for Parents of Children with Hyperactivity, Attention Deficit and Other Behavior and Learning Problems
W.G. Crook
Professional Books, 1991

Helping Your Hyperactive Child: From Effective Treatments and Developing Discipline and Self Esteem to Helping Your Family Adjust
John Taylor
Prima Publishing and Communication, 1990

He's Not There
Ann Colin, Ann Herbst
Viking Pengun, 1997

Honey, Are You Listening?
Fowler, Fowler
Thomas Nelson, Inc., 1995

How to Help Your Child Succeed In School – Strategies and Guidance for Parents of Children with ADHD and/or Learning Disabilities
Sandra Rief
Paul H. Brookes, 1997

How to Reach and Teach ADD/ADHD Children
Sandra Rief
Center for Applied Research in Education, 1993

The Hyperactive Child
Grant Martin
Chariot Victor Books, 1992

The Hyperactive Child, Adolescent, and Adult: Attention Deficit Disorder Through the Lifespan, 3rd ed.
Paul Wender, M.D.
Oxford University Press, 1987

The Hyperactive Child Book
Patricia Kennedy, Leif Terdal, Ph.D., Lydia Fusetti, M.D.
St. Martin's Press, 1994

The Hyperactive Child: What You Need to Know About Attention Deficit Hyperactivity Disorder
Grant Martin, M.D.
Victor Books, 1992

Hyperactive Children Grown Up, 2nd ed.
Gabrielle Weiss, Lily Trokenberg Hechtman
Guilford Publications, 1992

Hyperactivity: Why Won't My Child Pay Attention?
Sam Goldstein, Michael Goldstein
John Wiley & Sons, 1993

I Can't Sit Still - Educating and Affirming Inattentive and Hyperactive Children
Dorothy Davies Johnson, M.D., FAAP
ETR Associates, 1991

If Your Child is Hyperactive, Inattentive, Impulsive, Distractible. . . Helping the ADD / Hyperactive Child
Stephen Garber, Marianne Daniels Garber, Robyn Spizman
Villard Books, 1990

**Is Your Child Hyperactive? Inattentive? Impulsive? Distractible?
Helping the ADD / Hyperactive Child**
Stephen Garber, et al
Random House, 1995

Keys to Parenting a Child with Attention Deficit Disorder
Barry McNamara, Francine McNamara
Barrons Educational Series, 1993

Learning Disabilities and ADHD: A Family Guide to Living and Learning Together
Betty Osman
John Wiley and Sons, Inc., 1997

Life on the Edge: Parenting a Child with ADD/ADHD
David Spohn
Hazelden, 1998

The Link Between ADD and Addiction: Getting the Help You Deserve
Wendy Richardson, MA
Pinon Press, 1997

Living with ADD: A Workbook for Adults with Attention Deficit Disorder
M. Susan Roberts, Ph. D., Gerard Jansen, Ph.D.
New Harbinger, 1997

Living with ADHD: A Practical Guide to Coping with Attention Deficit Hyperactivity Disorder
Rebecca Kajander
Park Nicollet, 1995

Living with Attention-Deficit/Hyperactivity Disorder: Sometimes I Get All Scribbly
Maureen Neuville
PRO-ED, 1995

Living with a Challenging Child: Encouragement for Mothers of Children with ADD, Hyperactivity, or Other Behavioral Problems
Jayne Ray Garrison
Servant Publications, 1996

Lord, Help Me Love This Hyperactive Child
Evelyn Langston
Broadman and Holman Publishers, 1992

Management of Children and Adolescents with Attention Deficit Hyperactivity Disorder, 3rd ed.
Ronald Friedman, Guy Doyal
PRO-ED, 1992

Managing Attention and Learning Disorders: Super Survival Strategies
Elaine McEwan
Harold Shaw Publishers, 1997

Maybe You Know My Kid: A Parent's Guide to Identifying, Understanding and Helping Your Child with Attention Deficit Hyperactivity Disorder
Mary Cahill Fowler
Birch Lane Press, 1990

Medications for Attention Disorders (ADHD/ADD) and Related Medical Problems, 2nd ed.
Edna Copeland, Stephen Copps
Specialty Press, 1995

Meeting the ADD Challenge: A Practical Guide for Teachers
Steven Gordon, Michael Asher
Research Press, 1994

Mommy, I Can't Sit Sill: Coping with Hyperactive and Aggressive Children
Daniel O'Leary
New Horizon, 1989

A Parent's Guide to Attention Deficit Disorders
Lisa Bain
Dell Publishing, 1991

Moving Beyond A.D.D. / A.D.H.D.: An Effective, Holistic, Mind-Body Approach
Rita Kirsch Debroitner, Avery Hart
NTC Publishing Group, 1997

The Parent's Guide to Attention-Deficit Disorders: Intervention Strategies for the Home, 2nd ed.
Stephen McCarney, A.M. Bauer
Hawthorne, 1995

The Myth of the ADD Child: 50 Ways to Improve Your Child's Behavior and Attention Span Without Drugs, Labels, or Coercion
Thomas Armstrong
Plume, 1997

The Parents' Hyperactivity Handbook: Helping the Fidgety Child
David Paltin
Plenum Publishing, 1993

No More Ritalin: Treating ADHD Without Drugs
Mary Ann Block
Kensington Books, 1996

Performance Breakthroughs for Adolescents with Learning Disabilities or ADD: How to Help Students Succeed in the Regular Education Classroom
Geraldine Markel, Judith Greenbaum
Research Press, 1996

Out of the Fog: Treatment Options and Coping Strategies for Adult Attention Deficit Disorder
Kevin Murphy, Ph.D., Suzanne LeVert
Hyperion, 1995

Power Parenting for Children with ADD/ADHD: A Practical Parent's Guide for Managing Difficult Children
Grad Flick, Harvey Parker
Prentice Hall, 1996

Overload: Attention Deficit Disorder and the Addictive Brain
David Miller, Kenneth Blum, Ph.D.
Andrews McNeel Publishing, 1996

Put Yourself in Their Shoes: Understanding Teenagers with Attention Deficit Hyperactivity Disorder
Harvey Parker
Specialty Press, Inc., 1999

Parenting a Child with Attention Deficit/Hyperactivity Disorder
Nancy Boyles, Darlene Contadino
NTC Publishing, 1996

Re-Thinking ADHD: A Guide for Fostering Success with AD/HD at the College Level
Patricia Quinn, M.D., Anne McCormick (Eds.)
Advantage, 1998

Parenting the Overactive Child: Alternatives to Drug Therapy
Paul Lavin Lanham, M.D.
Madison, 1989

Rethinking Attention Deficit Disorders
Mariam Cherkes-Julkowski, Susan Sharp, Jonathan Stolzenberg
Brookline, 1997

Right-Brained Children In a Left-Brained World: Unlocking the Potential of Your ADD Child
Jeffrey Freed, M.A.T., Laurie Parsons
Simon and Schuster, 1997

The Ritalin-Free Child: Managing Hyperactivity and Attention Deficits Without Drugs
Diana Hunter
Consumer Press, 1995

Ritalin Free Kids
Judyth Reichenberg-Ullman, Robert Ullman
Prima Publishing, 1996

Ritalin Nation
Richard DeGranpre
W.W.Norton, 1998

Running on Ritalin: A Physician Reflects on Children, Society, and Performance in a Pill
Lawrence Diller
Bantam, 1998

Sit Down and Pay Attention! Coping with ADD Throughout the Life Cycle
Ronald Goldberg
PIA Press, 1991

Solving the Puzzle of Your Hard-to-Raise Child
William Crook, Laura Stevens
Random House, 1987

Stopping Hyperactivity: A New Solution
Patricia O'Dell, Patricia Cook
Avery Publishing Group, Inc., 1997

Strategies for Success: How to Help Your Child with ADHD or Learning Disability
Wilson Grant
Morris Publishing, 1996

Succeeding in College with Attention Deficit Disorders: Issues and Strategies for Students, Counselors and Educators
Jennifer Bramer, Ph.D.
Specialty Press, Inc., 1996

Success at Last: Helping Students with AD(H)D Achieve Their Potential
Constance Weaver (Ed.)
Heinemann, 1994

Survival Strategies for Parenting Your ADD Child: Dealing with Obsessions, Compulsions, Depression, Explosive Behavior and Rage
George Lynn
Underwood, 1996

Taming the Dragons: Real Help for Real School Problems
Susan Setley
Starfish Publishing, 1995

Teaching the Tiger: A Handbook for Individuals Involved in the Education of Students with ADD, TS or OCD
M.P. Dornbush, Ph.D., S.K. Pruitt, M.Ed.
Hope Press, 1995

Teenagers with ADD: A Parents' Guide
Chris Dendy
Woodbine House, 1995

Think Fast! The ADD Experience
Thomas Hartmann, Janie Bowman, Susan Burgess (Ed.)
Underwood Books, 1996

Total Concentration: How to Understand Attention Deficit Disorders with Treatment Guidelines for You and Your Doctor
Harold Levinson, M.D.
M. Evans and Co., Inc., 1992

Twelve Steps: A Guide for Adults with Attention Deficit Disorder
Friends in Recovery
R P I Publishing, Inc., 1996

Understanding ADHD
Christopher Green, Kit Chee
Fawcett Group Publishing, 1998

Understanding ADHD
William Bender
Prentice Hall, 1997

Understanding Girls with AD/HD
Kathleen Nadeau, Ellen Littman, Patricia Quinn
Advantage Books, 1999

Understanding and Managing Children's Classroom Behavior
Sam Goldstein
John Wiley and Sons, 1994

Understanding Your Hyperactive Child: The Essential Guide for Parents
Eric Taylor
Trafalgar Square, 1997

Voices from Fatherhood: Fathers, Sons and ADHD
Patrick Kilcarr, Ph.D., Patricia Quinn, M.D.
Brunner/Mazel, 1997

What is Attention Deficit Hyperactivity Disorder? ADHD: A Primer for Parents and Teachers
Keith Bauer
PER Publications, 1993

When Acting Out Isn't Acting: Understanding Attention-Deficit Hyperactivity and Conduct Disorders in Children and Adolescents
Lynne Weisberg, M.D.,Ph.D., Rosalie Greenberg,M.D.
PIA Press, 1988

Why Johnny Can't Concentrate: Coping with Attention Deficit Problems
Robert Moss, Helen Duff Dunlap
Bantam Books, 1996

Willie: Raising and Loving a Child with Attention Deficit Disorder
Ann Colin
Penguin, 1998

Windows into the A. D. D. Mind: Understanding and Treating Attention Deficit Disorders in the Everyday Lives of Children, Adolescents and Teenagers
Daniel Amen, M. D.
MindWorks Press, 1997

Women with Attention Deficit Disorder: Embracing Disorganization at Home and in the Workplace
Sari Solden
Underwood, 1995

You Don't Have to Hurt: Attention Deficit Disorder in Intimate Relationships
Daniel Amen, M. D.
MindWorks Press, 1997

You Mean I'm Not Lazy, Crazy, or Stupid?
Kate Kelly, Peggy Ramundo
Scribner, 1993

You and Your A.D.D. Child
Paul Warren, M.D., Jody Capehart, M.Ed.
Thomas Nelson Publishers, 1995

Your Hyperactive Child: Parent's Guide To Coping With Attention Deficit Disorder
Barbara Ingersoll, Ph.D.
MainStreet Books, 1988

Books for Youth

ADD and the College Student: A Guide for High School and College Students with Attention Deficit Disorder
Patricia Quinn, M.D.
Magination Press, 1994

Help4add@Highschool
Kathleen Nadeau
Advantage, 1998

ADHD: A Teenager's Guide
James Crist
Child's Work Child's Play, 1997

Help is On the Way
Marc Nemiroff, Ph.D., Jane Annunziata, Psy.D.
Magination Press, 1998

Adolescents and ADD: Gaining the Advantage
Patricia Quinn, M.D.
American Psychological Association, 1996

I Would if I Could: A Teenager's Guide to ADHD/Hyperactivity
Michael Gordon, Ph.D.
GSI Press, 1992

Attention Deficit Disorder
Wendy Moragne
Millbrook, 1996

I'm Somebody Too (for siblings)
Jeanne Gehret
Verbal Images Press, 1992

Coping with ADD/ADHD
Jaydene Morrison
Rosen Publishing Group, 1996

Joey Pigza Swallowed the Key
Jack Gantos
Farrar Strauss & Giroux, 1998

Distant Drums, Different Drummers: A Guide for Young People with ADHD
Barbara Ingersoll
Cape Publications, 1995

Jumpin' Jake Settles Down – A Workbook to Help Impulsive Children Learn to Think Before They Act (with Game)
Lawrence Shapiro, Ph.D.
1994

Eukee the Jumpy Jumpy Elephant
Cliff Corman, Esther Trevino
Specialty Press, Inc., 1995

Jumpin' Johnny Get Back to Work! A Child's Guide to ADHD/Hyperactivity
Michael Gordon
GSI Publications, 1991

Learning to Slow Down and Pay Attention: A Book for Kids About ADD, 2nd ed.
Kathleen Nadeau, Ellen Dixon
Magination Press, 1997

Making the Grade: An Adolescent's Struggle with ADD
Roberta Parker, Harvey Parker
Specialty Press, 1992

My Brother's A World-Class Pain: A Sibling's Guide to ADHD-Hyperactivity
Michael Gordon, Ph.D.
GSI Publications, 1992

Otto Learns About His Medicine: A Story About Medication for Children with ADHD
Matthew Galvin
Magination Press, 1995

Pay Attention, Slosh
Mark Smith, Gail Piazza
Albert Whitman and Co., 1997

Putting on the Brakes Activity Book for Young People with ADHD
Patricia Quinn, M.D., Judith Stern
American Psychological Association, 1993

Putting on the Brakes: Young People's Guide to Understanding Attention Deficit Hyperactivity Disorder (ADHD)
Patricia Quinn, M.D., Judith Stern, M.A.
Magination Press, 1991

Shelley, the Hyperactive Turtle
Deborah Moss
Woodbine House, 1989

What Do You Mean I Have Attention Deficit Disorder?
Kathleen Dwyer
Walker and Co., 1996

Slam Dunk: A Young Boy's Struggle with ADD
Roberta Parker
Specialty Press, 1996

Sometimes I Drive My Mom Crazy, But I Know She's Crazy About Me
Lawrence Shapiro
Center for Applied Psychology, 1993

A Teenager's Guide to ADD
Anton Amen, Sharon Johnson
Mindworks Press, 1996

Think Fast! The ADD Experience
Thom Hartmann, Janie Bowman (Eds.)
Underwood Books, 1996

Zipper, the Kid with ADHD
Caroline Janover
Woodbine House, 1997

Periodicals / Newsletters

ADDvance: A Magazine for Women with Attention Deficit Disorder
1001 Spring St., Suite 816
Bethesda, MD 20910
Ph: (888) 238-8588
Fax: (202) 966-1561
E-mail: editors@addvance.com
Web: http://www.addvance.com/

Attention!
CH.A.D.D.
8181 Professional Place, Suite 201
Landover, MD 20785
Ph: (800) 233-4050
        (301) 306-7070
Fax: (301) 306-7090
Web: http://chadd.org/

ADHD Report
Russell Barkley Ph.D. & Associates
Guilford Publications
72 Spring St.
New York, NY 10012
Ph: (800) 365-7006
        (212) 431-9800
Fax: (212) 966-6708
E-mail: news@guilford.com
Web: http://www.guilford.com

Videos

Video tapes can be very useful, but may a challenge to find, especially if they aren't new to the market. Try contacting the producers noted even if the tape isn't listed on their web site, book stores and your library.

A. D. D. from A to Z: A Comprehensive Guide to Attention Deficit Disorder
William Bender, Ph.D., Phillip Mclaughlin, Ed.D.
Sopris West, Inc., 1994
4093 Specialty Place
Longmont, CO 80504
Ph: (303) 651-2829
Fax: (888) 819-7767
E-mail: customerservice@sopriswest.com
Web :   http://www.sopriswest.com/
Characteristics of ADD, instructional strategies, medical interventions, parenting strategies.

A.D.D. – From A To Z: Understanding the Diagnosis and Treatment of Attention Deficit Disorder in Children and Adults
Edward Hallowell, M.D.
142 North Road
Sudbury, MA 01776
Ph: (978) 287-0810
Fax: (978) 287-5566
E-mail: ehallowell@aol.com
Web: http://www.drhallowell.com/
Symptoms, diagnosis, treatment methods.

ADD in the Classroom: Strategies for Teachers
Russell Barkley
Guilford Publications, 1994
72 Spring St.
New York, NY 10012
Ph: (800) 365-7006
        (212) 431-9800
Fax: (212) 966-6708
E-mail: info@guilford.com
Web: http://www.guilford.com
Help for teachers with ADHD students in the classroom.

A.D.D. – Stepping Out of the Dark
Lenae Madonna, Tom Demenkoff
Child Developmental Media, Inc.
5632 Van Nuys Blvd., Suite 286
Van Nuys, CA 91401
Ph: (800) 405-8942
Fax: (818) 994-6549
E-mail: info@childdevmedia.com
Web: http://www.childdevmedia.com/
Feel the frustration, the lack of attention and the confusion of ADD. Perspectives from families, a doctor, an adult, an educator.

ADHD in Adults
Russell A. Barkley, Ph.D.
Guilford Publications, 1994
72 Spring Street
New York, NY 10012
Ph: (800) 365-7006
        (212) 431-9800
Fax: (212) 966-6708
E-mail: info@guilford.com
Web: http://www.guilford.com/
Illustrates the impact ADHD has on adults.

ADHD – Inclusive Instruction & Collaborative Practices
Sandra Rief
Council for Exceptional Children, 1994
1110 North Glebe Road, Suite 300
Arlington, VA 22201-5704
Ph: (888) CEC-SPED
         (703) 620-3660
TTY(text): (703) 264-9446
Fax: (703) 264-9494
E-mail: service@cec.sped.org
Web: http://www.cec.sped.org
Techniques for teachers that are positive, practical, and educationally sound.

ADHD: What Can We Do?
Russell Barkley, Ph.D.
Guilford Publications, 1993
72 Spring St.
New York, NY 10012
Ph: (800) 365-7006
        (212) 431-9800
Fax: (212) 966-6708
E-mail: info@guilford.com
Web: http://www.guilford.com
Techniques for managing ADHD in the classroom, at home, and on family outings.

ADHD: What Do We Know?
Russell Barkley, Ph.D.
Guilford Publications, 1993
72 Spring Street
New York, NY 10012
Ph: (800) 365-7006
        (212) 431-9800
Fax: (212) 966-6708
E-mail: info@guilford.com
Web: http://www.guilford.com/
Causes and prevalence of ADHD, ways children with ADHD behave, other conditions that may accompany ADHD, long-term prospects for children with ADHD.

Adults with Attention Deficit Disorder
Thomas Phelan, Ph.D.
Ph: (800) 442-4453
Web: http://www.thomasphelan.com
Panel discusses ADD in adults: diagnosis, effects on home/work/life, effects on mood and self esteem. Diagnosis, effects on work, home, marriage, parenting, social life; impact on mood and self esteem, how to get help.

All About Attention Deficit Disorder: Symptoms, Diagnoses and Treatment
Thomas Phelan, Ph.D.
Ph: (800) 442-4453
Web: http://www.thomasphelan.com

Answers to ADD: The School Success Kit

John Taylor, Ph.D.
ADD-Plus
P.O. Box 1035
Sandpoint, Idaho 83864
Ph: (800) 847-1233
Fax: (208) 255-1387
Web: http://www.add-plus.com/
School success techniques for math, spelling, teacher-parent cooperation, distractibility and fidgetiness, testing and long-term assignments, homework.

Around the Clock: Parenting the Delayed ADHD Child

Joan Goodman, Susan Hoban
Guilford Publications, 1994
72 Spring Street
New York, NY 10012
Ph: (800) 365-7006
       (212) 431-9800
Fax: (212) 966-6708
E-mail: info@guilford.com
Web: http://www.guilford.com/
Challenges facing parents of children with both ADHD and developmental delay, learning to cope, achieving a meaningful relationship with the child.

Classroom Interventions for ADHD

George DuPaul, Gary Stoner
Produced by Steve Lerner
Guilford Publications, 1998
72 Spring Street
New York, NY 10012
Ph: (800) 365-7006
       (212) 431-9800
Fax: (212) 966-6708
E-mail: info@guilford.com
Web: http://www.guilford.com
Interventions to help students with ADHD enhance school performance while keeping the classroom functioning smoothly.

A Continuing Education Program on ADHD

William Bender, Phillip McLaughlin
The Council for Exceptional Children, 1995
1110 North Glebe Road, Suite 300
Arlington, VA 22201-5704
Ph: (888) CEC-SPED
       (703) 620-3660
TTY (text): (703) 264-9446
Fax: (703) 264-9494
E-mail: service@cec.sped.org
Web: http://www.cec.sped.org
Experiences of parents, teachers, professionals who provide service to children with ADD.

Educating Inattentive Children: A Guide for the Classroom

Sam Goldstein, Ph.D., Michael Goldstein, M.D.
Neurology, Learning and Behavior Center
230 South 500 East, Suite 100
Salt Lake City, Utah 84102
Ph: (801) 532-1484
Fax: (801) 532-1486
E-mail: info@samgoldstein.com
Web: www.samgoldstein.com
For teachers. Information to identify and evaluate classroom problems caused by inattention. Guidelines on how to efffectively teach ADD children.

It's Just Attention Disorder: A Video Guide for Kids

Sam Goldstein, Ph.D., Michael Goldstein, M.D.
Neurology, Learning and Behavior Center
230 South 500 East, Suite 100
Salt Lake City, Utah 84102
Ph: (801) 532-1484
Fax: (801) 532-1486
E-mail: info@samgoldstein.com
Web: www.samgoldstein.com
To help children and teens with ADD become active participants in their treatment. Claymation, advice from a former NBA coach on becoming a winner, interviews with children and teens with ADHD.

Jumpin' Johnny Get Back to Work!
Michael Gordon, Ph.D.
GSI Publications, Inc., 1994
P.O. Box 746
DeWitt, NY 13214
Ph: (800) 550-2343
Fax: (315) 446-2012
E-mail: addgsi@aol.com
Web: http://www.gsi-add.com/
Animated story of a boy with ADHD. For children.

Medication for ADD
Thomas Phelan, Ph.D., Jonathan Bloomberg, M.D.
Ph: (800) 442-4453
Web: www.thomasphelan.com
Effectiveness of medication for ADD, side effects.

A New Look at ADHD: Inhibition, Time, and Self Control
Russell A. Barkley
Produced by Steve Lerner
Guilford Publications, 2000
72 Spring Street
New York, NY 10012
Ph: (800) 365-7006
      (212) 431-9800
Fax: (212) 966-6708
E-mail: info@guilford.com
Web: http://www.guilford.com/
Dr. Barkley's alternative theory of ADHD as a disorder of self-regulation, not attention.

Success in College and Career with Attention Deficit Disorder
Jennifer Bramer, Ph.D., Wilma Fellman, M. Ed., LPC
Available through A.D.D. WareHouse
300 Northwest 70th Avenue, Suite 102
Plantation, FL 33317
Ph: (800) 233-9273
      (954)792-8100
Fax: (954) 792-8545
Appropriate school selection, resources on campus, communicating with instructors, study strategies.

Teen to Teen: The ADD Experience
Avail. Through Schlessinger Media, 1999
P.O. Box 580
Wynnewood, PA 19096
Ph: (800) 843-3620
      (610) 645-4000
Fax: (610) 645-4040
E-mail: comments@libraryvideo.com
Teenagers and young adults talk about their experiences coping with ADD. Grades 9 to adult.

Understanding Attention Deficit Disorder
Samel Epstein, M.D.
Connecticut Associaton for Children with Learning Disabilities
25 VanZant St., Unit 15-5
E. Norwalk, CT 06855
Ph: (203) 838-5010
Fax: (203) 866-6108
E-mail: cacld@juno.com
Web: http://www.cacld.org/
General introduction to ADHD: history, symptoms, methods of diagnosis. Special education, medication therapy, self esteem.

Why Won't My Child Pay Attention?
Sam Goldstein, Ph.D.
Neurology, Learning and Behavior Center
230 South 500 East, Suite 100
Salt Lake City, Utah 84102
Ph: (801) 532-1484
Fax: (801) 532-1486
E-mail: info@samgoldstein.com
Web: www.samgoldstein.com
Familiarizes parents with ADD behaviors and
problems they can cause in childhood. Effects on
children at home, school, in the community. Guidelines
to manage the problems.

Vendors

ADD/ADHD Online Newsletter
Web: http://users.nlci.com/nutrition/
Nutrition based.

ADD-Plus
P.O. Box 1035
Sandpoint, ID 83864
Ph: (800) 847-1233
Fax: (208) 255-1387
E-mail: addplus@hotmail.com
Web: http://www.add-plus.com/
Books and tapes on ADD.

A.D.D. Warehouse
300 NW 70th Ave., Suite 102
Plantation, FL 33317
Ph: (800) 233-9273
       (954) 792-8100
Fax: (954) 792-8545
E-mail: sales@addwarehouse.com
Web: http://www.addwarehouse.com
Books, tapes on ADD and other developmental
disorders.

One A.D.D. Place
Web: http://www.oneaddplace.com/
Materials, camps, services for ADD children.

Yes You Can Ministries
C/o 2965 West Comstock Dr.
Chandler, AZ 85224
Ph: (602) 820-4177
Web:
http://members.aol.com/ghales8071/yesyoucan/#homelist
Materials for parents of ADD/ADHD children with
Christian emphasis.

Web Sites
Also see "General Web Sites". Many have sections on ADD and ADHD, but they are not listed
separately below.

About.com (on ADD)
Web: http://add.miningco.com/msubinfo.htm
Series of articles on ADD.

Christian ADHD List
Web: http://www.christianadhd.com/loop.html#intro
Members encourage one another as they raise their ADD
children.

---- *Autism*

Developmental disorder that prevents a child from making sense of the world. Coherent ideas about his environment and behavior aren't fully formed. The biggest challenges are with social relationships, communication, understanding and imagination. Symptoms are different in each child, with a wide range of characteristics and developmental difficulties.

Also called (types)
- Autistic disorder
- High level language disorder
- Semantic-pragmatic disorder
- Infantile autism
- Childhood autism
- Childhood psychosis
- Pervasive developmental disorder (PDD)
- Classic autism - Used to describe those more severely disabled in social skills, language and communication. These cases are rare; most children have an assortment of symptoms and severity.
- Kanner's Autism - Refers to the minority of people with autism (25-30% of autistic population) who aren't mentally retarded. These people may become college educated and live independently, have a large vocabulary. Yet they may still have difficulties with social skills, have ritualistic behavior and desire for extreme constancy in their environment.

Frequency
- In the U.S., 4-5 children per 10,000 have classic autism, 17 per 10,000 have closely related conditions. Worldwide 5-15 per 10,000 are autistic.
- Autism is the 4th most common developmental disability, preceded by mental retardation, epilepsy, and cerebral palsy.
- Boys outnumber girls by 3 or 4 to 1.
- When girls are affected, they are more likely to be more seriously disabled, have lower IQs then boys.
- Children with the most severe form of autism probably make up only 2-3% of children with autism.
- A family with one child with autism has a 9% risk of having a second autistic child.
- Relatives of autistic people have a slightly greater chance of being autistic, but families with an autistic member tend to have relatives with speech disorders, learning difficulties, and other cognitive disabilities.

- The number of cases are on the increase, greater than can be attributed to simple awareness.
- Over 70% of persons with autism are mentally retarded.

Symptoms and Possible Effects

Little evidence of development delay during a child's first year of life. Symptoms begin to appear betweeen ages 2 and 5. Range of possible symptoms is wide:

Social relationships/behavior
- ❑ Young child's behavior may range from normal to unsoothable screaming.
- ❑ May not show preference for parents over others. However, some may become obsessively attached to one parent.
- ❑ Attention problems, abnormally high or low activity levels, tantrums, destructive behavior.
- ❑ Unable to develop relationships, understand social behavior and others' feelings.
- ❑ Tends to be a loner.
- ❑ Social approaches are one-sided and done to indulge unusual interests. May be passive about others' social approaches.
- ❑ Repetitive but aimless activities, such as running up and down, flicking, twirling, arranging objects.
- ❑ May avoid eye contact, or gaze excessively.
- ❑ Doesn't seek comfort when distressed nor "check in" with parents occasionally.
- ❑ Tends to be independent, keeping a distance or even hiding from others.

Communication
- ❑ Lack of development or use of language, gestures and body language.
- ❑ Has difficulty understanding and expressing emotion. Apathetic.
- ❑ Reverses pronouns (e.g., substitutes "you" for "I").
- ❑ Makes irrelevant factual comments or uses jargon that doesn't make sense.
- ❑ May talk a great deal but not have two-way conversations with others.
- ❑ May not respond to voices yet be aware of interesting sounds.
- ❑ Comprehension may be poor in spite of a large vocabulary.
- ❑ May repeat others' words, but not respond to questions.
- ❑ Learns phrases, sentences, jingles, rhymes, songs, even sophisticated chunks of language. May use illogical words.
- ❑ Understanding is literal. Unable to generalize.
- ❑ Humor, if present, is confined to slapstick, puns and wordplay.
- ❑ Child may remain mute; 40% don't speak.
- ❑ Voice pitch may be monotone or high-pitched. Can't comprehend the meaning of others' tones of voice.

Cognition
- ❑ Range of interests and activities is limited, often restricted to a few stereotyped repeated behaviors.
- ❑ May develop an intense interest in things such as electrical plugs, switches, appliances, wheels, lights. Conventional toys may be of little interest.
- ❑ 75% have mild to severe mental retardation. IQ scores fall in a broad range. A minority have normal or above average intellect.
- ❑ May have good rote memory.
- ❑ May mimic others, but not understand the purpose of an activity.
- ❑ Has a great need for constancy, becoming upset at changes in environments or schedule.
- ❑ May not engage in pretend play nor start play activities.

❑ Has difficulty spontaneously imitating and learning through imitation.
❑ Development rate or sequence of development may be different than that of other children.
❑ Those less affected may display special skills far exceeding those of others, referred to as *savant syndrome*. Examples include extraordinary memory, advanced numerical skills, sophisticated artistic or musical skills, mapping or calendaring skills.

Sensory sensitivities
❑ May enjoy intense movement such as spinning around or have an intense fear of movement.
❑ May focus on visual.
❑ Unusual or even explosive reactions to sensory stimuli, particularly sound.
❑ May be fascinated with lights, color patterns, logos, shapes or configuration of letters and words.
❑ May be preoccupied with scratching or rubbing certain surfaces.
❑ May avoid certain food textures.

Physical
❑ Requires little sleep, nights are interrupted.
❑ Toilet training may be slow.
❑ Eating habits, likes/dislikes are often extreme. May eat non-edible things.
❑ Unexplained high temperatures, transient rashes.
❑ Toe walking, hand regard and flapping, writhing movements of the fingers, body twirling, motor ritual, repetitive mannerisms.
❑ Insensitivity to physical dangers and pain.
❑ Seizures.
❑ Head banging.
❑ Doesn't extend arms to signal desire to be picked up.
❑ Obsessive attachment to objects.

Causes
Causes for the abnormal brain development that results in autism are uncertain, but theories include:

- Illnesses such as viruses, rubella, herpes simplex, candida albicans, meningitis, encephalitis.
- Some inherited disorders that are known to cause brain damage, e.g., tuberous sclerosis, neurofibromatosis, fragile-X syndrome, Rett's syndrome, mental retardation, untreated PKU, microcephaly, XYY syndrome.
- Prenatal infections, prematurity, birth trauma, toxemia.
- Injury that affects the central nervous system, such as trauma, anoxia, metabolic factors.

Diagnostic Processes
Although autism is caused by abnormal brain development, it can't be reliably detected by a brain scan or other definitive tests. Instead observations are gathered, such as:

- A child's behavior and development, use of language, level of understanding, social skills, play, sensory and perceptual abilities, use of imagination, attention level, intelligence.
- Diagnostic assessment tools.
- Medical history, early development.

DSM IV Diagnostic Criteria

Reprinted with permission from the *Diagnostic and Statistical Manual of Mental Disorders, Fourth Edition, Text Revision.* Copyright 2000 American Psychiatric Association.

A. A total of six (or more) items from (1), (2), and (3), with at least two from (1) and one each from (2) and (3):

(1) qualitative impairment in social interaction, as manifested by at least two of the following:

(a)   marked impairment in the use of multiple nonverbal behaviors such as eye-to-eye gaze, facial expression, body postures, and gestures to regulate social interaction
(b)   failure to develop peer relationships appropriate to developmental level
(c)   a lack of spontaneous seeking to share enjoyment, interests, or achievements with other people (e.g., by a lack of showing, bringing, or pointing out objects of interest)
(d)   lack of social or emotional reciprocity

(2) qualitative impairments in communication as manifested by at least one of the following:

(a)   delay in, or total lack of, the development of spoken language (not accompanied by an attempt to compensate through alternative modes of communication such as gesture or mime)
(b)   in individuals with adequate speech, marked impairment in the ability to initiative or sustain a conversation with others
(c)   stereotyped and repetitive use of language or idiosyncratic language
(d)   lack of varied, spontaneous make-believe play or social imitative play appropriate to developmental level

(3) restricted repetitive and stereotyped patterns of behavior, interests, and activities, as manifested by at least one of the following:

(a)   encompassing preoccupation with one or more stereotyped and restricted patterns of interest that is abnormal either in intensity or focus
(b)   apparently inflexible adherence to specific, nonfunctional routines or rituals
(c)   stereotyped and repetitive motor mannerisms (e.g., hand or finger flapping or twisting, or complex whole-body movements)
(d)   persistent preoccupation with parts of objects

B. Delays or abnormal functioning in at least one of the following areas, with onset prior to age 3 years:
(1) social interaction,
(2) language as used in social communication, or
(3) symbolic or imaginative play.

C. The disturbance is not better accounted for by Rett's Disorder or Childhood Disintegrative Disorder.

What Else Could it Be?
Children with autism have symptoms that mimic those of other conditions, such as those noted below. To properly diagnose a problem, these may need to be ruled out as causes for the problem.

- ✓ Adenyosuccinate lyase deficiency (disorder of nucleic acid metabolism)
- ✓ Angelman syndrome
- ✓ Asperger's disorder
- ✓ Attention deficit disorder
- ✓ Carnitine deficiency
- ✓ Childhood aphasia
- ✓ Childhood disintegrative disorder (Heller's syndrome)
- ✓ Deafness
- ✓ Developmental language disorders
- ✓ Expressive language disorder
- ✓ Sensory impairments
- ✓ Smith-Magenis syndrome (chromosome abnormality)
- ✓ Fetal alcohol effect
- ✓ Fragile X syndrome
- ✓ Galactosemia
- ✓ Hyperlexia
- ✓ Irlen syndrome / scotopic sensitivity syndrome (visual perception problems)
- ✓ Klinefelter syndrome (chromosome abnormality)
- ✓ Lactic acidosis – tendency to accumulate lactic acid in the blood
- ✓ Landau-Kleffner syndrome
- ✓ Mental retardation
- ✓ Mixed receptive-expressive language disorder
- ✓ Stereotypic movement disorder
- ✓ Tourette's syndrome
- ✓ Obsessive compulsive disorder
- ✓ PKU (phenylketronuria)
- ✓ Progressive nervous system disorders
- ✓ Prosopagnosia (inability to recognize faces)
- ✓ Rett's syndrome
- ✓ Schizophrenia
- ✓ Seizure disorder
- ✓ Selective mutism
- ✓ Semantic-pragmatic speech disorder
- ✓ Turner's syndrome (chromosome abnormality)
- ✓ Verbal apraxia

What Can Be Going on at the Same Time?
Autism may occur concurrently with:
- Mental retardation.
- Blindness, deafness.
- Epilepsy.

Treatment
- Recent research suggests that intense behavioral intervention (such as the Lovaas Method) between ages 2 and 5 can have a lasting positive effect. This is the time in which a child's brain growth and development occurs rapidly.
- Therapy for speech, cognition, social, behavior, general stimulation, and daily life tasks.
- As an adult, vocational training, job coaching, sheltered workshops, day treatment, residential placement.
- Initial yet promising attempts are currently underway with secretin coupled with vitamin therapy.
- There are no medications used expressly for autism. But some medications may use be used to help control symptoms such as aggression, tics, mood extremes, hyperactivity, attention span, social withdrawal, anxiety, sleep disturbances, self-injurious behavior, obsessive behavior. Controlling these factors may aid in learning.

- Sensory integration therapy.
- Facilitated communication with a keyboard or communications board.

Outcomes

- Lifelong condition, though progress varies among individuals.
- After age 5, there is often a marked improvement in social skills, especially in more able children. 50% gain social speech by this time.
- During age 6 to adolescence, many autistic children make considerable spontaneous improvement, with autistic features becoming less pronounced.
- By adolescence, the child's ability to be independent will depend on his intelligence and speech skills.
- Autistic children with mental retardation will behave like other children with mental retardation, but may have poorer language and social skills. Problem-solving abilities may be better, however.
- Even higher functioning autistic adults may still be awkward verbally, socially, and behaviorally. Their thinking will be literal. Most adults live in supervised living or at home, but can care for themselves and engage in daily living. Supported employment situations may be an option for some.

Who to Contact

Also refer to "Who Else to Contact." Organizations listed below target their work specifically toward autism.

Autism National Committee
P.O. Box 6175
North Plymouth, MA 02362-6175
Web: http://www.autcom.org
Protects and advances the rights of persons with autism, pervasive developmental disorder, related differences of communication and behavior.

Autism Research Institute
4182 Adams Ave.
San Diego, CA 92116
Ph: (619) 281-7165
Fax: (619) 563-6840
Web: http://www.autism.com/ari
Research and information on the causes of autism, methods of preventing, diagnosing and treating autism, severe behavioral disorders of childhood.

The Autism Research Foundation
P.O. Box 1571, GMF
Boston, MA 02205
Ph: (617) 414-5286
Fax: (617) 414-7207
E-mail: tarf@ladders.org
Web: http://www.ladders.org/tarf/
Researchers investigating the neurobiological underpinnings of autism and related disorders.

Autism Society of America
7910 Woodmont Ave., Suite 300
Bethesda, MD 20814-3015
Ph: (800) 3AUTISM
(301) 657-0881
Fax: (301) 657-0869
E-mail: info@autism-society.org
Web: http://www.autism-society.org/
Advocacy, public awareness, education, research, family support.

Center for the Study of Autism
P.O. Box 4538
Salem, OR 97302
Web: http://www.autism.org/
Provides information to parents, professionals.
Conducts research on various therapeutic interventions.

Cure Autism Now Foundation
5455 Wilshire Blvd., Suite 715
Los Angeles, CA 90036
Ph: (888) 8AUTISM
        (323) 549-0500
Fax: (323) 549-0547
Web: http://www.canfoundation.org
Parents, clinicians, scientists working to find
prevention and a cure for autism and related disorders.

Eden Institute Inc.
One Eden Way
Princeton, NJ 08540
Ph: (609) 987-0099
Fax: (609) 987-0243
E-mail: info@edenservices.org
Web: http://www.edenservices.org
Services for autistic individuals. Early intervention,
residential, employment services for adults, outreach.

Facilitated Communication Institute
Syracuse University
370 Huntington Hall
Syracuse, NY 13244-2340
Ph: (315) 443-9657
Fax: (315) 443-2274
E-mail: fcstaff@sued.syr.edu
Web: http://soeweb.syr.edu/thefci/
Research, public education, training scholarly
seminars.

Georgiana Institute
P.O. Box 210
Roxbury, CT 06783
Ph: (860) 355-1545
Fax: (860) 355-2443
E-mail: georgianainstitute@snet.net
Web: http://www.georgianainstitute.org/
Trains individuals on auditory integration training. AIT
addresses the hearing distortions, hyperacute hearing
which cause discomfort and confusion in
developmentally delayed children.

National Alliance for Autism Research
414 Wall St., Research Park
Princeton, NJ 08540
Ph: (609) 430-9160
        (888) 777-NAAR
Fax: (609) 430-9163
E-mail: naar@naar.org
Web: http://www.naar.org
Works to find causes, prevention, effective treatment
and cure of the autism spectrum disorders.

Society for Auditory Integration Training
P.O. Box 4538
Salem, OR 97302
E-mail: sait@teleport.com
Web: http://www.teleport.com/~sait/table.html#sai
Distributes information on auditory integration
training.

**University of California at Santa Barbara
Autism Research Center**
University of California, Santa Barbara
Graduate School of Eduation
Santa Barbara, CA 93106
Ph: (805) 893-2176
E-mail: ucsbautism@education.ucsb.edu
Web: http://education.ucsb.edu/~doniel/index.html
Works to understand, treat autism, improve education
efforts for children with autism, severe disabilities.

Recommended Reading

Activities for Developing Pre-Skill Concepts in Children with Autism
Toni Flowers
PRO-ED, 1987

Activity Schedules for Children with Autism: A Guide for Parents and Professionals
Lynn McClannahan, Ph.D., Patricia Krantz, Ph.D.
Woodbine House, 1998

Adapted Physical Education for Students with Autism
Kimberly Davis
Charles C. Thomas Publisher, 1990

Adults with Autism: A Guide to Theory and Practice
Hugh Morgan (Ed.)
Cambridge University Press, 1996

At Home with Autism: Three Families' Stories
Danielle Morse, Viki Garyhardt, R. Stewart Wallace
Potential Unlimited Publishing, 1998

Autism, 4th ed.
Laura Schreibman
Sage Publications, 1988

Autism and Asperger Syndrome
Uta Frith (Ed.)
Cambridge University Press, 1992

Autism: Information and Resources for Parents, Families, and Professionals
Richard Simpson, Paul Zionts
PRO-ED, 1992

Autism in Children and Adults: Etiology, Assessment and Intervention
Johnny Matson
Sycamore Publishing Co., 1994

Autism and the Development of Mind
Hobson
Lawrence Erlbaum, 1994

Autism: Explaining the Enigma
Uta Frith
Basil Blackwell, 1989

Autism: The Facts
Simon Baron-Cohen, Patrick Bolton
Oxford University, 1993

Autism: From Theoretical Understanding to Educational Intervention
Theo Peeters
Singular Press, 1997

Autism: From Tragedy to Triumph
Carol Johnson, Julia Crowder
Branden Publishing Co., 1997

Autism: Handle with Care! Understanding and Managing Behavior of Children and Adults with Autism, 2nd ed.
Gail Gillingham
Future Education, 1995

Autism: Identification, Education and Treatment
Dianne Berkell (Ed.)
Lawrence Erlbaum Assocs., Inc., 1992

Autism: An Introduction to Psychological Theory
Francesca Happe
Harvard University Press, 1998

Autism and Life in the Community: Successful Interventions for Behavioral Challenges
Marcia Smith
Paul H. Brookes, 1989

Autism: A Practical Guide for Those Who Help Others
John Gerdtz, Joel Bregman, M.D.
Continuum, 1990

Autism Preparing for Adulthood
Patricia Howlin
Routledge, 1996

Autism Through the Lifespan: The Eden Model
David Holmes
Woodbine House, 1998

Autism Treatment Guide
Elizabeth Gerlach
Four Leaf Press, 1993

Autism: Understanding the Disorder
Gary Mesibov, Lynn Adams, Laura Klinger
Plenum Press, 1997

Autistic Adults at Bittersweet Farms
Norman Giddan, Ph.D., Jane Giddan, MA (Eds.)
Haworth Press, Inc., 1991

Autistic Spectrum: A Guide for Parents and Professionals
Lorna Wing
Trans-Atl., 1997

Behavioral Intervention for Young Children with Autism: A Manual for Parents and Professionals
Catherine Maurice (Ed.)
PRO-ED, 1996

Behavioral Issues in Autism
Eric Schopler, Gary Mesibov (Eds.)
Plenum, 1994

Beyond Gentle Teaching: A Nonaversive Approach to Helping Those in Need
John McGee, Frank Manolascino
Plenum, 1991

Case Studies in Autism: A Young Child and Two Adolescents
Cheryl Seifert
University Press of America, 1990

Children With Autism: A Developmental Perspective (Developing Child Series)
Marian Sigman, Lisa Capps
Harvard University Press, 1996

Children with Autism: Diagnosis and Interventions to Meet Their Needs, 2nd ed.
Colwyn Trevarthen
Taylor and Francis, 1997

Children with Autism: A Parent's Guide
Michael Powers (Ed.)
Woodbine House, 1988

Comic Strip Conversations
Carol Gray
Future Education, 1994

Communication Unbound: How Facilitated Communication is Challenging Traditional Views of Autism and Ability-Disability
Douglas Biklen
Teachers College Press, 1995

Creating a Win-Win IEP for Students with Autism!
Beth Fouse
Future Horizons, 1996

Crossing Bridges: A Parent's Perspective on Coping After a Child is Diagnosed with Autism/PDD
Viki Satkiewicz-Gayhardt, Barbara Peerenboom, Roxanne Campbell, R.N.
Potential Unlimited Publishing, 1997

Dancing with Dragons: An Entire Family's Insights into a Disability
Gerard Mialaret
Future Education, 1996

Dancing in the Rain: Stories of Exceptional Progress by Parents of Children With Special Needs
Annabel Stehli
The Georgiana Organization, 1995

Emergence: Labeled Autistic
Temple Grandin, Margaret Scariano
Warner Books, Inc., 1996

Extraordinary People: Understanding Savant Syndrome
Darold Treffert, M.D.
Ballantine Books, 1989

Fighting for Darla: Challenges for Family Care and Professional Responsibility: The Case Study of a Pregnant Adolescent with Autism
Ellen Brantlinger
Teachers College Press, 1994

Fragile Success - Nine Autistic Children, Childhood to Adulthood
Virginia Sperry, Sally Provence
Shoe String, 1995

Frances Tustin
Sheila Spensley
Routledge, 1995

A Guide to Successful Employment for Individuals with Autism
Marcia Datlow Smith, Ph.D., Ronald Belcher, Ph.D., Patricia Juhrs
Paul H. Brookes, 1997

The Handbook of Autism and Pervasive Developmental Disorders, 2nd ed.
Donald Cohen, Fred Volkmar (Eds.)
John Wiley and Sons, Inc., 1997

Handle with Care: Understanding and Managing Behavior of Children and Adults with Autism, 3rd ed.
Gail Gillingham
Tacit Publishing, 1998

Hearing Equals Behavior
Guy Berard, M.D.
Keats Publishing, 1993

Helping the Child Who Doesn't Fit In
Marshall Duke, Ph.D, Stephen Nowicki, Ph.D.
Peachtree Publishers, Ltd., 1992

The Hidden Child: The Linwood Method for Reaching the Autistic Child
Jeanne Simons, Sabine Oishi
Woodbine House, 1987

Higher Functioning Adolescents and Young Adults With Autism: A Teacher's Guide
Joyce Stratton, Phyllis Coyne, Carol Gray
ProEd, 1996

High-Functioning Individuals with Autism
Eric Schopler, Gary Mesibov (Eds.)
Plenum Press, 1992

Higher Functioning Adolescents and Young Adults with Autism: A Teacher's Guide
Ann Fullerton, Georgiana Thomas, Phyllis Coyne, Joyce Stratton, Carol Gray
PRO-ED, 1996

Keys to Parenting the Child with Autism
Marlene Targ Brill
Barron's Educational Series, 1994

Laughing and Loving with Autism: A Collection of "Real Life" Warm & Humorous Stories
R. Wayne Gilpin (Ed.)
Future Horizons, 1993

Learning and Cognition in Autism
Eric Schopler, Gary Mesibov (Eds.)
Plenum Publishing, 1995

Let Me Hear Your Voice: A Family's Triumph Over Autism
Catherine Maurice
Fawcett, 1994

Like Color to the Blind: Soul Searching and Soul Finding
Donna Williams
Random House, Inc., 1996

Living with Autism: The Parents' Stories
Kathleen Dillon
Parkway Publishers, Inc., 1995

Mindblindness: An Essay on Autism and Theory of Mind
Simon Baron-Cohen
M I T Press, 1997

Mixed Blessings
William Christopher, Barbara Christopher
Abingdon, 1989

More Laughing and Loving with Autism
R. Wayne Gilpin
Future Horizons, 1994

Movement Differences and Diversity in Autism/Mental Retardation
Anne Donnellan, Ph.D.
D R I Press, 1995

Music Therapy for the Autistic Child, 2nd ed.
Juliette Alvin, Auriel Warwick
Oxford University Press, Inc., 1992

News From the Border: A Mother's Memoir of Her Autistic Son
Jane Taylor McDonnell, Paul McDonnell
Ticknor and Fields, 1993

Nobody Nowhere: The Extraordinary Autobiography of an Autistic
Donna Williams
Avon Books, 1994

Out of Silence: An Autistic Boy's Journey into Language and Communication
Russell Martin
Viking Penguin, 1995

Parent Survival Manual: A Guide to Crisis Resolution in Autism and Related Developmental Disorders
Eric Schopler
Plenum Press, 1995

A Parent's Guide to Autism: Answers to the Most Common Questions
Charles Hart
Simon & Schuster Trade, 1993

Preschool Education Program for Children with Autism
Sandra Harris, Jan Handleman (Eds.)
PRO-ED, 1996

Preschool Issues in Autism
Eric Schopler, Mary Van Bourgondien, Marie Bristol (Eds.)
Plenum Press, 1993

Reaching the Child with Autism Through Art
Toni Flowers
Future Horizons, 1996

The Riddle of Autism: A Psychological Analysis
George Victor
Jason Aronson Publishers, 1995

Right from the Start: Behavioral Intervention for Young Children with Autism: A Guide for Parents and Professionals
Sandra Harris, Ph.D., Mary Jane Weiss, Ph.D.
Woodbine House, 1998

Siblings of Children with Autism: A Guide for Families
Sandra Harris
Woodbine House, 1994

A Slant of Sun
Beth Kephart
W.W. Norton, 1998

Social Skills for Students with Autism, 2nd ed.
Richard Simpson, Gary Sasso, Debra Kamps, Brenda Myles
Council for Exceptional Children, 1997

Somebody Somewhere: Breaking Free From the World of Autism
Donna Williams
Random House, 1995

Son-Rise: The Miracle Continues
Barry Neil Kaufman
H. J. Kramer, 1995

Soon Will Come the Light: A View From Inside the Autism Puzzle
Thomas McKean
Future Horizons, 1994

The Sound of a Miracle: A Child's Triumph Over Autism
Annabel Stehli
Georgiana, 1997

Taming the Recess Jungle
Carol Gray, Jenison Public Schools, Michigan
Future Horizons, 1994

Targeting Autism: What We Know, Don't Know, and Can Do to Help Young Children With Autism and Related Disorders
Shirley Cohen
University California Press, 1998

Teach Me Language: A Language Manual for Children with Autism, Asperger's Syndrome & Related Developmental Disorders, 2nd ed.
Sabrina Freeman, Lorelei Dake
SKF Publisher, 1997

Teaching Children with Autism: Strategies to Enhance Communication and Socialization
Kathleen Ann Quill
Delmar Publishing, Inc., 1995

Teaching Children with Autism: Strategies for Initiating Positive Interactions and Improving Learning Opportunities
Robert Koegel, Ph.D., Lynn Kern Koegel, Ph.D. (Eds.)
Paul H. Brookes, 1995

Teaching Spontaneous Communication to Autistic and Developmentally Handicapped Children
Linda Watson (Ed.)
PRO-ED, 1989

There's A Boy in Here
Judy Barron, Sean Barron
Avon Books, 1992

Thinking in Pictures and Other Reports of My Life with Autism
Temple Grandin
Doubleday, 1995

A Treasure Chest of Behavioral Strategies for Individuals with Autism
Beth Fouse, Ph.D., Maria Wheeler
Future Horizons, 1997

Turning Every Stone: Autism with Love
Phyllis Lambert
Scots Plaid Press, 1990

The Ultimate Treasure Hunt: Finding the Child Inside
Adair Renning
Adair Renning, 1995

Understanding Other Minds: Perspectives from Autism
Simon Baron-Cohen, Helen Tager-Flusberg, Donald Cohen (Eds.)
Oxford University Press, Inc., 1993

Understanding and Teaching Children with Autism
Rita Jordan, Stuart Powell
John Wiley and Sons, 1995

Unlocking the Potential of Secretin
V. Beck, G. Beck
Autism Research Institute, 1998

Visual Strategies for Improving Communication: Practical Supports for School and Home
Linda Hodgdon
Quirk Robe, 1995

When Snow Turns to Rain: One Family's Struggle to Solve the Riddle of Autism
Craig Schulze
Woodbine House, 1996

Winter's Flower, 2nd ed.
Ranae Johnson
Rain Tree, 1992

Without Reason: A Family Copes with Two Generations of Autism
Charles Hart
Signet, 1989

Working Together for a Brighter Future: A Unique Approach for Educating High – Functioning Students with Autism
Marilyn Hays
Future Horizons, 1996

The World of the Autistic Child: Understanding and Treating Autistic Disorders
Bryna Siegel
Oxford University Press, 1996

Books for Youth

Andy and His Yellow Frisbee
Mary Thompson
Woodbine House, 1996

Joey and Sam
Illana Katz, Edward Ritvo
Real Life Storybooks, 1993

Are You Alone on Purpose?
Nancy Werlin
Ballantine Books, 1994

Little Rainman
Karen Simmons
Future Horizons, 1996

The Babysitters Club: Kristy and the Secret of Susan
Ann Martin
Scholastic Inc., 1996

Mori's Story: A Book About a Boy with Autism
Zachary Gartenberg
Lerner Publications, 1998

Captain Tommy
Abby Word Messner
Future Horizons, 1999

Russell is Extra Special: A Book About Autism for Children
Charles Amenta III, M.D.
Magination Press, 1992

Ian's Walk: A Story about Autism
Laurie Lears
Albert Whitman & Company, 1998

Talking to Angels
Esther Watson
Harcourt Brace and Co., 1996

Videos

Video tapes can be very useful, but may a challenge to find, especially if they aren't new to the market. Try contacting the producers noted even if the tape isn't listed on their web site, book stores and your library.

A is for Autism
Available through Films for the Humanities and Sciences, 1994
Ph: (800) 257-5126
Web: http://www.iidc.indiana.edu/
Glimpse into autism spectrum disorders with words, drawings, music by people with autism.

Activating Communication Therapy: Autism
Center for Speech and Language Disorders, 1993
Ph: (630)530-8551
Web: http://www.iidc.indiana.edu/
Communication difficulties experienced by children with autism. Strategies for increasing communication efforts.

Autism

"The Doctor is In" Series
Dartmouth-Hitchcock Medical Center
Available through Fanlight Productions
4196 Washington St, Suite 2
Boston, MA 02131
Ph: (800) 937-4113
         (617) 469-4999
Fax: (617) 469-3379
E-mail: fanlight@fanlight.com
Web: http://www.fanlight.com/index.htm
Temple Grandin, Ph.D., describes growing up autistic.

Autism Awareness for Law Enforcement / Community Service Personnel

Harrisburg Chapter of the Autism Society of America, 1998
Order through Autism Society of America
Ph: (800) 3AUTISM
Behaviors associated with autism spectrum disorders, recommendations for how community members and law enforcement agencies should interact with these individuals.

Autism: Being Friends

Indiana Resource Center for Autism, 1991
2853 E. Tenth St.
Bloomington, IN 47408-2696
Ph: (812) 855-6508
Ph: (800) 437-7924
TTY: (812) 855-9396
Fax: (812) 855-9630
E-mail: prattc@indiana.edu
Web: http://www.iidc.indiana.edu/
Elementary school children's disability awareness education.

Autism: Learning More than Ever Before

Autism Research Institute
4182 Adams Ave.
San Diego, CA 92116
Fax: (619) 563-6840
Web: http://www.autism.com/ari
Bernard Rimland on early intervention, inclusion, aversives, vitamin treatment.

Autism Perspectives

Continuing Education Programs of America, 1996
Media/Publications Division
P.O. Box 52
Peoria, IL 61650
Ph: (309) 263-0310
Web: http://www.autism.com/cont_ed_prog/
Panel discussion on autism, pervasive developmental disorders.

Autism: A World Apart

Karen Cunninghame
Los Angeles Chapter, Autism Society of America
Available through Fanlight Productions
4196 Washington St, Suite 2
Boston, MA 02131
Ph: (800) 937-4113
         (617) 469-4999
Fax: (617) 469-3379
E-mail: fanlight@fanlight.com
Web: http://www.fanlight.com/index.htm
Three families show life with an autistic child.

Behind the Glass Door: Hannah's Story

Karen Pascal, Windborne Productions, 2000
Available through Fanlight Productions
4196 Washington St, Suite 2
Boston, MA 02131
Ph: (800) 937-4113
         (617) 469-4999
Fax: (617) 469-3379
E-mail: fanlight@fanlight.com
Web: http://www.fanlight.com/index.htm
Follow one family through five years of work with their autistic child and applied behavioral analysis.

Breaking the Silence Barrier

Thirteen/WNET, 1996
Order through Films for the Humanities and Sciences
Ph: (800) 257-5126
Creative technologies used to help people with autism, traumatic brain injuries, learning, speech disabilities.

Breakthrough: How to Reach Students with Autism
Karen Sewell, Attainment Company, 1998
Available through Child Development Media
5632 Van Nuys Blvd., Suite 286
Van Nuys, CA 91401
Ph: (800) 405-8942
Fax: (818) 994-6549
E-mail: info@childdevelopmentmedia.com
Web: http://www.childdevmedia.com/
Teaching methods for working with autistic children.

Bridges for Children with Autism
Helen Bloomer, 1997
Available through Child Development Media
5632 Van Nuys Blvd., Suite 286
Van Nuys, CA 91401
Ph: (800) 405-8942
Fax: (818) 994-6549
E-mail: info@childdevelopmentmedia.com
Web: http://www.childdevmedia.com/
Four tapes. Introduction to applied behavior analysis
(ABA) for children with autism.

But He Knows His Colors: Characteristics of Autism in Children Birth to Three
Univ. of New Mexico Health Sciences Center, 1995
Available through Child Development Media
5632 Van Nuys Blvd., Suite 286
Van Nuys, CA 91401
Ph: (800) 405-8942
Fax: (818) 994-6549
E-mail: info@childdevelopmentmedia.com
Web: http://www.childdevmedia.com/
Behaviors. Importance of early diagnosis, intervention.

Careers – Opportunity for Growth
Temple Grandin, Ph.D.
Future Horizons, 1999
721 W. Abram Street
Arlington, TX 76013
Ph: (800) 489-0727
Fax: (817) 277-2270
E-mail: info@futurehorizons-autism.com
Web: http://www.futurehorizons-autism.com/
Dr. Grandin's career journey as an autistic person.

Come Back Jack
Robert Parish, 1999
Come Back Jack Video
P.O. Box 44
Terrace Park, OH 45174
E-mail: backjack@fuse.net
Web: www.comebackjack.com
Parents responding to the autism diagnosis of their son.

Day by Day: Raising the Child with Autism/PDD
Joan Goodman, Susan Hoban, 1992
Available through Child Development Media
5632 Van Nuys Blvd., Suite 286
Van Nuys, CA 91401
Ph: (800) 405-8942
Fax: (818) 994-6549
E-mail: info@childdevelopmentmedia.com
Web: http://www.childdevmedia.com/
Lives of two preschool children with autism/PDD.

Discreet Trial Training
New York Families for Autistic Children, Inc.
Ph: (718) 641-6711
How to establish an applied behavior analysis program
using discreet trial teaching.

Every Step of the Way: Toward Independent Communication
Facilitated Communication Institute, Syracuse Univ.
370 Huntington Hall
Syracuse, NY 13244-2340
Ph: (315) 443-9657
Fax: (315) 443-2274
E-mail: fcstaff@sued.syr.edu
Web: http://soeweb.syr.edu/thefci/
Individuals working toward independent typing.

Making Contact – Sensory Integration & Autism
Continuing Education Programs of America
Media/Publications Division
P.O. Box 52
Peoria, IL 61650
Ph: (309) 263-0310
Web: http://www.autism.com/cont_ed_prog/
Sensory integration activities, benefits.

Understanding Autism
NewsCart Productions, Inc.
Available through Fanlight Productions
4196 Washington St, Suite 2
Boston, MA 02131
Ph: (800) 937-4113
        (617) 469-4999
Fax: (617) 469-3379
E-mail: info@fanlight.com
Web: http://www.fanlight.com/index.htm
Therapists, teachers, parents of children with autism
discuss symptoms, behavior modification.

Medications – Fact or Fiction
Temple Grandin, Ph.D.
Future Horizons, 1999
721 W. Abram Street
Arlington, TX 76013
Ph: (800) 489-0727
Fax: (817) 277-2270
E-mail: info@futurehorizons-autism.com
Web: http://www.futurehorizons-autism.com/
Medications available for people with autism.

Visual Thinking of a Person with Autism
Temple Grandin, Ph.D.
Available through Future Horizons, 1998
721 W. Abram Street
Arlington, TX 76013
Ph: (800) 489-0727
Fax: (817) 277-2270
E-mail: info@futurehorizons-autism.com
Web: http://www.futurehorizons-autism.com/
How autistic people think in pictures, adjusting for
this learning style.

A Sense of Belonging: Including Students with Autsim in Their School Community
Kim Davis, Cathy Pratt
Indiana Institute on Disability and Community, 1997
2853 E. Tenth St.
Bloomington, IN 47408-2696
Ph: (812) 855-6508
Ph: (800) 437-7924
TTY: (812) 855-9396
Fax: (812) 855-9630
E-mail: prattc@indiana.edu
Web: http://www.iidc.indiana.edu/
Value of inclusion. Strategies for teaching students with
autism.

Writing Social Stories
Carol Gray
Available through Future Horizons
721 W. Abram Street
Arlington, TX 76013
Ph: (800) 489-0727
Fax: (817) 277-2270
E-mail: info@futurehorizons-autism.com
Web: http://www.futurehorizons-autism.com/
Workshop.

Sensory Challenges and Answers
Temple Grandin
Available through Future Horizons
721 W. Abram Street
Arlington, TX 76013
Ph: (800) 489-0727
Fax: (817) 277-2270
E-mail: info@futurehorizons-autism.com
Web: http://www.futurehorizons-autism.com/
Sensory challenges facing people with autism.

Periodicals / Newsletters

Advocate Newsletter
Autism Society of America
7910 Woodmont Ave., Suite 300
Bethesda, MD 20814-3015
Ph: (800) 3AUTISM
       (301) 657-0881
Fax: (301) 657-0869
E-mail: info@autism-society.org
Web: http://www.autism-society.org/
Available with membership.

The ANDI News
Autism Network for Dietary Intervention (ANDI)
P.O. Box 17711
Rochester, NY 14617-0711
Web: http://www.autismndi.com/
Dietary intervention, information, advice, recipes.

Autism Research Review International
Autism Research Institute
4182 Adams Ave.
San Diego, CA 92116
Ph: (619) 281-7165
Fax: (619) 563-6840
Web: http://www.autism.com/ari/newslet.html
Reviews recent work on autism.

Focus on Autism and Other Developmental Disabilities
Autism Society of America
7910 Woodmont Ave., Suite 300
Bethesda, MD 20814-3015
Ph: (800) 3AUTISM
       (301) 657-0881
Fax: (301) 657-0869
E-mail: info@autism-society.org
Web: http://www.autism-society.org/
Practical elements of management, treatment, planning, education for persons with autism, PDD.

Journal of Autism and Developmental Disorders (JADD)
Autism Society of America
7910 Woodmont Ave., Suite 300
Bethesda, MD 20814-3015
Ph: (800) 3AUTISM
       (301) 657-0881
Fax: (301) 657-0869
E-mail: info@autism-society.org
Web: http://www.autism-society.org/
Current issues in autism and related disorders.

NAARRATIVE
National Alliance for Autism Research
414 Wall St., Research Park
Princeton, New Jersey 08540
Ph: (888) 777-NAAR
       (609) 430-9160
Fax: (609) 430-9163
E-mail: naar@naar.org
Web: http://www.naar.org/
Available to donors. Information about autism research, medical interventions.

The Sound Connection
Society for Auditory Intervention Techniques
P.O. Box 4538
Salem, OR 97302
Web:
http://www.teleport.com/~sait/table.html#sait
Auditory integration training, auditory interventions.

Web Sites

Also see "General Web Sites". Many have sections on autism, but they are not listed separately below.

Autism Biomedical Information Network
Web: http://www.autism-biomed.org/
Science-based information on autism.

Autism Home Page
Web: http://members.spree.com/autism/
Collection of scientific and developmental articles.

**Autism, PDD, Hyperlexia, Asperger's:
Therapy and Special Education**
Web: http://members.tripod.com/~Rsaffran/index.html
Large collection of information.

Autism-PDD Resources Net
Web: http://www.autism-pdd.net/
Broad range of autism-related information.

Autism Resources
Web: www.autism-resources.com
Collection of information on autism.

Autism Resources
Web: http://www.unc.edu/~cory/autism-info/
Large collection of information on autism.

Vendors

Autism Treatment Center of America
Son-Rise Program
2080 S Undermountain Road
Sheffield, MA 01257
Ph: (413) 229-2100
Fax: (413) 229-3202
E-mail: sunrise@option.org
Web: http://www.option.org/
Home-based/child-centered programs enabling children to improve in all areas of development.

Future Horizons
721 W. Abram St.
Arlington, TX 76013
Ph: (800) 489-0727
Fax: (817) 277-2270
E-mail: info@futurehorizons-autism.com
Web: http://www.futurehorizons-autism.com
Books, videos, conferences, more on autism/PDD.

Indiana Resource Center for Autism
Indiana Institute on Disability and Community
2853 E. Tenth Street
Bloomington, IN 47408-2696
Ph: (812) 855-6508
TT: (812) 855-9396
Fax: (812) 855-9630
E-mail: prattc@indiana.edu
Web: http://www.isdd.indiana.edu/~irca/
Large listing of video tapes.

PC Enterprise of Iowa
Ph: (888) 446-9272
E-mail: logit@iowapc.com
Web: http://www.iowapc.com/
Log-It software for recording discreet trial training therapy.

---- *Bipolar Disorder (Manic Depression)*

A brain disorder that causes cyclical mood swings from euphoria and high energy to depression and anger, and then back again. The length of time that it takes to complete a cycle can vary, from minutes to years. Typically, a person with bipolar disorder will have eight to ten episodes of mania or depression in a lifetime. Rapid cyclers may have many more. Milder forms of the illness are far more common than full-blown bipolar disorder.

Also called
- Manic depression.
- Hypomania.
- Rapid cycling bipolar disorder.
- Schizoaffective disorder (in which one straddles the line between schizophrenia and bipolar disorder.)

Frequency
- At least 2 million Americans suffer from bipolarity.
- 3 to 4% of the general population account for the milder forms of the illness.
- Onset is typically between ages 18-44, (20-30 being most common), but may occur either earlier or later in life. Infrequently seen before adolescence.
- Often begins with serious depression lasting for weeks or months. First manic episode may not appear until several years afterward. Less often, a manic episode is the first sign. Mania can erupt within hours, but frequently takes weeks to unfold.

Symptoms and Possible Effects
Manic symptoms
- ❑ Mood is happy, silly, euphoric, excited, enthusiastic.
- ❑ Unusually high self esteem.
- ❑ High energy and activity level, getting by on little sleep, distractible, jumping from one thing to the next, often to irrelevant things.
- ❑ Increased, pressured talking, racing thoughts, jumping between topics, joking, hard to understand.
- ❑ Risky behavior, not believing that they will be hurt.
- ❑ Outgoing, overly friendly.

❑ Feeling highly creative, starting projects but not completing them.
❑ Seeking adventure, often on a whim.
❑ Increased social activity.
❑ Heightened sexual drive and related sprees.
❑ May damage job or social relationships.
❑ Paranoia, feelings of being watched or controlled.
❑ Buying sprees.
❑ Annoyance with anyone interfering or disagreeing.
❑ Losing touch with reality and become increasingly psychotic, hearing voices encouraging eratic behavior.
❑ Irritability and paranoia.
❑ Delusions of grandeur such as having a relationship with a well-known person. Preoccupation with wealth and success.
❑ Poor judgment.
❑ Drinking to calm down.
❑ Insomnia.
❑ Pressured writing.
❑ Others seem slow.
❑ Inappropriate behavior.
❑ Feeling superior.
❑ Driving dangerously.
❑ Making unnecessary phone calls.
❑ More sensitive than usual.
❑ Inability to concentrate.
❑ Anxiety, feeling of being wound up, difficulty being still.
❑ Easily distracted by unimportant comments or events.
❑ Over or under eating.

Depressive symptoms
❑ Depression, sadness, crying.
❑ Loss of enjoyment in favorite activities.
❑ Headaches, stomachaches.
❑ Low energy level.
❑ Poor concentration, boredom.
❑ Oversleeping.
❑ Overeating.
❑ Self-doubt, hopelessness.

Some variations on bipolar disorder include:

Mixed states
Symptoms that are at odds with each other: elation and ecstasy mixed with irritability, anger and rage. They are very critical and complain a good deal, acting manipulative and obnoxious. They may be depressed and possibly suicidal. This mixture of behavior reflects both extremes of the illness coming out at one time. So the manic mood, rather than pleasant and exciting, is depressing and antagonistic.

Rapid cycling

Experiencing at least four complete mood cycles in a year. Some rapid cyclers can complete a mood cycle within days, some more rarely in hours. More common in women than men. Although the shifts from one state to another are usually gradual, they can also come suddenly, giving the impression that the person is dangerous and unpredictable.

Cyclothymia

Less severe form of bipolar disorder, with short and irregular cycles of depression and mania (may be days or weeks.) Neither the depression nor mania involved is extreme enough to be termed bipolar disorder. However, many people with cyclothymia eventually develop full-blown major depressive or manic episodes. Cyclothymia often begins in the teens or early childhood, appearing to be hyperactivity or a personality disorder. They may cycle from depression to mania day to day. Symptoms are similar to bipolar disorder, the difference being intensity.

Unipolar mania

A form of bipolar disorder in which the person has manic highs or recurring acute psychosis, but little depression. Mania can cause some people to become psychotic.

In children
- Younger children generally show intense, rapid cyclic symptoms.
- Irritability, anger and rage are prevalent.
- Depression may appear as withdrawal and inhibited behavior, extreme agitation or rage.
- May have intense interests, concentrating on things that they like for hours.
- Willful and self-directed.
- May be quite distractible with "boring" things.
- Attracted to visual-motor tasks and drawing, which is done with detail and imagination.
- Impulsive, may shoplift, abuse substances, have difficulties with the law or aggression.

Causes
- Unknown, but general belief is that it's caused by abnormal brain functioning.
- Genetic, chemical, hormonal, psychological, social and developmental factors may play a role.
- Manic-like episodes can be caused by somatic antidepressant treatment (e.g., medication, electroconvulsive therapy, light therapy) but are not bipolar disorder.
- Stress may trigger an episode but is not a cause of the illness.

What Else Could it Be?
Children with bipolar disorder have symptoms that mimic those of other conditions, such as those noted below. To properly diagnose a problem, these may need to be ruled out as causes for the problem.

- ✓ ADHD
- ✓ Addison's disease
- ✓ Antisocial behavior
- ✓ Cushing's syndrome
- ✓ Major depression
- ✓ Mood disorder due to a medical condition or substance abuse
- ✓ Multiple sclerosis
- ✓ Neurological problems such as Huntington's disease, brain tumors, encephalitis
- ✓ Panic attacks
- ✓ Porphyria (an inherited copper metabolism disorder)
- ✓ Schizophrenia
- ✓ Thyroid, liver or kidney disease
- ✓ Vitamin B-12 deficiency

Diagnostic Processes
Diagnosis can only be made through observation over time. Depends on recognizing the manic phase.

DSM IV Diagnostic Criteria
Reprinted with permission from the *Diagnostic and Statistical Manual of Mental Disorders, Fourth Edition, Text Revision.*
Copyright 2000 American Psychiatric Association.

For manic episode:
A. A distinct period of abnormally and persistently elevated, expansive, or irritable mood, lasting at least 1 week (or any duration if hospitalization is necessary).

B. During the period of mood disturbance, three (or more) of the following symptoms have persisted (four if the mood is only irritable) and have been present to a significant degree:
    (1) inflated self esteem or grandiosity
    (2) decreased need for sleep (e.g., feels rested after only 3 hours of sleep)
    (3) more talkative than usual or pressure to keep talking
    (4) flight of ideas or subjective experience that thoughts are racing
    (5) distractibility (i.e., attention too easily drawn to unimportant or irrelevant external stimuli)
    (6) increase in goal-directed activity (either socially, at work or school, or sexually) or psychomotor agitation
    (7) excessive involvement in pleasurable activities that have a high potential for painful consequences (e.g., engaging in unrestrained buying sprees, sexual indiscretions or foolish business investments)

C. The symptoms do not meet criteria for a Mixed Episode.

D. The mood disturbance is sufficiently severe to cause marked impairment in occupational functioning or in usual social activities or relationships with others, or to necessitate hospitalization to prevent harm to self or others, or there are psychotic features.

E. The symptoms are not due to the direct physiological effects of a substance (e.g., a drug of abuse, a medication, or other treatment) or a general medical condition (e.g., hyperthyroidism).

Treatment
Bipolar disorder is one of the most treatable psychiatric illnesses through:
- Medication.
- Psychotherapy.
- Education.
- Hospitalization if one:

- ➢ Can't care for him or herself
- ➢ Is at risk for suicide
- ➢ May harm others
- ➢ Doesn't have a safe, supportive living environment
- ➢ Needs detoxification from drugs or alcohol
- ➢ Has other mental or medical needs

- ➢ Doesn't improve in outpatient therapy
- ➢ Develops psychotic symptoms
- ➢ Has lost a sense of judgment
- ➢ Is out of control
- ➢ Has lost touch with reality

Outcomes
- Bipolar illness tends to be chronic and recurrent. Without treatment a manic episode can last as long as three months, and a depressive episode longer. With treatment episodes are milder and shorter. Even those on medication can have break through episodes of mania or depression, sometimes provoked by stress.
- The more intense the symptoms, the more likely that medication will be successful.
- Untreated mania may result in exhaustion and collapse through such problems as a heart attack, cerebral hemorrhage, dehydration.
- Untreated bipolar patients frequently attempt suicide.

Who to Contact
Also refer to "Who Else to Contact." Organizations listed below target their work specifically toward bipolar disorder. Also see section on depression.

Lithium Information Center
Madison Institute of Medicine
7617 Mineral Point Road, Suite 300
Madison, WI 53717
Ph: (608) 827-2470
Fax: (608) 827-2479
E-mail: mim@healthtechsys.com
Web:
http://www.healthtechsys.com/mimlithium.html
Information about the biomedical uses of lithium and other treatments for bipolar disorder.

National Depressive and Manic-Depressive Association (NDMDA)
730 N. Franklin St., Suite 501
Chicago, IL 60610-7204
Ph: (800) 826-3632
(312) 642-0049
Fax: (312) 642-7243
E-mail: nbunch@ndma.org
Web: http://www.ndmda.org/
Education on the nature of depressive and manic-depressive illness as treatable medical diseases; self-help for patients and families.

Recommended Reading

Agents in My Brain: How I Survived Manic Depression
Bill Hannon, Karen Dickson
Open Court Publishing Co., 1997

The Bipolar Child: The Definitive and Reassuring Guide to Childhood's Most Misunderstood Disorder
Demitri Papolos, M.D., Janice Papolos
Broadway Books, 1999

Bipolar Disorder: A Guide for Patients and Families
Francis Mondimore
John Hopkins University Press, 1999

Bipolar Puzzle Solution: A Mental Health Client's Perspective
Bryan Court, Gerald Nelson. M.D.
Accelerated Development Publishers, 1996

A Brilliant Madness: Living with Manic Depressive Illness
Patty Duke Austin, Gloria Hochman
Bantam Books, 1992

Call Me Anna
Patty Duke
Bantam Books, 1988

**Carbamazepine and Manic Depression:
A Guide, rev. ed.**
Janet Medenwald, M.D., John Greist, M.D., James
Jefferson, M.D.
Dean Foundation, 1996

**Cognitive-Behavioral Therapy for Bipolar
Disorder**
Monica Ramirez Basco, A. John Rush
Guilford Publications, 1996

**The Depression Workbook: A Guide for
Living with Depression and Manic Depression**
Mary Ellen Copeland, M.S., M.A.
New Harbinger Publications, 1992

Divalproex and Manic Depression: A Guide
James Jefferson, M.D., John Greist, M.D.
Lithium Information Center, 1996

**Hidden Epidemic: The Ups and Downs of
Manic Depression**
Vernon White
Morris Publishing, 1995

**Key to Genius: Manic Depression and the
Creative Life**
D. Jablow Hershman, Julian Lieb
Prometheus Books, 1988

**Lithium and Manic Depression: A Guide, rev.
ed.**
John Bohn, M.D., James Jefferson, M.D.
Lithium Information Center, 1996

**Living Without Depression and Manic
Depression: A Workbook for Maintaining
Mood Stability**
Mary Ellen Copeland
New Harbinger Publications, 1994

**A Mood Apart: The Thinker's Guide to
Emotion and Its Disorders**
Peter Whybrow, M.D.
Harper Perennial, 1998

The Looney Bin Trip
Kate Millett
Simon and Schuster, 1990

Moodswing, rev. ed.
Ronald Fieve, M.D.
Bantam Books, 1997

**On Mood Swings: The Psychobiology of Elation
and Depression**
Susanne Schad-Somers, S.P.
Plenum Press, 1990

**Surviving the Crisis of Depression and Bipolar
(Manic-Depression) Illness: Layperson's Guide
to Coping with Mental Illness Beyond the Time
of Crisis and Outside the Hospital**
Mark Halebsky
Personal and Professional Growth, 1997

Manic Depression and Creativity
D. Jablow Herscgnab, Julian Lieb
Prometheus Books, 1998

Manic Depression: Illness or Awakening
Robert Kelly
Knowledge Unlimited Publishers, 1995

**Touched by Fire: Manic Depressive Illness and
the Artistic Temperament**
Kay Redfield Jamison
Free Press, 1993

Overcoming Depression and Manic Depression (Bipolar Depression): The Non-Drug Approach
Paul Wider
Wider Pubs, 1993

We Heard the Angels of Madness: A Family Guide to Coping with Manic Depression
Diane Berger, Lisa Berger
William Morrow, 1992

Schizophrenia and Bipolar Disease: Often Misdiagnosed, Often Mistreated
Herbert Wagemaker
Ponte Vedra Pub., 1996

Win the Battle: The 3-Step Lifesaving Formula to Conquer Depression and Bipolar Disorder
Bob Olson
Chandler House, 1999

Videos

Video tapes can be very useful, but may a challenge to find, especially if they aren't new to the market. Try contacting the producers noted even if the tape isn't listed on their web site, book stores and your library.

Breaking the Dark Horse: A Family Copes With Manic Depression
Two Tents Media, 1994
Looks at one woman's struggle with manic depression and its effect on her family.

Understanding and Communicating with a Person Who is Experiencing Mania
Nurseminars, Inc.
12204 W. Sunridge Dr.
Nine Mile Falls, WA 99026
Ph: (509) 468-9848
Fax: (509) 466-6586
E-mail: marymoller@psychiatricwellness.com
Web: http://www.psychiatricwellness.com/nurseminars.html

Web Sites

Also see "General Web Sites". Many have sections on bipolarity, but they are not listed separately below.

Bipolar Disorder
Web: http://www.frii.com/~parrot/bip.html
Collection of information.

Pendulum Resources
Web: http://www.pendulum.org
Collection of information.

---- *Cerebral Palsy*

Cerebral palsy (C.P.) refers to a group of problems that can occur in a child's development from conception to age 5 as a result of brain injury during pregnancy or delivery (congenital C.P.) or an injury or illness after birth (acquired C.P.) Neurological, motor, development, and physical problems are possible. In its mildest form, C.P. may involve only minor muscle spasticity. More severe cases may result in immobility, loss of vision and hearing, and even mental retardation, though this is rare.

Frequency
- Affects 500,000-700,000 children and adults in the U.S. One of the most common congentical disorders.
- Affects approximately 1 in 200 children. This number is rising, however, with the survival rate of premature babies. Their risk of cerebral palsy is 50% higher than that of a full-term baby.

Types
Cerebral palsies are divided in to four groups based on the part of the brain that sustains the injury. The type of C.P. that a child has may change over time.

Spastic C.P.
60% of those with C.P. Spasticity refers to extreme muscle tightness, even to the point of being paralyzed. These children have stiff and jerky movements, difficulty in changing positions, tend to drop things. Learning disabilities and mental retardation are not the rule, but are not uncommon.

Subtypes of spastic C.P. are based on the parts of the body affected:

- *Diplegia* - affects one side of the body, mainly the child's legs, though arms may be affected to a lesser extent. Walking may be difficult. Because these children's upper bodies are usually not affected they can hold themselves upright and use their arms and hands. Occasionally, a child will have the use of their arms but not their legs.

- *Hemiplegia* - affects both arms or both legs, or an arm and leg on one side of the body. Many children with hemiplegia are able to walk and run, although awkwardly.

- *Quadriplegia* - affects all limbs, either equally or to a greater degree in the arms.

- *Monoplegia* - affects only one limb (very rare).

- *Triplegia* - affects three limbs (very rare).

Athetoid (Dystonic) C.P.
20% of those with C.P. A severe form of C.P. in which muscle tone varies across the entire body between too high (extreme stiffness) and too low (extreme floppiness). Children with athetoid C.P. have trouble holding themselves upright to sit or walk. They make large, random motor movements with their face, arms, and upper body, and have difficulty reaching for and hanging onto things.

However, a large percent of persons with athetoid C.P. have above average intelligence.

Ataxic C.P.
10% of those with C.P. Children may have balance and coordination problems, shaky hand movements, irregular speech. They also often have very poor balance and have an unsteady walk.

Mixed C.P.
10% of those with C.P. A mixture of other subtypes, for example spastic/athetoid (most common) or athetoid/ataxic (the least common.) Different parts of a child's body may be affected, depending on the part of the brain that was damaged and the extent of the damage. Muscle tone may be high in some parts of the body, but low in others.

Symptoms and Possible Effects
- Spasticity (increased muscle tone or reaction).
- Seizures (about half the children).
- Self-injurious behavior.
- Visual impairment/blindness.
- Hearing loss.
- Swallowing difficulties, food aspiration, drooling.
- Dental caries.
- Sleep disorders.
- Abnormal speech. Dysarthria is common, i.e., difficulty controlling the muscle and air flow needed to talk.
- Impaired motor skills involving any of the body's muscle groups, especially the arms and legs.
- Difficulty controlling facial expressions.
- Lack of coordination, difficulty in movement.
- Mental abilities range from normal functioning to severe retardation.
- 25-50% of children also have some form of learning disabilities.

Causes
- 25% of cases are from an intrauterine problem (e.g., virus, infection, exposure to radiation, drugs, chromosomal abnormalities, developmental brain abnormalities, anemia, other illnesses, lack of proper nutrition, alcohol exposure, premature delivery).

- 40% of cases are caused by lack of oxygen or a brain injury during birth or shortly after (e.g., meningitis, poisoning, head trauma). Oxygen loss can be caused by premature separation of the placenta from the wall of the uterus, awkward birth position of the baby, labor that is too long or too abrupt, interference with circulation in the umbilical cord.
- Maternal infections while the child is in utero, such as German measles/rubella, diabetes, radiation, toxemia.
- Premature birth, low birth weight.
- A-B-O blood type incompatibility between mother and infant.
- Multiple births.
- Infection that attacks an infant's nervous system.
- Intracranial bleeding.
- Ataxic CP is caused by damage to cerebellum.
- Causes during infancy include brain infection, viruses (e.g., meningitis or encephalitis), head trauma, loss of oxygen, brain tumor, cerebral vascular lesions. Brain scarring may occur up to the age of 5 and result in cerebral palsy.

What Can Be Going On at the Same Time?
The symptoms of C.P. depend on the area of the brain affected and the extent of the damage.

- Mental retardation.
- Seizures.
- Visual and auditory problems. A large number of children have a *strabismus*, a condition in which eyes don't align proprerly due to differences in the left and right eye muscles.
- Blindness.
- Behavior problems.
- Epilepsy or seizures.
- Deafness.
- Mental impairment. One third are not impaired, one third are mildly impaired, and the remaining third are moderately to severely impaired.
- Failure to thrive is common in children with moderate to severe C.P.
- Sensation and perception problems.

Diagnostic Processes
For the full-term baby with no risk factors, it may be difficult to diagnose cerebral palsy before the first year of age. Significant delays in normal developmental (e.g., reaching for toys, sitting, walking) are considered, as are abnormal muscle tone and movements, the persistence of infantile reflexes.

If a child is only mildly delayed, a diagnosis may not be possible until she is a year old, and the full extent of the disability may be not seen for yet another year.

For children at high risk for cerebral palsy, however, cerebral palsy may be diagnosed much earlier.

Treatment
Prebirth prevention:
- The mother is healthy before conception.
- The mother receives early, continual prenatal care.
- The mother has all needed immunizations before becoming pregnant.

Newborns are:
- Treated for jaundice if necessary.
- Protected from accidents or injury.

A child may benefit from therapy to ease the symptoms of C.P.:
- Physical therapy to help develop muscle control and maintain balance.
- Speech and language therapy.
- Occupational therapy.
- Recreation therapy.
- Neurodevelopmental therapy.
- Point pressure therapy.
- Hydrotherapy.
- Neuromuscular electrical stimulation.
- Exercise programs can improve control of movement and prevent deformities.
- Surgery to release tight muscle tendons which cause spasticity.
- Medications may help prevent seizures and ease spasticity.

Outcomes

The damage that causes C.P. does not get worse with age. However, the effects of C.P. can cause additional problems later; uncorrected posture, for example, can cause stress on other parts of the body, resulting in new problems. Some children lose some of the evidence of being affected by C.P. as they get older. Having C.P. doesn't necessarily prevent one from leading a full and independent life.

Who to Contact

Also refer to "Who Else to Contact." Organizations listed below target their work specifically toward cerebral palsy.

American Academy for Cerebral Palsy and Developmental Medicine
6300 North River Road, Suite 727
Rosemont, IL 60018-4226
Ph: (847) 698 1635
Fax: (847) 823-0536
E-mail: woppenhe@ucla.edu
Web: http://www.aacpdm.org/home_basic.html
Studies C.P., other childhood onset disabilities, promotes professional education for the treatment and management of these conditions.

Motion Analysis and Motor Performance Laboratory
University of Virginia, Health Sciences Center
2270 Ivy Road
Charlottesville, VA 22903
Ph: (804) 982-0848
E-mail: dvc2d@virginia.edu
Web: http://www.med.virginia.edu/medcntr/gaitlab/home.html
Studies neuromuscular disorders and spinal injuries.

Capital Association for Conductive Education
2445 Army-Navy Dr., 3rd Floor
Arlington, VA 22206
Ph: (703) 920-0600
E-mail: CapitalCE@aol.com
Web: http://members.aol.com/jimceleste/cond_ed/index.html
Promotes conductive education, learning system for children with motor disorders.

National Ataxia Foundation
2600 Fernbrook Lane, Suite 119
Minneapolis, MN 55447
Ph: (763) 553-0020
Fax: (763) 553-0167
E-mail: naf@ataxia.org
Web: http://www.ataxia.org/
Information, research on hereditary ataxia.

United Cerebral Palsy Association
1660 L St., NW, Suite 700
Washington, DC 20036
Ph: (800) USA-5-UC
       (202) 776-0406
TTY: (202) 973-7197
Fax: (202) 776-0414
E-mail: ucpnatl@ucpa.org
Web: http://www.ucpa.org/
Information and services for people with C.P.

United States Cerebral Palsy Athletic Association
200 Harrison Ave.
Newport, RI 02840
Ph: (401) 792-7130
Fax: (401) 792-7132
E-mail: uscpaa@mail.bbsnet.com
Web: http://www.uscpaa.org/
Individualized sports training, competitive opportunities for athletes with C.P. and related challenges.

Recommended Reading

Cerebral Palsy
Nathan Aaseng
Franklin Watts Inc., 1991

Each of Us Remembers the Day We Learned Our Child had Cerebral Palsy
Sally Weiss
United Cerebral Palsy Associations, Inc., 1993

Cerebral Palsy: A Complete Guide for Caregiving
Steven Bachrach, M.D., Freeman Miller, M.D.
John Hopkins University Press, 1998

Gait Analysis in Cerebral Palsy
James Gage
Cambridge University Press, 1991

Children with Cerebral Palsy: A Parent's Guide, 2nd ed.
Elaine Geralis (Ed.)
Woodbine House, 1998

Keys to Parenting a Child with Cerebral Palsy
Jane Faulkner Leonard, Margaret Myers, Sherri Cadenhead
Barron's Educational Series, Inc., 1997

Coping with Cerebral Palsy: Answers to Questions Parents Often Ask
Jay Schleichkorn
PRO-ED, 1996

Management of Motor Disorders of Children with Cerebral Palsy
David Scrutton (Ed.)
Cambridge University Press, 1991

Cerebral Palsy: A Complete Guide for Caregiving
Steven Bachrach, M.D., Freeman Miller, M.D.
John Hopkins University Press, 1998

More than an Average Guy: The Story of Larry Patton
Janet Kastner
Life Enrichment Publishers, 1989

Children with Cerebral Palsy: A Parent's Guide, 2nd ed.
Elaine Geralis (Ed.)
Woodbine House, 1998

The Natural History of Cerebral Palsy
Bronson Crothers, Richmond Paine
Cambridge University Press, 1991

Coping with Cerebral Palsy: Answers to Questions Parents Often Ask
Jay Schleichkorn
PRO-ED, 1996

Neurophysiological Basis for the Treatment of Cerebral Palsy, rev. ed.
Karel Bobath
Cambridge University Press, 1997

Training Guide to Cerebral Palsy Sports: The Recognized Training Guide of the United States Cerebral Palsy Athletic Association, 3rd ed.
Jeffery Jones (Ed.)
Human Kinetics Publishers, 1988

Uncommon Voyage: Parenting a Special Needs Child in the World of Alternative Medicine
Laura Shapiro Kramer, Seth Kramer
Faber and Faber, 1996

For Youth

Andy Opens Wide
Nan Holcomb
Jason and Nordic, 1990

I'm Joshua and "Yes, I Can!"
Joan Whinston
Joshua Books

Barry's Sister
Lois Metzger
S&S Children's, 1992

Imagine Me on a Sit-Ski!: A Concept Book
Nadine Bernard Westcott
Albert Whitman and Co., 1994

Danny and the Merry-Go-Round
Nan Holcomb
Jason and Nordic Pub., 1992

It's Your Turn at Bat
Barbara Aiello
Twenty-First Century Books, 1988

Dinosaur Hill
Diana Loski
Writer's Press, 1995

Mine for Keeps
Jean Little
Viking Chi, 1995

Eddie's Blue Winged Dragon
Carole Adler
Putnam Publishing Group, 1988

Sara's Secret
Suzanne Wanous
Lerner Publications, 1995

Going Places: Children Living with Cerebral Palsy
Thomas Bergman
Gareth Stevens Inc., 1991

Smile from Andy
Nan Holcomb
Jason and Nordic, 1992

Howie Helps Himself
Joan Fassler
Albert Whitman and Co., 1991

Under the Eye of the Clock: The Life Story of Christopher Nolan
Christopher Nolan, John Carey
St. Martin's Press, 1987

I'm the Big Sister Now
Michelle Emmert
Albert Whitman and Co., 1991

Yes, I Can: Challenging Cerebral Palsy
Doris Sanford
Multnomah Press, 1993

Web Sites
Also see "General Web Sites". Many have sections on cerebral palsy, but they are not listed separately below.

Cerebral Palsy: A Multimedia Tutorial for Children and Parents
Web:
http://www.people.virginia.edu/~smb4v/tutorials/cp/cp.htm
Primer on cerebral palsy.

Mariposa Ministry
Web: http://www.satcom.net/mariposa/
Explores what it means to live with a physical disability.

---- *Depression*

A mood disorder in which one feels hopeless or desperate. Depression can occur as a result of current circumstances or a chemical imbalance and can last for varying periods of time with different intensities and outcomes.

Also called / types:
- Anhedonia
- Atypical depression
- Bipolar disorder
- Cyclothymia
- Double depression
- Dysthymia
- Endogenous depression
- Low-grade depression
- Major depression
- Manic depression
- Melancholic depression
- Monopolar disorder
- Postpartum depression
- Primary depression
- Psychotic depression
- Reactive depression
- Seasonal affective disorder
- Secondary depression
- Unipolar disorder
- Winter blues, winter depression

Frequency
- 1 in 20 Americans suffer from depression severe enough to need medical treatment.
- Affects 2-5 times as many woman as men.
- Less than 1% of preschool children suffer from depression.
- 10% of children experience major depression before age 15 that lasts for a year. For boys, this rate is constant for several years. For girls, the rate increases to 16% during ages 14-16.
- By age 18, 20% of teens have suffered at least one episode of major depression.
- Median age of onset of major depressive episodes is 24.

- Rates of depression worldwide are rapidly increasing.
- Dysthymia is about half as common as major depression, but lasts longer (up to 5 years.) The presence of dysthymia increases the likelihood that a person will experience major depression.
- Seasonal affective disorder accounts for 1 in 3 cases of depression, with more women diagnosed than men.

Suicide
- At least 10% of people with major depression end their lives by suicide.
- 500,000 teens attempt suicide annually.
- The third leading cause of death, behind unintentional injury and homicide.
- 11% of high school students admit to having made at least one suicide attempt.
- 60% of people who succeed at their suicide have made a previous attempt.
- Adolescent girls outnumber boys in attempts (3-4 times more), but boys outnumber girls in success (3-4 times).
- Suicidal behavior is less common before puberty, with the incidences increasing and peaking at age 15, then trailing off again by late teens.
- Suicide rates are significantly higher among teens who abuse alcohol or drugs. 40% of all teen suicides are done while under the influence of drugs or alcohol.
- The suicide rates of those with mental illness are 12 times higher than for the rest of the population.
- White males and females account for 90% of suicides in the U.S.

Symptoms and Possible Effects
- ❑ May express guilt, self-reproach over many things, some imagined.
- ❑ Decreased concentration, thoughts of death, anxiety; nightmares.
- ❑ Play, fantasies and drawing themes may show depression.
- ❑ Prone to hear voices.
- ❑ Tearful, sad, irritable. Low self esteem.
- ❑ Symptoms of major depression in children and adolescents match those of adults.
- ❑ Stomach aches, headaches.
- ❑ Loss of interest in pleasurable activities, school, play.
- ❑ Low energy, fatigue, poor concentration, listlessness.
- ❑ May revert to childlike behaviors, e.g., thumb sucking.
- ❑ Phobias or unwarranted fears.
- ❑ Refusal to go to school.
- ❑ Angry, destructive behavior.
- ❑ Mood and behavior changes.

Teenagers
- ❑ Teens show depression differently than adults, being extremely angry, irritable, rebellious. They may act out their feelings through school problems, truancy, sexual activity, drinking, drug abuse, stealing, running away from home. May be hyperactive.
- ❑ Restless, irritable, argumentative.
- ❑ Poor school performance.
- ❑ Social withdrawal.
- ❑ Obsessed with spending time with friends.

Adolescents
- ❑ Antisocial behavior, increased difficulty in school, perhaps dropping out.
- ❑ Drug, alcohol abuse.
- ❑ Depression can occur as they try to separate from their parents and learn to make their own decisions.
- ❑ Frequently express anger toward parents.

School-age children
- ❑ Though rare under age 10, suicide is not impossible.
- ❑ Irritable, pick fights, talk back, throw tantrums, are argumentative.
- ❑ Complain of aches and pains.
- ❑ May feel guilty because they fear their negative feelings might actually harm their parents.
- ❑ May cry over things that would ordinarily not upset them.
- ❑ More easily bothered by things.
- ❑ May appear more fragile and unhappy. May stop smiling.
- ❑ Guilt and hopelessness may be present, but not obvious.
- ❑ Refusal to attend school.
- ❑ Some children, notably girls, may suffer silently, looking like "good" children.
- ❑ The younger the child, the longer the depression.
- ❑ May have fewer close friends and their friendships don't last as long as those of other children.
- ❑ Shy, likely to be teased.
- ❑ Low self esteem.
- ❑ May do poorly in school. Depressed children may be placed at levels below their capabilities. Their difficulty with concentration leads to lack of interest, distraction, fatigue, and inability to do homework.

Preschoolers
- ❑ May have suicidal thoughts and high-risk activities, such as throwing themselves in front of cars or jumping out of windows.
- ❑ Tantrums, clinginess, regression in speech, toilet training.
- ❑ May occur as a result of abuse, neglect, trauma.

Infants
- ❑ Withdrawal, lose interest in things around them, may stop eating. Infants may suffer depression if they experience early separation from their mothers, neglect or only superficial care.

Atypical depression
- ❑ Many of the vegetative symptoms seen in major depression are reversed in atypical depression.
- ❑ Agitation.
- ❑ Unmotivated.
- ❑ Overeats, oversleeps, gains weight rapidly.
- ❑ Feels worse at the end of the day.
- ❑ Feels controlled by external events.
- ❑ Sensitive to rejection, especially romantic.
- ❑ Can last for years or a lifetime.

Cyclothymia

❑ Chronic mood disorder in which one's mood alternates between elation and depression. The cause of mood swings usually isn't related to one's external environment.

❑ Sometimes considered a type of bipolar disorder, but differs in that the individual is not greatly impaired at work or socially during hypomanic episodes. Also called *cyclic disorder.*

❑ Anxiety due to rapid mood changes.

❑ In the elation phase, one has little need for sleep, an inflated self-concept, talks excessively, and has a high sex drive. In the depressive phase, one's self-concept declines, she withdraws from people, has decreased sex drive, and a negative attitude toward goals.

❑ Is associated with young adulthood.

❑ More girls are affected than boys.

❑ Tends to be a long-lasting condition.

❑ Treated with medications, psychotherapy.

Dysthymia or chronic depression

❑ Low grade, long-term depression that can go on for years or a lifetime.

❑ Poor appetite or overeating.

❑ Insomnia or excessive sleeping.

❑ Low energy, fatigue.

❑ Low self esteem.

❑ Poor concentration, difficulty making decisions.

❑ Feelings of hopelessness.

❑ In children, disobedient behavior is the most prevalent feature.

❑ Energy is used for work, with none left for leisure and family/social activities.

❑ May develop as a result of a pre-existing, chronic condition, such as ADHD, an eating disorder, anxiety disorder, or other chronic health challenge.

❑ Usually begins in childhood, adolescence or early adult life.

❑ Almost always accompanied by other psychiatric conditions.

❑ Referred to as "depressive personality".

❑ Often preceeds full depression by as much as 3 years.

Double depression

❑ Major depressive episode occurring after two years of dysthymia.

❑ Frequently dysthymic symptoms return after the major depressive episode ends.

❑ The longer the major depression, the more likely dysthymia will return.

Major depression

❑ Lasts for months. If untreated, it tends to recur, each episode lasting longer and intensifying.

❑ Depressed or cranky, irritable for no obvious reason. Unable to tolerate frustration; has angry outbursts. Usually more apparent at home than in other settings. Picks fights with family members. Mood may fluctuate during a day. Feels lonely, unloved, self pitying.

❑ Has little interest or pleasure in most activities (referred to as "anhedonia.") Feels that everything is boring or dumb.

❑ May lose interest in friends and social activities.

❑ Significant weight loss or gain, significant change in appetite. Those who become big eaters crave and may hoard carbohydrates and junk food. Carbohydrate craving is especially likely in those who suffer from seasonal affective disorder.

❑ Insomnia, excessive sleeping. These children, many of whom also suffer from anxiety disorders, can't tolerate sleeping alone. Switch days and night sleep patterns. Have bad dreams. Aren't refreshed by sleep.

❑ Physical restlessness or slowed body movement and speech. May be restless, fidgety, pace, wring hands, fiddle nervously with clothes, hair, etc.

❑ Fatigue, low energy may vary in a predictable pattern over the day, morning being the hardest. Even small tasks feel overwhelming. Child may lie around, stare at the TV.

❑ Low self esteem, excessive guilt. Reluctant to try new activities. Critical of own performance. May have an "I don't care" attitude.

❑ Sensitive to criticism and brood over any slight.

❑ Evaluate the world in negative terms.

❑ Have difficulty thinking, concentrating, making decisions.

❑ School performance drops.

❑ Recurrent thoughts of death or suicide. Adolescents may gravitate toward music and literature that focus on these things.

❑ Delusions are rare but point to bipolar disorder. Auditory hallucinations are fairly common in younger children who suffer from depression.

❑ Depressed youth are anxious. They develop unreasonable fears, worry.

❑ Boys are more likely to act out aggressively or destructively. Girls are more likely to be sexually promiscuous or develop eating disorders. Alternately, both may lose interet in sex.

❑ Self-destructive behaviors (lying, stealing, fighting, skipping class, or running away from home) to avoid facing their feelings.

❑ Fearful, overwhelmed.

❑ Fear being alone.

❑ Preoccupation with failure, illness, other unpleasant things.

❑ Unexplained anxiety, panic attacks.

❑ Vague aches and pains, heaviness in chest.

❑ Constipation.

Seasonal affective disorder (S.A.D.)

A special kind of depression that occurs in the wintertime. Not the same as the winter blues or cabin fever, in which people feel housebound and restless. S.A.D is a response to the winter's decreased sunlight. As a result, light therapy is the prime treatment method. S.A.D.'s hallmarks are depressed mood and fatigue, which run annually from around September to April, but are worst in the darkest months of the year. Conversely, most S.A.D. sufferers experience elation, even hypomania in the summer. Additional possible symptoms:

❑ Sleep problems. One oversleeps but doesn't feel refreshed after sleeping. Getting out of bed is a challenge and a daytime nap is needed.

❑ Overeating, carbohydrate craving, weight gain.

❑ Depression. Normal tasks become difficult. One feels hopeless, guilty, desperate, anxious.

❑ Low energy, low productivity.

❑ Pain in joints, stomach problems, low resistance to infection.

❑ Withdrawal from social activities. Behavioral problems.

❑ Irritable. Feels indifferent to events and people.

❑ Females report worsening of premenstrual symptoms.

❑ S.A.D. requires professional evaluation and treatment. Treatment typically is light therapy which changes a person's circadian rhythms. Light therapy consists of a set of fluorescent bulbs installed in a box with a diffusing screen, and set up on a table or desk top at which one can sit.

Triggers and signs of depression, potential suicide

❑ Holidays.
❑ Beginning or ending therapy for depression.
❑ Negative experience with others (e.g., parents, teachers, boss).
❑ Natural events.
❑ Substance abuse.
❑ Death fantasy.
❑ Bipolar disorder, depression, other psychiatric conditions.
❑ Poor view of the future.
❑ Desire to escape or control others.
❑ Family history of suicidal behavior.
❑ Family dysfunction.
❑ Poor social skills, few friends.
❑ Stressful life events.
❑ Low self esteem.
❑ Talking about suicide, threatening it overtly or in veiled terms.
❑ Prior suicide attempts.
❑ Severe mood problems.
❑ Excessive alcohol consumption or substance abuse.
❑ Dramatic change in eating or sleeping habits.
❑ Dramatic drop in school performance.
❑ Sudden loss of interest in activities and possessions, giving possessions away.
❑ Extreme restlessness or irritability.
❑ Feelings of hopelessness, worthlessness, self-hatred.
❑ Personality change.
❑ Disregard for appearance.
❑ Preoccupation with death or morbid themes.
❑ Acquisition of a means of suicide, e.g., rope, gun, hose.
❑ Social failure, trouble with family life.
❑ Sudden elevation of mood in a depressed child.
❑ Increased accidents or multiple physical complaints with no medical basis.
❑ Loss of a friend, relative or parent.
❑ Sudden or dramatic changes in behavior.
❑ Withdrawal from friends.
❑ Making a will.
❑ Taking unusual risks.
❑ Fatigue.
❑ Self-mutilation.

Causes

▪ 90% of the teens who commit suicide have a psychiatric diagnosis, most often a form of mood disorder, alcohol or substance abuse.
▪ The neurotransmitter, serotonin, is involved in sleep and mood regulation. If serotonin levels fall too low, one's mood drops, needs for sleep and food diminish, activity levels and speech slow down, self esteem is damaged. Antidepressants help restore normal levels of serotonin.

- Some physical illnesses will produce depression, which typically disappears after the illness is treated:
  - Hypothyroidism can produce severe depression and occurs more frequently than is thought, especially among women.
  - Anemia.
  - Hormone therapies.
  - Chronic illnesses such as AIDS or MS which drain one's immune system.

- 60% of teens who commit suicide have one or more of the following in their history:
  - A mother who had no prenatal care for the first 5 months of her pregnancy.
  - A mother who had a chronic disease during her pregnancy.
  - Respiratory distress for more than one hour after birth.
  - Over supply of vitamin C or D.
  - Life events, trauma, stress.
  - Struggles involved with learning and other disabilities.

What Can Be Going On at the Same Time?

50% of adolescents who are clinically depressed also have an anxiety disorder. In 85% of cases, the anxiety disorder came first.

What Else Could it Be?

Children with depression have symptoms that mimic those of other conditions, such as those noted below. To properly diagnose a problem, these may need to be ruled out as causes.

- ✓ ADHD
- ✓ Adjustment disorder with depressed mood
- ✓ Bereavement
- ✓ Manic episodes

- ✓ Mood disorder due to a general medical condition
- ✓ Sadness
- ✓ Substance-induced mood disorder

Diagnostic Processes

Mood disorders in children and adolescents are hard to diagnose because:

- Children have difficulty expressing their feelings.
- Symptoms take on different forms in children than adults.
- They are often accompanied by other psychiatric disorders that overshadow depression.
- Physicians tend to think of depression and bipolar disorder as illnesses of adulthood.

Steps in diagnosis include:
- Looking at the child's history of:
  - Development (pregnancy, labor, delivery, newborn behavior, development)
  - Medical concerns
  - Temperament, fears
  - Education.
- Conducting a medical and neurological exam to rule out other illnesses.
- Looking at family life.
- Interviewing parents and the child in different sessions.

DSM IV Diagnostic Criteria (for major depressive episodes)

Reprinted with permission from the *Diagnostic and Statistical Manual of Mental Disorders, Fourth Edition, Text Revision.* Copyright 2000 American Psychiatric Association.

A. Five (or more) of the following symptoms have been present during the same 2-week period and represent a change from previous functioning; at least one of the symptoms is either (1) depressed mood or (2) loss of interest or pleasure.

    (1) depressed mood most of the day, nearly every day, as indicated by either subjective report (e.g., feels sad or empty) or observation made by others (e.g., appears tearful). NOTE: In children and adolescents, can be irritable mood.

    (2) markedly diminished interest or pleasure in all, or almost all, activities most of the day, nearly every day (as indicated by either subjective account or observation made by others)

    (3) significant weight loss when not dieting or weight gain (e.g., a change of more than 5% of body weight in a month), or decrease or increase in appetite nearly every day. Note: In children, consider failure to make expected weight gains.

    (4) insomnia or hypersomnia nearly every day

    (5) psychomotor agitation or retardation nearly every day (observable by others, not merely subjective feelings of restlessness or being slowed down)

    (6) fatigue or loss of energy nearly every day

    (7) feelings of worthlessness or excessive or inappropriate guilt (which may be delusional) nearly every day (not merely self-reproach or guilt about being sick)

    (8) diminished ability to think or concentrate, or indecisiveness, nearly every day (either by subjective account or as observed by others)

    (9) recurrent thoughts of death (not just fear of dying), recurrent suicidal ideation without a specific plan, or a suicide attempt or a specific plan for committing suicide.

B. The symptoms do not meet criteria for a Mixed Episode.

C. The symptoms cause clinically significant distress or impairment in social, occupational, or other important areas of functioning.

D. The symptoms are not due to the direct physiological effects of a substance (e.g., a drug of abuse, a medication) or a general medical condition (e.g., hypothyroidism).

E. The symptoms are not better accounted for by Bereavement, i.e., after the loss of a loved one, the symptoms persist for longer than 2 months or are characterized by marked functional impairment, morbid preoccupation with worthlessness, suicidal ideation, psychotic symptoms, or psychomotor retardation.

Treatment

- Medication.
- Therapy such as psychotherapy, behavior, cognitive, family, counseling.
- Light therapy for seasonal affective disorder.
- Hospitalization.
- Exercise for light to moderate depression.
- In the case of suicide threats, keeping communication lines open, setting limits, providing support, ensuring a child's safety, getting professional help immediately.

- Electroconvulsive treatment. Though controversial, it can be effective in reducing suicide risk, and can be helpful when other treatments have failed.
- Taking prompt action to prevent depressive behaviors from becoming habits, to avoid interference with a child learning to become independent, develop competence and establish an identity.

Outcomes
At least half the children who experience a clinical depression will have subsequent bouts as an adult.

Who to Contact
Also refer to "Who Else to Contact." See "Bipolar Disorder" for organizations related specifically to that disorder. Organizations listed below target their work toward depression and suicide.

American Association of Suicidology
4201 Connecticut Ave NW, Suite 408
Washington, DC 20008
Ph: (202) 237-2280
Fax: (202) 237-2282
E-mail: ajkulp0124@ix.netcom.com
Web: http://www.suicidology.org/
Promotes research, public awareness, education for professsionals and volunteers.

American Foundation for Suicide Prevention
120 Wall St., 22nd Floor
New York, NY 10005
Ph (888) 333-AFSP
(212) 363-3500
E-mail: inquiry@afsp.org
Web: http://www.afsp.org
Supports research, provides information, professional education, publicity. Supports programs to advance knowledge of suicide and prevention.

Depressed Anonymous
P.O. Box 17471
Louisville, KY 40217
Ph: (502) 459-6700
E-mail: info@depressedanon.com
Web: http://www.depressedanon.com
Therapeutic resources for depressed individuals and those recently discharged from health facilities.

Depression After Delivery Support Groups
P.O. Box 59973
Renton, Washington 98058
Ph: (206) 283-9278
Web: http://www.behavenet.com/dadsgwa/
Support, education, referral for women and families coping with mental health issues associated with childbearing, during and after pregnancy.

Depression and Related Affective Disorders Association (DRADA)
Meyer 3-181
600 North Wolfe St.
Baltimore, MD 21287-7381
Ph: (410) 955-4647
(202) 955-5800
E-mail: drada@jhmi.edu
Web: http://www.med.jhu.edu/drada
Self-help groups, education and information, research.

National Foundation for Depressive Illness, Inc.
P.O. Box 2257
New York, NY 10116
Ph: (800) 239-1265
Web: http://www.depression.org/
Educates the public and professionals about depression, its consequences and its treatability.

Suicide Awareness Voices of Education (SA/VE)
7317 Cahill Road, Suite207
Minneapolis, MN 55424-0507
Ph: (952) 946-7998
(800) 784-2433 Hotline
E-mail: save@winternet.com
Web: http://www.save.org
Educates about suicide and its prevention.

Recommended Reading

100 Ways to Overcome Depression
Frank Minirth, Paul Meier, States Skipper
Fleming H. Revell Co., 1993

Adolescent Suicidal Behavior
David Curran
Hemisphere Publishing Corp., 1987

Adolescent Suicide
Paul Robbins
McFarland, 1997

Adolescent Suicide: Recognition, Treatment and Prevention
Gordon Garfinkel, M.D., Gordon Northrup, M.D. (Eds.)
Haworth Press, Inc., 1990

Adolescent Suicide: A School-Based Approach to Assessment and Intervention
William Kirk
Research Press, 1993

After Suicide: A Ray of Hope
Eleanora "Betsy" Ross
Lynn Publications, 1990

Andrew, You Died Too Soon: A Family Experience of Grieving and Living Again
Corinne Chilstrom
Augsburg Fortress, 1994

Anorexia, Murder and Suicide
David Malan
Butterworth-Heinemann, 1997

Anxiety and Depression in Adults and Children
Keith Dobson
Sage Publications, Inc., 1995

Ask the Doctor: Depression
Vincent Friedewald
Andrews McMeel Publishing, 1998

Assessment and Management of the Suicidal Adolescent
Lawrence Clayton, Ph.D.
Essential Med. Info. S., 1990

Assessment and Prediction of Suicide
Ronald Maris, John Maltsberger, Alan Berman, Robert Yufit (Eds.)
Guilford Publications, 1992

Awakening from Depression: A Mind-Body Approach to Emotional Recovery
Jerome Marmorstein, Nanette Marmorstein
Woodbridge, 1991

The Beast: A Journey Through Depression
Tracy Thompson
Plume, 1996

Beat Depression with St. John's Wort
Steven Bratman
Prima Publishing, 1987

Befriending Your Teenager: How to Prevent a Crisis from Happening
William Grimbol
Augsburg Fortress Pubs., 1991

Being Present in the Darkness: Using Depression as a Tool for Self-Discovery
Cheri Huber
Perigee, 1996

Ben's Story: The Symptoms of Depression, ADHD, and Anxiety That Caused His Suicide
Trudy Carlson
Benline Press, 1998

The Best Little Girl Says Good-bye:
A Therapist Grieves
Blanche Goodwin
Routledge, 1996

Beyond the Darkness: My Near-Death Journey
to the Edge of Hell and Back
Angie Fenimore
Bantam Books, 1995

Black Sun: Depression and Melancholia
Julia Kristeva
Columbia University Press, 1991

Breaking the Patterns of Depression
Michael Yapko, Ph.D.
Doubleday & Co., 1998

Breaking the Silence: A Guide to Help
Children with Complicated Grief: Suicide,
Homicide, Aids, Violence, and Abuse
Linda Goldman
Accelerated Development, 1996

Can I Get a Witness? For Sisters, When the
Blues is More Than a Song
Julia Boyd
E.P. Dutton, 1998

Childhood Depression: School-Based
Intervention
Kevin Stark
Guilford Publications, 1990

The Childhood Depression Sourcebook
Jeffrey Miller, Ph. D.
Lowell House, 1999

Children Who Don't Want to Live
Israel Orbach
Jossey-Bass Publishers, 1988

Choosing to Live: How to Defeat Suicide
through Cognitive Therapy
Thomas Ellis, Cory Newman
New Harbinger Publications, 1996

The Complete Idiot's Guide to Beating the Blues
Ellen McGrath, Marcela Kogan
Macmillan Publishing, 1999

Conquering Depression: Heavenly Wisdom
from God Illumined Teachers
St. Herman Press
Saint Herman of Alaska Brotherhood, 1996

Contagious Emotions: Staying Well When Your
Loved One is Depressed
Ronald Podell, M.D., Porter Shimer
Pocket Books, 1993

Contemplating Suicide: The Language of Ethics
and Self-Harm
Gavin Fairbairn
Routledge, 1995

Coping with Depression: The Common Cold of
the Emotional Life
Siang-Yang Tan, John Ortberg
Baker Books, 1995

Coping with Suicide: A Resource Book for
Teenagers and Young Adults, rev. ed.
Judie Smith
Rosen Publishing Group, 1989

Counseling the Depressed
Archibald Hart, Ph. D.
Word Publishing, 1994

Counseling for Depression
Paul Gilbert
Sage Publications, Inc., 1992

The Cruelest Death: The Enigma Of Adolescent Suicide
David Lester
Charles Press Publishers, 1993

Dealing with Depression Naturally: The Drugless Approach to the Condition That Darkens Millions of Lives
Syd Baumel
Keats Publishing, Inc., 1995

Cruelty of Depression
Jacques Hassoun, M.D.
Addison Wesley Longman, 1997

Death by Denial: Preventing Suicide in Gay and Lesbian Teenagers
Gary Remafedi (Ed.)
Alyson Publications, Inc., 1994

Cry of Pain: Understanding Suicide and Self-Harm
Mark Williams
Viking Penguin, 1997

Defeat Depression: Understand Your Sadness—and Banish It Forever!
Frank Bruno, Ph.D.
Macmillan Publishing Co., Inc., 1997

Cure by Crying: How to Cure Your Own Depression, Nervousness, Headaches, Violent Temper, Insomnia, Marital Problems, Addictions…
Thomas Stone
Cure by Crying, 1995

Denial is Not a River in Egypt: How to Overcome Depression, Addiction, Compulsion and Feel Terrific!
Sandi Bachom
Hazelden Foundation, 1998

Dare to Live: A Guide to the Prevention and Understanding of Teenage Suicide and Depression
Michael Miller, Debra Whalley Kidney
Beyond Words Publishing, 1988

Depression
Constance Hammen
Taylor & Francis, 1997

Dark Clouds, Silver Linings
Archibald Hart
Focus on the Family, 1993

Depression and Antidepressants: A Guide, rev. ed.
John Greist, M.D., James Jefferson, M.D., Dilek Tunali, M.D.
Dean Foundation Information Centers, 1997

Dealing with Depression in 12 Step Recovery
Jack O.
Hazelden Foundation, 1990

Depression and Anxiety Management
John Preston, Ph.D.
New Harbinger Publications, 1993

Dealing with Depression: Five Pastoral Interventions
Richard Dayringer, Ph.D.
Harrington Park Press, 1995

Depression in Children and Adolescents
Harold Koplewicz, Emily Klass (Eds.)
Gordon and Breach Science Pubs., Inc., 1993

Depression in Children and Adults
Kedar Dwivedi, Ved Varma (Eds.)
Singular Press, 1997

Depression: Cured at Last
Sherry Rogers
Prestige Publishers, 1997

Depression and Families: Impact and Treatment
Gabor Keitner, M.D. (Ed.)
American Psychiatric Press, 1990

Depression: How It Happens, How It's Healed
John Medina, Ph.D.
New Harbinger Publications, 1998

Depression Sourcebook
Brian Quinn
Lowell House, 1998

Depression and Suicide in Children and Adolescents: Prevention, Intervention, and Postvention
Philip Patros, Tonia Shamoo
Allyn and Bacon, 1989

Depression and Suicide: Special Education Students at Risk
Eleanor Guetzloe
Council for Exceptional Children, 1991

Depression: Theories and Treatments: Psychological, Biological, and Social Perspectives
Arthur Schwartz, Ruth Schwartz
Columbia University Press, 1993

Depression: The Way Out of Your Prison, 2nd ed.
Dorothy Rowe
Routledge, 1996

Depression: What Families Should Know
Elaine Fantle Shimberg
Ballantine Books, Inc., 1996

Depression in the Young: What We Can Do to Help Them
Trudy Carlson
Benline Press, 1998

Depression: Your Questions Answered
Sue Breton
Element Books, 1996

Depressive States and Their Treatment
Vamk Volkan (Ed.)
Jason Aronson, 1994

Diet-Behavior Relationships: Focus on Depression
Larry Christensen
American Psychological Assn., 1996

Down With Gloom! Or How to Defeat Depression
Brice Pitt
American Psychiatric Press, 1994

The Encyclopedia of Suicide
Glen Evans, Norman Farberow
Facts on File, Inc., 1988

Essential Papers on Suicide
John Maltsberger
New York University Press, 1996

Everything to Live For
Susan White-Bowden
White-Bowden Assoc., 1993

Everything You Need to Know about Teen Suicide
Jay Schleifer
Rosen Publishing Group, 1993

Everything You Need to Know to Understand and Live with Depression
Charles Mellon, M.D.
Genetics Heritage, 1996

Feel Well Again: Three Hundred Fifty Questions and Answers about Depression and Anxiety
Mercedes Leidlich
Maupin House Publishing, 1991

The Freedom from Depression Workbook
Leslie Carter, Ph.D., Frank Minirth, M.D.
Thomas Nelson Inc., 1995

From the Brink of Suicide into the Presence of Jesus and His Holy Smiling Angel
Simeon Johnson
Vantage Press, Inc., 1998

From Sad to Glad, rev. ed.
Nathan Kline, M.D.
Ballantine, 1987

Getting Up When You're Feeling Down: A Woman's Guide to Overcoming and Preventing Depression
Harriet Braiker
Pocket Books, 1990

Gift of the Dark Angel: A Woman's Journey through Depression toward Wholeness
Ann Keiffer
LuraMedia, 1991

God is Close to the Brokenhearted: Good News for Those Who are Depressed
Rachel Callahan, Rea McDonnell
St. Anthony Messenger Press, 1997

Good Mood: The New Psychology of Overcoming Depression
Julian Simon
Open Court Press, 1993

The Good News About Depression: Breakthrough Medical Treatments That Can Work for You
Mark Gold, M.D.
Bantam, 1995

Good Women Get Angry: A Woman's Guide to Handling Her Anger, Depression, Anxiety, and Stress
Gary Oliver, Ph.D., H. Norman. Wright
Servant Publications, 1995

The Grieving Child: A Parent's Guide
Helen Fitzgerald
Simon & Schuster Trade, 1992

Growing Up Sad: Childhood Depression and its Treatment
Leo Cytryn, M.D., Donald McKnew, M.D.
W.W. Norton and Co., NY, 1998

Hand-Me-Down Blues
Michael Yapko
Golden Books Co., 1999

A Handbook for the Understanding of Suicide
Seymour Perlin (Ed.)
Jason Aronson, Inc., 1994

Happiness is a Choice: The Symptoms, Causes and Cures of Depression
Frank Minirth, Paul Meier
Baker Books, 1994

Healing After the Suicide of a Loved One
Ann Smolin, John Guinan
Simon & Schuster Trade, 1993

Healing Depression: A Guide to Making Intelligent Choices about Treating Depression
Catherine Carrigan
Heartsfire Books, 1997

Help Me, I'm Sad: Recognizing, Treating, and Preventing Childhood and Adolescent Depression
David Fassler, Lynne Dumas
Viking Penguin, 1997

Helping Your Child Cope with Depression and Suicidal Thoughts
Tonia Shamoo, Philip Patros
Jossey-Bass Publishers, 1997

Helping Your Depressed Child
Lawrence Kerns, Adrienne Lieberman
Prima Publishing, 1993

Helping Your Depressed Teenager: A Guide for Parents and Caregivers
Gerald Oster, Ph.D., Sarah Montgomery, MSW
John Wiley and Sons, 1994

Helplessness: On Depression, Development, and Death, 2nd ed.
Martin Seligman
W. H. Freeman & Co., 1992

High Times / Low Times: How to Cope with Teenage Depression
John Meeks, M.D.
Hazelden, 1988

How to Cope with Depression: A Complete Guide for You and Your Family
J. Raymond DePaulo, Jr., M.D., Keith Ablow, M.D.
Fawcett Group, 1989

How to Heal Depression
Harold Bloomfield, M.D., Peter McWilliams
Prelude Press, 1994

How to Help Someone Who Is Depressed or Suicidal: Practical Suggestions From a Survivor
John Cook
Rubicon Press, 1993

How You Can Survive When They're Depressed
Anne Sheffield
Harmony Books, 1999

Human Dimension of Depression: A Practical Guide to Diagnosis, Understanding, and Treatment
Martin Kantor
Greenwood Publishing Group, Inc., 1992

Hypericum & Depression
Harold Bloomfield, M.D., Mikael Nordfors, M.D., Peter McWilliams
Prelude Press, 1996

I Can See Tomorrow: A Guide For Living with Depression
Patricia Owen, Ph.D.
Hazelden Foundation, 1995

I Don't Know Who You Are Anymore: A Family's Struggle With Depression
Kellie Branson, Dale Babcock, M.S.
Legendary Publishing, 1992

I Don't Want to Talk About It: Overcoming the Secret Legacy of Male Depression
Terrence Real
Simon and Schuster Trade, 1998

If You Think You Have Depression
Roger Granet, M.D., Robin Karol Levinson
Dell, 1998

If You Think You Have Seasonal Affective Disorder
Clifford Taylor , M.D., Robin Levinson
Dell, 1998

The Impact of Suicide
Brian Mishara (Ed.)
Springer Publishing Company, Inc., 1995

In the Shadow of God's Wings: Grace in the Midst of Depression
Susan Gregg-Schroeder
Upper Room, 1997

In the Wake of Suicide: Stories of the People Left Behind
Alexander Victoria
Jossey-Bass Publishers, 1998

Is Your Child Depressed?
Joel Herskowitz, M.D.
Pharos Books, 1988

A Joy I'd Never Known
Jan Dravecky, Connie Neal
Zondervan Publishing House, 1996

Kid Power Tactics for Dealing with Depression
Nicholas Dubuque, Susan Dubuque
Center for Applied Psychology, Inc., 1996

Life After Grief: A Soul Journey after Suicide
Jack Clarke
Personal Pathways Press, 1989

Life After Suicide: A Ray of Hope for Those Left Behind
E. Betsy Ross
Plenum Press, 1997

Life After Suicide: A Survivor's Grief Experience
Terence Barrett, Ph.D.
Aftermath Research, 1989

Life Happens: A Teenager's Guide to Friends, Failure, Sexuality, Love, Rejection, Addiction, Peer Pressure, Families, Loss, Depression, Change and Other Challenges of Living
Kathy McCoy, Charles Wibbelsman
Berkley Publishing Group, 1995

Living with Grief: After Sudden Loss, Suicide, Homicide, Accident, Heart Attack, Stroke
Kenneth Doka, Ph.D. (Ed.)
Taylor and Francis, 1996

Living Without Depression and Manic Depression: A Workbook for Maintaining Mood Stability
Mary Ellen Copeland
New Harbinger, 1994

Lonely, Sad and Angry: A Parent's Guide to Depression in Children and Adolescents
Barbara Ingersoll, Ph.D., Sam Goldstein, Ph.D.
Doubleday, 1995

Making Sense of Suicide: An In-Depth Look at Why People Kill Themselves
David Lester
Charles Press Publishers, 1997

A Mother's Story
Gloria Vanderbilt
Alfred A. Knopf, Inc., 1997

My Child, Let Me Take the Wheel!: Dealing with Depression
Lila Burrows, Don Pratt, Fran Pratt
Son-Rise Publications and Distribution Co., 1991

Natural Prozac: Leaning to Release Your Body's Own Anti-Depressants
Joel Robertson, Tom Monte
Harper San Francisco, 1997

A New Lease on Life
John Chabot
Fairview Press, 1997

No One Saw My Pain: Why Teens Kill Themselves
Andrew Slaby, M.D., Lili Garfinkel
W. W. Norton and Co., Inc., 1994

No Time to Say Goodbye: Surviving the Suicide of a Loved One
Carla Fine
Doubleday and Co., Inc., 1997

Not with My Life I Don't: Preventing Your Suicide and That of Others
Howard Rosenthal
Accelerated Development, 1988

Nurturing Happiness: Natural Ways to Relieve and Prevent Depression
Linda App
Windmill Press of Alexandria, 1997

On the Edge of Darkness: Conversations about Conquering Depression
Kathy Cronkite
Doubleday, 1994

Once Upon a Suicide
Judy Hollar
Libra Publishers, Inc., 1990

The Optimistic Child: A Proven Program to Safeguard Children From Depression and Build Lifelong Resistance
Martin Seligman, Ph.D.
Harper Perennial, 1997

Out of the Blue: Depression and Human Nature
David Cohen
W. W. Norton, 1995

Out of the Nightmare: Recovery from Depression and Suicidal Pain
David Conroy, Ph.D.
New Liberty Press, 1991

Overcoming Depression
Richard King Mower, Ph.D.
Deseret Book Co., 1993

Overcoming Depression: The Definitive Resources for Patients and Families Who Life with Depression and Manic Depression, 3rd. ed.
Demitri Papolos, Janice Papolos
Harper Collins Publisher, 1997

Overcoming Depression and Manic Depression (Bipolar Depression) the Non-Drug Approach
Paul Wider, M.A.
Wider Pubs., 1993

Overcoming Depression: Practical Stages Towards Recovery
Caroline Shreeve
Thorson, 1994

Overcoming Depressive Living Syndrome: How to Enjoy Life, Not Just Endure It
Earnest Larsen, Cara Macken
Liguori Publishing, 1996

A Parent's Guide to Childhood and Adolescent Depression
Patricia Shapiro
Dell Publishing, 1994

A Parent's Guide to Suicidal and Depressed Teens: Help for Recognizing if a Child is in Crisis and What to Do about It
Kate Williams
Hazelden Foundation, 1995

Parent's Survival Guide to Childhood Depression
Susan Dubuque
Center for Applied Psychology, Inc., 1996

Pastoral Care of Depression: A Guidebook
Binford Gilbert
Haworth Press, Inc., 1997

Patterns of Suicide and Homicide in America
David Lester
Nova Science Pubs., Inc., 1994

Perspectives on College Student Suicide
Ralph Rickgarn
Baywood Publishing Company, Inc., 1994

Physical Activity and Mental Health
William Morgan, Ed.D. (Ed.)
Taylor and Francis, Inc., 1996

The Physiology of Psychological Disorders: Schizophrenia, Depression, Anxiety, and Substance Abuse
James Hollandsworth
Plenum Press, 1990

Please Listen to Me: Your Guide to Understanding Teenagers and Suicide
Marion Crook, B.Sc.N.
Self Counsel Press, Inc., 1992

Pressed Down but Not Forgotten
H. Curtis Lyon, John Juern
Northwestern Publishing House, 1993

Preventing Adolescent Suicide
David Capuzzi, Larry Golden
Accelerated Development, 1988

Preventing Teenage Suicide: The Living Alternative Handbook
Polly Joan
Human Sciences Press, Inc., 1987

Preventing Youth Suicide - A Handbook for Educators and Human Service Professionals
Marcia McEvoy, Alan McEvoy
Learning Publications, Inc., 1994

The Prevention of Depression: Research and Practice
Ricardo Munoz, Yu-Wen Ying
Johns Hopkins University Press, 1993

Preventive Strategies on Suicide
Rene Diekstra (Ed.)
Brill Acad., 1995

Prozac Nation: Young and Depressed in America
Elizabeth Wurtzel
Riverhead Books, 1997

Questions and Answers About Depression and its Treatment: A Consultation with a Leading Psychiatrist
Ivan Goldberg, M.D.
The Charles Press, 1993

Questions and Answers About Suicide
David Lester, Ph.D.
Charles Press, 1989

A Reason to Live
Melody Beattie (Ed.)
Tyndale House Publishers, 1991

Recovery from Depression
Dale Ryan, Dale Ryan
InterVarsity Press, 1993

Religion and Suicide in the African-American Community
Kevin Early
Greenwood Publishing Group, Inc., 1992

Restless Mind, Quiet Thoughts: A Personal Journal
Paul Eppinger, Charles Eppinger
White Cloud, 1994

Review of Suicidology, 1997
Ronald Maris, Morton Silverman, Silva Canetto (Eds.)
Guilford Publications, 1997

Reviving Ophelia: Saving the Selves of Adolescent Girls
Mary Pipher, Ph.D.
Putnam Publishing Group, 1994

Seasonal Affective Disorder: Winter Depression: Who Gets It, What Causes It, How to Cure It, rev. ed.
Angela Smyth, Chris Thompson
Thorsons Pub., 1992

Seasons of the Mind: Why You Get the Winter Blues and What You Can Do About It
Norman Rosenthal, M.D.
Bantam Books, 1989

Secret Strength of Depression, 2nd ed.
Frederic Flach, M.D.
Hatherleigh Press, 1995

Shadow on My Soul: Overcoming Addiction to Suicide
Paula Quinn, Ph.D.
Knowledge, Ideas and Trends, Inc., 1995

Silent Grief: Living in the Wake of Suicide
Christopher Lukas, Henry Seiden
Jason Aronson, Inc., 1997

Slaying the Giant: Practical Help for Understanding Preventing and Overcoming Depression
French O'Shields
Hem Of His Garment, 1995

Speaking of Sadness: Depression, Disconnection, and the Meanings of Illness
David Karp
Oxford University Press, 1997

A Special SCAR: The Experiences of People Bereaved by Suicide
Alison Wertheimer
Routledge, 1991

Step Back from the Exit: Forty-Five Reasons to Say No to Suicide
Jillayne Arena
Zebulon Press, 1996

Stephen Lives! His Life, Suicide and Afterlife
Anne Puryear
Pocket Books, 1997

The Storm Within
Mark Littleton
Tyndale House Publishers, 1994

Suicidal Behaviors: Diagnosis and Management
H. Resnik (Ed.)
Jason Aronson, Inc., 1994

Suicidal Mind
Edwin Shniedman
Oxford University Press, Inc., 1996

The Suicidal Patient: Recognition, Intervention, Management
Victor Victoroff
Jason Aronson, Inc., 1996

Suicidal Youth: School-Based Intervention and Prevention
John Davis, Jonathan Sandoval
Jossey-Bass Publishers, 1991

Suicide
Laura Dolce
Chelsea House, 1992

Suicide
Robert Long (Ed.)
H. W. Wilson, 1995

Suicide
David Wilkerson
Spirit Press, 1997

Suicide Across the Life Span: Premature Exits, 2nd ed.
Judith Stillion, Eugene McDowell
Hemisphere Publishing Corp., 1996

Suicide in African Americans
David Lester
Nova Science Pub., 1998

Suicide in Alcoholism
George Murphy
Oxford University Press, Inc., 1992

Suicide in America
Herbert Hendin
W. W. Norton and Co., Inc., 1995

Suicide in American Indians
David Lester
Nova Sci. Press, 1997

Suicide: Prevention, Intervention, Postvention
Earl Grollman
Beacon Press, 1988

Suicide Prevention in Schools
Antoon Leenaars, Susanne Wenckstern
Hemisphere Publishing Corp., 1991

Suicide of a Child: For Parents Whose Child Has Completed Suicide
Adina Wrobleski
Centering Corp., 1993

Suicide: A Christian Response: Five Crucial Considerations for Choosing Life
Timothy Demy, Gary Stewart (Eds.)
Kregel Publications, 1997

Suicide: Closing the Exits
Ronald, V. Clarke, David Lester
Springer Verlag, 1989

Suicide: The Constructive/Destructive Self
Coletta Klug (Ed.)
Edwin Mellen Press, 1996

Suicide in Creative Women
David Lester
Nova Science Pub., 1993

Suicide: The Forever Decision
Paul Quinnet
Crossroad, 1987

Suicide: Guidelines for Assessment, Management, and Treatment
Bruce Bongar (Ed.)
Oxford University Press, 1992

Suicide: Individual, Cultural, International Perspectives
Antoon Leenaars, Ronald Maris, Yashitomo Takahashi (Eds.)
Guilford Publications, 1997

Suicide Intervention in the Schools
Scott Poland
Guilford Publications, 1989

Suicide: Knowing When Your Teen is at Risk
T. Mitchel Anthony
Regal Books, 1991

Suicide as a Learned Behavior
David Lester
Charles C. Thomas Pub., 1987

The Suicide of My Son: A Story of Childhood Depression
Trudy Carlson
Benline Press, 1995

Suicide: A Preventable Tragedy
Dorothy Francis
E.P. Dutton, 1989

Suicide Prevention in the Schools: Guidelines for Middle and High School Settings
David Capuzzi
American Counseling Assn., 1994

Suicide Prevention: Toward the Year 2000
Morton Silverman, Ronald Maris (Eds.)
Guilford Publications, 1995

Suicide as Psychache: A Clinical Approach to Self-Destructive Behavior
Edwin Shneidman
Jason Aronson, Inc., 1995

Suicide and the School: A Practical Guide to Suicide Prevention
Patrick McKee, Richard Barbe, R. Wayne Jones
LRP Publications, 1993

Suicide: Some Things We Know, and Some We Do Not
M. Russell Ballard
Deseret Book Co., 1996

Suicide: Survivors: A Guide for Those Left Behind, 2nd ed.
Adina Wrobleski
SA\VE, 1994

Suicide Survivors' Handbook: A Guide for the Bereaved and Those Who Wish to Help Them
Trudy Carlson
Benline Press, 1995

**Suicide: The Ultimate Rejection?
A Psycho-Social Study**
Colin Pritchard
Taylor and Francis, Inc., 1995

Suicide and the Unconscious
Antoon Leenaars, David Lester (Eds.)
Jason Aronson, Inc., 1996

Suicide: Understanding and Responding
Herbert Brown, Douglas Jacobs (Eds.)
International Universities Press, 1993

Surviving the Crisis of Depression and Bipolar (Manic-Depression) Illness: Layperson's Guide to Coping with Mental Illness Beyond the Time of Crisis and Outside the Hospital
Mark Halebsky
Personal and Professional Growth, 1997

Surviving the Epidemic of Suicide
Bill Steele
PPI Publishing, 1994

Survivors of Suicide
Rita Robinson
Newcastle Publishing Company, Inc., 1992

Treating Anger, Anxiety, and Depression in Children and Adolescents: A Cognitive-Behavioral Perspective
Jerry Wilde, Ph.D.
Accelerated Development, 1995

Teen Suicide: Too Young to Die
Cynthia Copeland Lewis
Enslow Pub., 1994

Treating Suicidelike Behavior in a Preschooler
Paul Trad, M.D.
International Universities Press, 1993

Teenage Depression
Herman Silverstein
Franklin Watts, 1990

Treatment of Suicidal People (Death Education, Aging, and Health Care)
John Maltsberger, Antoon Leenaars
Hemisphere Publishing Corp., 1994

Teenage Depression and Drugs
Solomon Snyder
Chelsea House Publishers, 1995

Undercurrents: A Life Beneath the Surface
Martha Manning
Harper San Francisco, 1995

Teenage Depression and Suicide
John Chiles
Chelsea House, 1992

Understanding Depression
Donald Klein, M.D., Paul Wender, M.D.
Oxford University Press, 1993

Ten Days to Self Esteem
David Burns
Quill Trade Paperbacks, 1993

Understanding Depression
Paul Robbins
McFarland and Company, Inc. Publishers, 1993

A Time to Listen: Preventing Youth Suicide
Patricia Hermes
Harcourt Brace Jovanovich, 1991

Understanding Depression
Siang-Yang Tan, John Ortberg
Baker Books, 1995

Teenage Suicide
Sandra Gardner, Gary Rosenberg
Julian Messner, 1992

Understanding and Preventing Teen Suicide
Warren Colman
Children's Press, 1990

Tragedy to Triumph
Reuel Nygaard
Life Journey Books, 1994

Understanding Your Teenager's Depression: Issues, Insights and Practical Guidance for Parents
Kathleen McCoy, Ph.D.
Berkley Publishing Group, 1994

The Transmission of Depression in Families and Children: Assessment and Intervention
Pirooz Sholevar (Ed.)
Jason Aronson, Inc., 1994

Undoing Depression: What Therapy Doesn't Teach You and Medication Can't Give You
Richard O'Connorr, Ph.D.
Little, Brown and Co., 1997

Waking Up Alive: The Descent, the Suicide Attempt, and the Return to Life
Richard Heckler, Ph.D.
Ballantine Books, Inc., 1996

The Way Up From Down
Priscilla Slagle, M.D.
St. Martin's Press, Inc., 1992

What the Blues is All About: Black Women Overcoming Stress and Depression
Angela Mitchell, Gladys Croom
Perigree, 1998

What to Do When Someone You Love Is Depressed
Mitch Golant, Ph.D., Susan Golant
Villard, 1997

What of the Night? A Journey through Depression and Anxiety
Jeffrey Knowles
Herald Press, 1993

When the Blues Won't Go Away: New Approaches to Dysthymic Disorder and Other Forms of Chronic Low-Grade Depression
Robert Hirschfeld, M.D., Susan Meltsner
Macmillan, 1991

When It Hurts to Live: Devotions for Difficult Times
Kathleen Kern
Faith and Life Press, 1995

When Living Hurts
Sol Gordon, Ph.D.
Dell Books, 1989

When Someone You Love is Depressed
Laura Rosen, Ph.D., Xavier Amador, Ph.D.
Free Press, 1997

When Words Are Not Enough: The Women's Prescription for Depression and Anxiety
Valerie Davis Raskin, M.D.
Broadway Books, 1997

Why Do I Feel This Way? What Every Woman Needs to Know about Depression
Brenda Poinsett
NavPress Publishing Group, 1996

Why Suicide? Answers to 200 of the Most Frequently Asked Questions about Suicide, Attempted Suicide, and Assisted Suicide
Eric Marcus
Harper San Francisco, 1995

Willow Weep for Me: A Black Woman's Journey Through Depression: A Memoir
Meri Nana-Ama Danquah
W.W. Norton & Co., 1998

Win the Battle: The 3-Step Lifesaving Formula to Conquer Depression and Bipolar Disorder
Bob Olson, Melissa Olson
Chandler House Press, 1999

Winning: How Teens (and Other Humans) Can Beat Anger and Depression
Lew Hamburger
Vantage Press, Inc., 1997

Winter Blues: Seasonal Affective Disorder: What It Is and How to Overcome It, rev. ed.
Norman Rosenthal, M.D.
Guilford Publications, Inc., 1998

A Woman Doctor's Guide to Depression: Essential Facts and Up-to-the-Minute Information on Diagnosis, Treatments, and Recovery
Jane Ferber, Suzanne LeVert
Hyperion, 1997

Women, Anger and Depression: Strategies for Self-Empowerment
Lois Frankel, Ph.D.
Health Communications, Inc., 1992

Women and Suicidal Behavior
Silva Sata Canetto
Spring Publishing, 1995

You Are Not Alone
Julia Thorne, Larry Rothstein
Harper Perennial, 1997

You Can Beat Depression: A Guide to Recovery, 2nd ed.
Jack Preston
Impact Publishers, 1996

You Can Choose to Be Happy: "Rise Above" Anxiety, Anger, and Depression
Tom Stevens, Ph.D.
Wheeler-Sutton Publishing, 1998

You Mean I Don't Have to Feel This Way? New Help for Depression, Anxiety and Addiction
Collete Dowling
Scribner's, 1991

When Feeling Bad is Good
Ellen McGrath
Henry Holt and Co., 1992

Wrestling with Depression: A Spiritual Guide to Reclaiming Life
William Hulme, Lucy Hulme
Augsburg Fortress Publishers, 1995

You Are Not Alone
Julia Thorne, Larry Rothstein
Harper Collins, 1993

You Can Beat Depression: A Guide to Prevention and Recovery, 2nd ed.
John Preston, Psy.D.
Impact Publishers, 1996

You Can Feel Good Again: Common-SenseTherapy for Releasing Depression and Changing Your Life
Richard Carlson
NAL/Dutton, 1994

Youth Suicide: A Comprehensive Manual for Prevention and Intervention
Barbara Barrett Hicks
National Educational Service, 1990

Youth Suicide Prevention Programs: A Resource Guide
U.S. Dept. of Health and Human Services
1992

Youth Suicide: What the Educator Should Know
Eleanor Guetzloe
Council for Exceptional Children, 1989

Books for Youth

After Suicide: Young People Speak Up
Susan Kuklin
Putnam Publishing, 1994

Amazing Gracie
A.E. Cannon
Dell Publishing Co., Inc., 1993

Coping with Depression
Sharon Carter, Lawrence Clayton, Ph.D.
Hazelden Foundation, 1997

Dead Serious: A Book for Teenagers About Teenage Suicide
Jane Mersky Leder
Atheneum, 1987

Dear Uncle Dave
Yuri Norton
Shirley Baldwin Waring Publishers, 1993

Depression
Alvin Silverstein, Virginia Silverstein
Enslow Pub., 1997

Depression
Cathie Cush
Raintree Steck-Vaughn Publisher, 1993

Depression is the Pits, But I'm Getting Better: A Guide for Adolescents
Jane Garland, Bonnie Garland
Magination Press, 1997

Depression: Psychological Disorders and Their Treatment (Encyclopedia of Health)
Dianne Hales
Chelsea House Pub., 1995

Don't Be S.A.D.: A Teenage Guide to Handling Stress, Anxiety and Depression
Susan Newman
Silver Burdett Press, 1991

Drugs and Depression
Beth Wilkinson
Hazelden Foundation, 1997

Emotional Disorders
M. Nikki Goldman
Marshall Cavendish, 1994

Encyclopedia of Depression
Roberta Roesch
Facts on File, 1991

Everything You Need to Know about Depression, 2nd ed.
Eleanor Ayer
Rosen Group, 1997

First Came the Owl
Judith Benet Richardson
Henry Holt and Co., Inc., 1998

Happiness is a Choice for Teens
Paul Meier, Jan Meier
Thomas Nelson Inc., 1997

I Never Knew Your Name
Sherry Garland
Houghton Mifflin, 1994

Life Happens: A Teenager's Guide to Friends, Failure, Sexuality, Love, Rejection, Addiction, Peer Pressure, Families, Loss, Depression, Change and Other Challenges of Living
Kathy McCoy, Charles Wibbelsman
Berkley Publishing Group, 1995

The Power to Prevent Suicide: A Guide for Teens Helping Teens
Richard Nelson, Judith Galas
Free Spirit Publishing, Inc., 1994

Teenage Suicide
Nicki Goldman
Benchmark Books, 1996

A Reason to Live
Donalyn Powell
Bethany House, 1989

Teen Suicide: A Book for Friends, Family, and Classmates
Janet Kolehmainem, Sandra Handwerk
Lerner Group, 1989

Sad Days, Glad Days: A Story about Depression
DeWitt Hamilton
Albert Whitman and Co., 1995

Teen Suicide: Is It Too Painful to Grow Up?
Eleanor Ayer
Twenty-First Century Books, Inc., 1995

Straight Talk About Anxiety and Depression
Michael Maloney, M.D., Rachel Kranz
Facts on File, 1991

Teens and Depression
Gail Stewart
Lucent Books, 1998

Straight Talk about Teenage Suicide
Bernard Frankel, Ph.D., Rachel Kranz
Facts on File, Inc., 1994

When Living Hurts
Sol Gordon
U A H C Press, 1994

Suicide
Adam Woog
Lucent Books, 1997

When Nothing Matters Anymore: A Survival Guide for Teens
Bev Cobain
Free Spirit Press, 1998

Suicide
Stephen Flanders
Facts on File, Inc., 1991

Working Together Against Teen Suicide
Toby Axelrod
Rosen Group, 1996

Suicide
Leslie McGuire
Rourke Book Co., 1990

You'll Miss Me When I'm Gone
Stephen Roos
Delacorte Press, 1988

Teen Suicide
Judith Galas
Lucent Books, 1994

Videos

Video tapes can be very useful, but may be a challenge to find, especially if they aren't new to the market. Try contacting the producers noted even if the tape isn't listed on their web site, book stores and your library.

Carrie's Story
Depression and Related Affective Disorders
Association (DRADA), 1990
Meyer 3-181
600 North Wolfe Street
Baltimore, MD 21287-7381
Ph: (410) 955-4647
Web: http://ww2.med.jhu.edu/drada/
A teenager and her family cope with her depression, with explanation of the illness.

Day for Night:Recognizing Teenage Depression
Depression and Related Affective Disorders
Association (DRADA), 1999
Meyer 3-181
600 North Wolfe Street
Baltimore, MD 21287-7381
Ph: (410) 955-4647
Web: http://ww2.med.jhu.edu/drada/
Teenagers relate their experiences with depression and/or manic-depressive illness, treatments and recovery,encourage other teens to seek help. Professional explanations and tips about recognizing and treating these illnesses.

Dead Blue: A Film About Surviving Depression
Avail. through Schlessinger Media, 1997
P.O. Box 580
Wynnewood, PA 190960
Ph: (800) 843-3620
      (610) 645-4000
Fax: (610) 645-4040
E-mail: comments@libraryvideo.com
Web: http://www.libraryvideo.com/sm_home.asp
Three prominent survivors of clinical depression - "60 Minutes" correspondent Mike Wallace, psychologist Martha Manning and Pulitzer Prize-winning author William Styron – discuss their struggles with depression.

Depression
Avail. through Schlessinger Media, 1999
P.O. Box 580
Wynnewood, PA 19096
Ph: (800) 843-3620
      (610) 645-4000
Fax: (610) 645-4040
E-mail: comments@libraryvideo.com
Web: http://www.libraryvideo.com/sm_home.asp
Explanation of depression, suicidal thinking, treatments.

Depression: Beyond the Darkness
Avail. through Schlessinger Media, 1990
P.O. Box 580
Wynnewood, PA 19096
Ph: (800) 843-3620
      (610) 645-4000
Fax: (610) 645-4040
E-mail: comments@libraryvideo.com
Web: http://www.libraryvideo.com/sm_home.asp
Treatments for depression and their controversies. Grades 9 to adults.

Depression: On the Edge
Avail. through Schlessinger Media, 1998
P.O. Box 580
Wynnewood, PA 19096
Ph: (800) 843-3620
      (610) 645-4000
Fax: (610) 645-4040
E-mail: comments@libraryvideo.com
Web: http://www.libraryvideo.com/sm_home.asp
Teen angst - from normal "blues" to clinical depression and suicide to show how and where teens can get help if needed. Grades 7-adult.

Depressive Illness: What You Need to Know

Depression and Related Affective Disorders Assn., 1991
Meyer 3-181
600 North Wolfe Street
Baltimore, MD 21287-7381
Ph: (410) 955-4647
Web: http://ww2.med.jhu.edu/drada/
Information and personal experiences.

It's Never Too Late: Coping with Depression

Avail. through Schlessinger Media, 1999
P.O. Box 580
Wynnewood, PA 19096
Ph: (800) 843-3620
        (610) 645-4000
Fax: (610) 645-4040
E-mail: comments@libraryvideo.com
Web: http://www.libraryvideo.com/sm_home.asp
Suicide epidemic in communities. Grades 7-12.

A Patient's Perspective-Dick Cavett

Depression and Related Affective Disorders Assn., 1993
Meyer 3-181, 600 North Wolfe Street
Baltimore, MD 21287-7381
Ph: (410) 955-4647
Baltimore, MD 21287-7381
E-mail: drada@jhmi.edu
Web: http://www.med.jhu.edu/drada

A Patient's Perspective-Mike Wallace

Depression and Related Affective Disorders Assn., 1992
Meyer 3-181, 600 North Wolfe Street
Baltimore, MD 21287-7381
Ph: (410) 955-4647
Baltimore, MD 21287-7381
E-mail: drada@jhmi.edu
Web: http://www.med.jhu.edu/drada

Taking Control of Depression: Mending the Mind

Wood Knapp Video, 1991
Avail. through Schlessinger Media
P.O. Box 580
Wynnewood, PA 19096
Ph: (800) 843-3620
        (610) 645-4000
Fax: (610) 645-4040
E-mail: comments@libraryvideo.com
Web: http://www.libraryvideo.com/sm_home.asp
Ed Asner teaches about depression. Grades 9-adult.

Teenage Depression and Suicide

Avail. through Schlessinger Media, 1991
P.O. Box 580
Wynnewood, PA 19096
Ph: (800) 843-3620
        (610) 645-4000
Fax: (610) 645-4040
E-mail: comments@libraryvideo.com
Web: http://www.libraryvideo.com/sm_home.asp
Famous people who were suicidal teens. Grades 7-up.

Why Isn't My Child Happy?
A Video Guide About Childhood Depression

Sam Goldstein
Neurology, Learning and Behavior Center
230 South 500 East, Suite 100
Salt Lake City, Utah 84102
Ph: (801) 532-1484
Fax: (801) 532-1486
E-mail: info@samgoldstein.com
Web: www.samgoldstein.com
Causes, warning signs, treatments, guidelines to help.

Vendors

Apollo Light Systems
369 S. Mountain Way Dr.
Orem, UT 84058
Ph: (800) 545-9667
          (801) 226-2370
Fax: (801) 226-414
E-mail: info@apollolight.com
Web: www.apollolight.com
Light boxes.

Bio-Brite, Inc.
4350 East West Highway, Suite 401W
Bethesda, MD 20814
Ph: (800) 621-5483
Fax: (301) 961-5943
E-mail: biobrite@aol.com
Web: http://www.biobriteinc.com/
Light boxes and visors.

Hughes Lighting Technologies
34 Yacht Club Dr.
Lake Hopatcong, NJ 07849
Ph: (800) 544-4825
          (973) 663-1214
Fax: (973) 663-3496
E-mail: prices@hlt.com
Web: http://www.hlt.com
Light boxes and devices.

Sphere One, Inc.
461 Main St.
Box 1013
Silver Plume, CO 80476
Ph: (212) 208-4438
E-mail: questions@sphereone.com
Web: http://www.sphereone.com
Light boxes, ion generators.

The Sun Box Company
19217 Orbit Dr.
Gaithersburg, MD 20879-4149
Ph: (800) 548-3968
          (301) 869-5980
Fax: (301) 977-2281
E-mail: sunbox@aol.com
Web: www.sunboxco.com
Light boxes and devices.

Web Sites

Also see "General Web Sites". Many have sections on depression, but they are not listed separately below.

Dr. Ivan's Depression Central
Ivan Goldberg
Web: http://www.psycom.net/depression.central.html
Large collection of information.

Have a Heart's Depression Resource
Web: http://www.have-a-heart.com
Collection of information from the author of a book on depression.

Wings of Madness
Web: http://www.wingofmadness.com/whatis.htm
Collection of information on depression.

The Write Brain: Steven Thow's Mental Health Resources – Depression/Bipolar Disorder
Web: http://www.mhsource.com/wb/thow9903.html

Periodicals / Newsletters

Smooth Sailing

Depression and Related Affective Disorders
Association (DRADA)
Meyer 3-181
600 North Wolfe St.
Baltimore, MD 21287-7381
Ph: (410) 955-4647
E-mail: drada@jhmi.edu
Web: http://ww2.med.jhu.edu/drada/
Articles by mental-health professionals, descriptions of
personal experiences with depression or manic-
depressive illness, book reviews.

Surviving Suicide

American Association of Suicidology
4201 Connecticut Ave., NW, Suite 408
Washington, DC 20008
Ph: (202) 237-2280
Fax: (202) 237-2282
E-mail: debbiehu@ix.netcom.com
Web: http://www.suicidology.org/

---- Down Syndrome

Congenital disorder caused by a chromosomal abnormality that affects a child physically and mentally. Second most common birth defect (second to cerebral palsy) and is the leading known cause of mental retardation. The severity of the affects varies by child.

There are three forms of Down syndrome:

- **Nondisjunction or Trisomy 21** (95% of those with Down syndrome) Caused by a faulty cell division which results in an embryo with three #21 chromosomes. Before or at conception, if either the egg's or sperm's chromosome #21 fails to separate, the result is an extra chromosome. Normal human cells have 46 chromosomes. Children with Down syndrome have 1 extra.

- **Mosaicism** (2% of those with Down syndrome) The 21st chromosome fails to separate after fertilization, resulting in an extra chromosome in only some of the cells. Some cells have 46 chromosomes and other cells have 47. Those with Mosaic Down syndrome are less affected by the traits of Down syndrome than those with Trisomy 21.

- **Translocation** (3% of those with Down syndrome) Part of the 21st chromosome breaks off during cell divison and attaches to another chromosome. The total number of chromosomes in a person with translocation is 46, even though the presence of the extra part causes the traits of Down syndrome in these people. In 1/3 of the translocation cases, one parent is a carrier.

Also called
Mongolism

Frequency
1 in 700-800 births

Symptoms and Possible Effects
- ❑ Almond-shaped eyes with Brushfield spots (fine white spots on the edge of the iris.)
- ❑ Epicanthic fold of the upper eyelid.
- ❑ Congenital cataracts.

❑ Eyes, nose, mouth are close together. Flat facial profile.

❑ Mouth is small, tongue is large. Some children keep their mouth open with their tongue slightly protruding. As child gets older, the tongue may become furrowed. Palete is narrow.

❑ Eruption of baby teeth is usually delayed. High incidence of missing primary and permanent teeth. Increased frequency of gum disease. Jaws are small.

❑ Nose is small, nasal bridge depressed. Deviated septums are common.

❑ Snore during sleep, have episodes when they don't breathe, are restless sleepers, may be tired during daytime.

❑ Ears are somewhat small and abnormally shaped, ear canals are narrow. Hearing problems.

❑ Excessive skin about the neck.

❑ Joint laxity, low muscle tone. Poor connective tissue. Hyperflexibility (an excessive ability to extend the joints.) Motor delays.

❑ Head is somewhat smaller, back is slightly flattened. Soft spots of the skull (fontanels) are frequently larger and take longer to close. In the midline where the bones of the skull meet, there is often an additional soft spot (false fontanel.)

❑ May be areas of missing hair.

❑ Widely spaced nipples.

❑ Congenital heart disease, which is the most serious health problem seen in Down syndrome.

❑ Mental retardation. IQ is typically 40-60 at school age.

❑ Seizure disorders, infantile spasms.

❑ Thyroid disfunction.

❑ Skeletal anomalies. Scoliosis in some children, round shoulders. Small features, short stature. Depressed or protruding chest bone. If child has enlarged heart due to congenital heart disease, chest may appear fuller on the side of the heart. Some may be missing 1 of their 12 ribs. Small skull.

❑ Some infants thrive poorly. Increasing weight gain is noted in adolescents and older persons.

❑ Conduct disorders, adjustment reactions. Adolescents may suffer from depression.

❑ Increased frequency of infections, especially those involving the head, neck and respiratory tract including sinuses, ears, and airway. Reduced numbers of T cells. Increased incidence of leukemia in childhood.

❑ Epilepsy, celiac disease.

❑ Hands and feet tend to be small and stubby. The first finger is often curved slightly inward. Toes are extremely short. In most there is a wide space between the first and second toes with a crease running between them on the sole of the foot. Many have flat feet. Dysplastic middle phalanx of the fifth finger, fifth finger has one flexion furrow instead of two. Single palmar crease on hands, abnormal finger prints.

❑ Skin is usually fair and may be mottled during infancy and early childhood. Skin is dry and hands and face may chap easily.

❑ Gastrointestinal problems such as blockage of the food pipe, connection of the food pipe with the air pipe, a narrowing of the outlet of the stomach, blockage of the bowel adjacent to the stomach, absence of certain nerves in some parts of the bowel, absence of the anal opening.

❑ Sensory, perceptual, physical and cognitive problems that affect development of communication.

❑ Language development problems.

❑ Difficulty learning.

Causes

The cause of **nondisjunction** is unknown, though it appears to be related to a mother's age. However, 80% of children born with Down syndrome are born to women under 35 years of age (due to higher fertility rates.) Nondisjunction can also come from the father, though less frequently (15% of the time.) Environmental factors haven't been ruled out, but not confirmed yet.

A mother's age is not linked to the risk of **translocation,** however. Most cases are chance events, but in about one-third of cases, one parent is a carrier of a translocated chromosome.

Diagnostic Processes

The diagnosis of Down syndrome is usually suspected after birth as a result of the baby's appearance.

Procedures available to pregnant women to help determine the likelihood that their baby will have Down syndrome:

- **Screening tests** which measure the risk of a baby having Down syndrome. Commonly used screening tests between 15 and 20 weeks of gestation are the Triple Screen and the Alpha-fetoprotein Plus. These tests measure quantities of various substances in the blood (alpha-fetoprotein, human chorionic gonadotropin and unconjugated estriol). Screening tests are often done with a detailed sonogram. These tests are only able to accurately detect about sixty percent of unborn babies with Down syndrome.

- **Diagnostic tests** tell whether or not the baby actually has Down syndrome. The procedures available for prenatal diagnosis are chorionic villus sampling (CVS), amniocentesis, and percutaneous umbilical blood sampling (PUBS).

Treatment

- No cure, efforts are focused on decreasing its incidence and treating the associated health problems.
- Early intervention to improve sensorimotor and social development, tactile stimulation, oral, visual and auditory stimulation.
- "Smart drugs" such a piracetam are intended to boost intelligence.

Outcomes

Some physical features may change over time, such as:

- Epicanthal folds or initially abundant neck tissue will become less prominent.
- Motor skills improve over time; significant physical disabilities are rarely evident by school age.
- Alzheimer disease later in life.

Who to Contact
Also refer to "Who Else to Contact." Organizations listed below target their work specifically toward Down syndrome.

National Down Syndrome Congress (NDSC)
7000 Peachtree-Dunwoody Road, NE
Lake Ridge 400 Office Park
Bldg. #5 - Suite 100
Atlanta, GA 30328
Ph: (800) 232-6372
       (770) 604-9500
Fax: (404) 633-2817
E-mail: NDSCcenter@aol.com
Web: http://www.ndsccenter.org/
Organization for parents of children with Down syndrome, teachers and medical professionals.

National Down Syndrome Society (NDSS)
666 Broadway
New York, NY 10012
Ph: (800) 221-4602
       (212) 460-9330
Fax: (212) 979-2873
Web: http://www.ndss.org/
Supports research on Down syndrome, publishes materials, referrals, events.

Recommended Reading

Adolescents with Down Syndrome: Toward a More Fulfilling Life
Siegfried Pueschel, M.D., Ph.D., J.D., M.P.H., Mária Sustrová, M.D., Ph.D. (Eds.)
Paul H. Brookes, 1997

Another Season
Gene Stallings, Sally Cook
Little, Brown and Co., 1997

Babies with Down Syndrome: A New Parents' Guide, 2nd ed.
Karen Stray-Gundersen (Ed.)
Woodbine House, 1995

Bethy and the Mouse: A Father Remembers His Children with Disabilities
Donald Bakely
Brookline Books, 1997

Biomedical Concerns in Persons with Down Syndrome
Siegfried Pueschel, Jeanette Pueschel (Eds.)
Paul H. Brookes, 1994

Bittersweet Baby
Jolie Kanat
CompCare Publishers, 1987

Camille's Children: 31 Miracles and Counting
Camille Geraldi, Carol Burris
Andrews and McMeel, 1996

Children with Down Syndrome:
A Developmental Perspective
Dante Cicchetti, Marjorie Beeghly (Eds.)
Cambridge University Press, 1990

Chris Burke: The Young Actor Who Has Down Syndrome
Helen Monsoon Geraghty
Chelsea House, 1994

Communication Skills in Children with Down Syndrome: A Guide for Parents
Libby Kumin, Ph.D., CCC-SLP
Woodbine House, 1994

Connecting Students: A Guide to Thoughtful Friendship Facilitation for Educators & Families
C.B. Schaffner, B. E. Buswell
PEAK Parent Center, Inc., 1992

Count Us In: Growing Up with Down Syndrome
Jason Kingsley, Mitchell Levitz
Harcourt Brace, 1993

Differences in Common: Straight Talk on Mental Retardation, Down Syndrome, and Life
Marilyn Trainer
Woodbine House, 1991

Down Syndrome: Advances in Medical Care
Ira Lott, Ernest McCoy (Eds.)
Wiley-Liss, 1992

Down Syndrome: Birth to Adulthood (Giving Families an Edge)
John Rynders, J. Margaret Horrobin
Love Pub. Co., 1997

Down Syndrome: The Facts
Mark Selikowitz
Oxford University Press, Inc., 1997

Down Syndrome: Living and Learning in the Community
Lynn Nadel, Donna Rosenthal (Eds.)
Wiley-Liss, 1995

Down Syndrome: A Resource Handbook
Carol Tingey
College Hill Press, 1988

Down Syndrome: Successful Parenting of Children with Down Syndrome
John Unruh, Ph.D.
Fern Ridge Press, 1994

Down Syndrome Moving Thru Life
Yvonne Burns, Pat Gunn (Eds.)
Singular Publishing Group, Inc., 1993

Down Syndrome: Now What Do I Do?
Anne Squires, Andrew Squires
Indian Orchard Publishing Co., 1990

Down Syndrome: Today's Health Care Issues
Ira Lott
Wiley and Sons, Inc., 1993

Down's Syndrome: Psychological, Psychobiological, and Socio-Educational Perspectives
Jean Rondal, Juan Perera, Lynn Nadel, Annick Comblain (Eds.)
Singular Publishing Group, Inc., 1996

Expecting Adam: A True Story of Birth, Rebirth, and Everyday Magic
Martha Beck
Random House, 1999

Fine Motor Skills in Children with Down Syndrome: A Guide for Parents and Teachers
Maryanne Bruni
Woodbine House, 1998

Gross Motor Skills in Children with Down Syndrome: A Guide for Parents and Professionals
Patricia Winders
Woodbine House, 1997

Keys to Parenting a Child with Down Syndrome (Barron's Parenting Keys)
Marlene Targ Brill, M.Ed.
Barron's Educational Series, Inc., 1993

Life as We Know It: A Father, a Family, and an Exceptional Child
Michael Berube
Random House, Inc., 1998

Medical Care in Down Syndrome: A Preventive Medicine Approach
Paul Rogers, Mary Coleman, Sue Buckley
Marcel Dekker, Inc., 1992

Medical and Surgical Care for Children with Down Syndrome: A Guide for Parents
D. Van Dyke, M.D., Philip Mattheis, M.D., Susan Schoon Eberly, M.A., Janet Williams, R.N., Ph.D. (Eds.)
Woodbine House, 1995

New Approaches to Down Syndrome
Brian Stratford, Pat Gunn (Eds.)
Cassell Academic, 1996

A Parent's Guide to Down Syndrome: Toward a Brighter Future
Siegfried Pueschel, et. al
Paul H. Brookes, 1990

Schooling Children with Down Syndrome: Toward an Understanding of Possibility
Christopher Kliewer
Teachers College Press, 1998

Teaching the Infant with Down Syndrome: A Guide for Parents and Professionals, 2nd ed.
Marci Hanson
PRO-ED, 1996

Teaching Reading to Children with Down Syndrome: A Guide for Parents and Teachers
Patricia Logan Oelwein
Woodbine House, 1994

Thumbs Up, Rico!
Maria Testa
Albert Whitman and Co., 1994

Understanding Down Syndrome: An Introduction for Parents
Cliff Cunningham
Brookline Books, 1995

Veronica's First Year
Jean Sasso Rheingrover
Albert Whitman and Co., 1996

The Young Person with Down Syndrome: Transition from Adolescence to Adulthood
Siegfried Pueschel
Paul H. Brookes, 1988

Yoga for the Special Child
Sonia Sumar
Special Yoga Publications, 1998

<u>Books for Youth</u>

Are There Stripes in Heaven?
Lee Klein
Paulist Press, 1994

Be Good to Eddie Lee
Virginia Fleming
Putnam Pub., 1997

Barnaby's Birthday
John Fitzgerald, Lyn Fitzgerald
McGraw, 1994

Becca and Sue Make Two
Sandra Haines
Writer's Press Service, 1995

Big Brother Dustin
Alden Carter
Albert Whitman and Co., 1997

Buddy's Shadow
Shirley Becker
Jason and Nordic Pubs., 1992

Chris Burke: He Overcame Down Syndrome
Greg Lee
Rourke Co., 1993

Chris Burke: Star of Life Goes On
Bob Italia
Abdo and Daughters, 1992

Cookie
Linda Kneeland
Jason and Nordic, 1995

The Falcon's Wing
Dawna Lisa Buchanan
Orchard Books, 1992

Finding a Friend
Zilpha Booth
Windswept House Publishers, 1996

For Love of Jeremy
Hazel Krantz
Lodestar Books, 1990

How Smudgie Came
Nan Gregory
Walker & Co., 1997

Loving Ben
Elizabeth Laird
Delacorte Press, 1989

The Man Who Loved Clowns
June Rae Wood
Hyperion Books for Children, 1995

My Sister Annie
Bill Dodds
Boyds Mills Press, 1997

Our Brother Has Downs Syndrome
Shelley Cairo, Jasmine Cairo, Tara Cairo, Irene McNeil
Firefly Books, Ltd., 1993

We'll Paint the Octopus Red
Stephanie Stuve-Bodeen
Woodbine House, 1998

Where's Chimpy?
Berniece Rabe
Albert Whitman and Co., 1991

Periodicals / Newsletters

Down Syndrome Quarterly
Denison University
Granville, OH 43023
Fax: (740) 587-6601
Web: http://www.denison.edu/dsq
Interdisciplinary journal devoted to advancing the state
of knowledge on Down syndrome. Covers all areas of
medical, behavioral, and social scientific research.

Videos
Video tapes can be very useful, but may a challenge to find, especially if they aren't new to the market.
Try contacting the producers noted even if the tape isn't listed on their web site, book stores and your
library.

Bittersweet Waltz
Produced by L. Safan, 1993
National Down Syndrome Society
666 Broadway
New York, NY 10012
Ph: (800) 221-4602
      (212) 460-9330
Fax: (212) 979-2873
Web: http://www.ndss.org/
An educational tool for parents seeking to have their
child included in a regular elementary classroom.

Choices
Comforty Media Concepts
2145 Pioneer Road
Evanston, IL 60201
Ph: (708) 475-0791
Fax: (708) 475-0793
E-mail: comforty@comforty.com
Web: http://www.comforty.com/
Introduction to the philosophy and practice of
inclusion. Four personalized stories about how
inclusion has affected the lives of people with
disabilities, including people with Down syndrome.

Down Syndrome: A Parental Perspective
Produced by Dartmouth-Hitchcock Medical Center
Available through Learner Managed Designs, Inc.
P.O. Box 747
Lawrence, KS 66044
Ph: (800) 467-1644
      (785) 842-9088
Fax: (785) 842-6881
E-mail: info@lmdusa.com
Web: http://www.lmdusa.com/
How parents of children with Down syndrome maintain
a focus on quality-of-life needs.

Early Use of Total Communication: Parents' Perspective on Using Sign Language with Young Children with Down Symdrome
Produced by Betsy Gibbs, Ph.D., Ann Springer, CCC-SLP
Paul H. Brookes, 1993
P.O. Box 10624
Baltimore, MD 21285-0624
Ph: (800) 638-3775
Fax: (410) 337-8539
E-mail: custserv@brookespublishing.com
Web: http://www.pbrookes.com/
How simultaneously using speech and sign language
helps children with Down syndrome to communicate.

Educating Peter
Produced by T. Goodwin, G. Wurzburg
Direct Cinema Limited, 1992
P. O. Box 10003
Santa Monica, CA 90410
Ph: (800) 525-0000
         (310) 636-8200
E-mail: info@directcinemalimited.com
Web: www.directcinema.com
Follows a child with Down syndrome through a year of inclusion in a public school.

Inclusion: Bernardsville Beginnings
National Down Syndrome Society, 1993
666 Broadway
New York, NY 10012
Ph: (800) 221-4602   -
         (212) 460-9330
Fax: (212) 979-2873
Web: http://www.ndss.org/
Follows a girl through her first full year in a first grade inclusion program. It is a step-by-step account of teaching staff preparation and classroom experience.

Like Any Child: Raising a Child with Down Syndrome
Produced by Kim Sheridan
Child Development Media, Inc.
5632 Van Nuys Blvd., Suite 286
Van Nuys, CA 91401
Ph: (800) 405-8942
Fax: (818) 994-6549
E-mail: info@childdevelopmentmedia.com
Web: http://www.childdevmedia.com/
The positive and enriching experiences of raising a child with Down Syndrome.

A Promising Future
666 Broadway
New York, NY 10012
Ph: (800) 221-4602
         (212) 460-9330
Fax: (212) 979-2873
Web: http://www.ndss.org/
For new or expecting parents of babies with Down syndrome. The experiences and advice of parents, developmental pediatricians and other professionals.

Sean's Story: Ready for School
Produced by ABC News, 1994
Ph: (800) 913-3434
Two different outlooks on the education of children with Down syndrome: inclusion versus a special school.

Web Sites

Also see "General Web Sites". Many have sections on Down syndrome, but they are not listed separately below.

Disability Solutions
Web: http://www.teleport.com/~dsolns/
Resources published by the Enoch-Gelbard Foundation.

Down Syndrome
Web: http://www.nas.com/downsyn/index.html
Information, resources, vendors.

Down Syndrome Amongst Us
Web: http://www.pirchei.co.il/specl_ed/down/index.htm
Collection of articles on Down syndrome.

Down Syndrome: Health Issues
Web: http://www.ds-health.com/
Pediatrician's site with information on Down syndrome.

---- *Eating Disorders*

Intense preoccupation with food as a way to deal with an emotional problem. The result is a negative, all-consuming way of life. Affecting primarily girls, eating disorders take on various forms and can change over time.

Types

Eating disorder types can occur alone or in combination:

- **Anorexia nervosa** - Intense fear of gaining weight in spite of already being thin. Through self-imposed starvation or light eating, one doesn't eat enough to maintain an ideal weight and health, and becomes thin to the point of damaging one's health.

- **Bingeing** - Rapid consumption of large amounts of food (typically secretively) in a short time, a few hours or days. One feels out of control and ashamed of his or her behavior, yet may be afraid of becoming overweight. Therefore, purging may follow a binge.

- **Bulimia** - Purging through self-induced vomiting, or using laxatives or diuretics to lose weight or counteract overeating.

- **Compulsive overeating** - Eating more than one's body requires, followed by guilt or shame.

- **Pica** - Craving non-food items, such as dirt, clay, paint chips, plaster, chalk, cornstarch, laundry starch, baking soda, coffee grounds, cigarette ashes, burnt match heads, rust, etc.

Frequency

- Over 60 million Americans suffer from dysfunctional eating.
- Affects 1-4% of girls age 15-24.
- 95% of those affected with eating disorders are female, in their late teens and early twenties, tending to be successful. They usually are of average weight.
- Only 5-10% of people with anorexia and bulimia are male.
- About 2% of the population is anorexic. 95% of those affected are female.
- Males in professions where weight is important (dance, modeling, jockeying) tend to have a higher rate of eating disorders.

- 4% of college-aged women suffer from bulimia.
- 10-15 % of the people with bulimia are male.
- 20% of bulimics abuse alcohol or drugs.
- 85% of compulsive eaters are women of all ages.

Symptoms and Possible Effects

Anorexia nervosa
- ☐ Onset is in early adolescence.
- ☐ Intense fear of becoming fat, even if one is already too thin.   Distorted body image.
- ☐ Excessive dieting, voluntary starvation. Denial of being hungry in spite of eating little.
- ☐ Large weight loss (15-25%) in a short time. Failure to gain weight during a growth period.
- ☐ Diet goals become continually more aggressive.
- ☐ One spends a good deal of time alone, preferring to eat alone. Refuses to eat with others in public.
- ☐ Ritualistic about food preparation, using special utensils, weighing food, arranging food on the plate or pushing it around without eating it. May collect recipes, cook for others, claim vegetarianism.
- ☐ Obsessiveness about exercise.
- ☐ Excellence in schoolwork becomes important. Perfectionism, obsession with self-control and order. Reasoning becomes "all or nothing."
- ☐ Aggressive behavior, depression.
- ☐ Hair is dry, patchy.
- ☐ Skin is dry, takes on a gray or yellow tone. Layer of fine, downy hair emerges. May break out.
- ☐ Bones and teeth may fall out or stop growing.   Osteoporosis, damaged bone growth.
- ☐ Heart failure, irregular heart beat, kidney failure, liver damage, electrolyte abnormalities, thyroid conditions, low blood pressure.
- ☐ Stomach distress, bowel dysfunction, hypoglycemia, abdominal pain, constipation, bloat, diarrhea.
- ☐ Low level of vitamins, loss of protein.
- ☐ Swelling of the legs, loss of muscle mass, loss of fatty tissue causing girls' breasts and hips to diminish.
- ☐ Sunken eyes, "chipmunk-like" face.
- ☐ Numbness and tingling in hands, feet, face, continually feeling cold, low tolerance for cold weather.
- ☐ Hormonal imbalance, loss of menstrual cycles, sexual dysfunction. Avoids sexual activity / intimacy.
- ☐ Loss of concentration, irritability, insomnia, hyperactivity, brain atrophy, headaches, fatigue, dizziness, fainting spells.
- ☐ Dehydration, frequent thirst, lowered body temperature, bruises, infections that don't heal.
- ☐ Use of laxatives or diuretics to lose weight.
- ☐ Feelings of guilt and self-loathing. Severe mood changes. Depression.
- ☐ Regular weighing.   Compulsive and excessive exercise.
- ☐ Withdrawal from others. Fear of control by others.
- ☐ Avoidance of drugs or alcohol.
- ☐ Denial of symptoms, resistance to treatment.

Anorexia athletica (activity anorexia)
- ☐ Compulsive exercising beyond the requirements for good health.
- ☐ Fanatic attitude about weight and diet, sacrificing time from school, work, and relationships to exercise.
- ☐ Challenge of exercise becomes the focus, not the fun.

❑ Self-worth is defined in terms of performance, yet achievements aren't satisfying and goals are raised.
❑ Behavior is justified by defining oneself as a dedicated athlete.

Bingeing
❑ Intense food cravings.
❑ Rapid eating until uncomfortably full.
❑ Eating alone out of embarrassment of how much one is eating. Lies about how much was eaten.
❑ Feelings of self-disgust.
❑ Alternate periods of heavy eating with periods of rigid dieting.
❑ Being overweight, though claiming to be on a diet.
❑ Eating is done in a rushed, urgent manner.
❑ History of failed diets.
❑ Food is purchased and eaten secretly.
❑ Foods eaten may be favorites from childhood, foods avoided on a diet, sweet or starchy foods, foods not even liked.
❑ Emotional eating, in response to bad or good news, boredom, nervousness, frustration, anger, loneliness. May be out of control in other areas of life, overly emotional, have mood swings.
❑ Shame of perceived eating and weight control failure. Unable to cope with stress.
❑ Avoidance of conflicts.
❑ Anxious feelings.
❑ Days are planned around eating or avoiding food.
❑ Avoidance of scales, discussions of weight, recreational activities that might expose parts of the body or require physical movement.
❑ Eating with buddies and having special rituals for food and eating.
❑ Fear of being left alone with food.
❑ Irregular menstrual periods, hormonal imbalances, constipation.
❑ Unusual weight changes.
❑ Feelings of being too hot.
❑ Fast or irregular heart beat.
❑ Exhaustion.
❑ Water retention.
❑ Weight fluctuations.
❑ Hypertension (high blood pressure).
❑ Fatigue.

Bulimia nervosa
❑ Comfort is found in food, which becomes an escape from circumstances in one's life.
❑ Self worth determined by weight.
❑ Purging is used for weight control. Self-induced vomiting, use of diuretics or laxatives to control weight.
❑ Possibly accompanied by binge eating.
❑ Preoccupation with body shape and weight; overly concerned with others' opinions of one's body.
❑ Near normal weight unless anorexia is also present.
❑ Large quantities of food are eaten without weight gain.
❑ Difficulty expressing negative feelings, problems regulating behavior. Low self esteem, depression.
❑ Disappearance into the bathroom, notably after meals.
❑ Secret eating evidenced by hidden wrappers, empty pantry shelves, missing money.
❑ Abuse of alcohol or drugs.

❑ Syrup of Ipecac used to induce vomiting. Regular use, even for a short time, can cause life-threatening problems.

❑ Shoplifting, promiscuity, abuse of credit cards to finance binges.

❑ Callused skin, bruised knuckles from self-inducing vomiting.

❑ Bags under one's eyes.

❑ Dehydration, electrolyte imbalances which can lead to cardiac arrhythmia and possible sudden death.

❑ Hypoglycemia, spontaneous regurgitation, abdominal cramps, gastric ruptures, hernias, kidney failure.

❑ Swollen or infected salivary glands making one's face and throat puffy. Broken blood vessels in face.

❑ Damaged tooth enamel, numerous cavities, tooth loss, severe gum disease.

❑ Fainting spells, rapid or irregular heartbeat.

❑ Tremors and blurred visions following episodes of vomiting.

❑ Menstrual periods can be normal, irregular, or even absent.

❑ Fatigue, muscle aches, sore throat, dizziness, fainting.

❑ Depression, alcohol and drug use is common as a way to "self medicate" to compensate for low neurotransmitter levels that result from purging.

❑ Awareness that habits aren't normal, yet fears not being able to stop.

❑ Feelings of embarrassment, deceit. Alternately wants and fears relationships. Will often ask for help once embarrassment is overcome.

Compulsive overeating
❑ Intense food cravings.

❑ Binges and weight gain.

❑ Eating in a rushed, urgent manner, to the point of uncomfortable fullness.

❑ Repeated diet failures.

❑ Small amounts eaten in public.

❑ Secret eating, lying about how much one eats.

❑ Fatigue, depression, embarrassment over weight and limited physical and social activities.

❑ Awareness that bingeing is abnormal, but fears food habits aren't controllable.

❑ Feelings that self-image is determined by weight and size.

❑ Family disturbances.

❑ Obsessions, compulsions, aggressive behavior, self-mutilation, elevated pain tolerance, menstrual changes, insomnia.

❑ Low self esteem from shame.

❑ Inability to cope with stress. Avoid conflicts or problems. Anxiety. Mood fluctuatations due to weight gain or loss.

❑ Avoidance of scales, discussions of weight, recreational activities that might expose parts of the body or require physical movement.

❑ Fluid imbalances, dehydration.

❑ Bowel infections and disfunction.

❑ High blood pressure.

❑ Fatigue.

Causes
▪ U.S. culture is obsessed with "perfect bodies" which sets expectations that many people try to meet, but can't. An eating disorder can be attempt to attain a perfect body or be a response to feeling that one's body isn't adequate.

challenges with friends and families, often of major importance in the life of a girl age 15-24, can also add fuel to the fire.

- Once started, eating disorders become self-perpetuating. Excessive dieting can turn into anorexia, which can bring on purging behavior, and then potential bingeing before purging.
- Some victims, particularly those of anorexia, feel unworthy of good things in life and so they deprive themselves of eating. Some feel angry yet seek approval and fear criticism; they don't know how to express their anger in acceptable ways. They may be dealing with painful emotions and looking for ways in which to gain control or over their lives. Some are avoiding sexuality, others are responding to sexual abuse. Some feel weak, victimized, and resentful. Feelings are locked inside and turn against themselves in the form of starving or bingeing.
- One may be reacting to the way she feels in relation to her family: alone, misunderstood, criticized for her appearance, overprotected. Her family may be rigid or ineffective at solving conflict. Families may have high expectations for their daughters to be successful or to look a certain way. A girl may feel her needs have no value or that her parents disapprove of her.
- Girls whose mothers are overly concerned about their own appearance and weight are more at risk for eating disorders.
- Some may be trying to develop a sense of identity by building a socially acceptable and admired body.
- Many of the females who suffer from eating disorders come from upwardly mobile families, but it's seen in all socio-economic classes.
- Eating triggers the same chemicals in the brain that regulate mood. Once a person begins to starve, binge, or purge, their brain chemistry changes, thus prolonging the problem. Both undereating and overeating activates brain chemicals that produce feelings of peace and euphoria. Eating disorders may be a way for some to "self medicate" anxiety and depression.
- Some may use their eating disorder as a way to handle situations for which they are unsure of how else to handle (e.g., change in the nuclear family, moving to a new school.)
- Repeated "diet-fail-diet" cycles. Eating disorders can be a way to stay on the diet or clean up after a diet failure. The problem is that each failure lowers self esteem and may strengthen one's resolve to be successful the next time, no matter what.

Compulsive eating
May also be caused by food allergies that produce a crave-crash cycle.

Pica
- Usually found in pregnant women, or those whose diets are lacking in minerals found in the non-food items.
- Those with psychiatric disturbances may eat non-food items, as well as those whose ethnic customs include eating such things.

Males
- Being overweight as a child.
- Dieting.
- Participation in a sport that values thinness (track, horse racing) or that includes weight categories for participation (wrestling, body building).
- Having a job that demands thinness, such as entertaining or modeling.
- Men who are gay are more at risk for eating disorders.

What Else Could it Be?

Children with eating disorders may have symptoms that mimic those of other conditions, such as those noted below. To properly diagnose a problem, these may need to be ruled out as causes for the problem.

✓ Borderline personality disorder
✓ Depersonalization disorder
✓ Depression

✓ Drug or alcohol abuse
✓ Major affective disorder
✓ Post traumatic stress disorder

Mimic anorexia nervosa:

✓ Body dystrophic disorder
✓ Obsessive-compulsive disorder
✓ Schizophrenia

✓ Social phobia
✓ Superior mesenteric artery syndrome

Mimic bulimia nervosa:

✓ Kleine-Levin syndrome

DSM IV Diagnostic Criteria

Reprinted with permission from the *Diagnostic and Statistical Manual of Mental Disorders, Fourth Edition, Text Revision.* Copyright 2000 American Psychiatric Association.

For anorexia nervosa:

A. Refusal to maintain body weight at or above a minimally normal weight for age and height (e.g., weight loss leading to maintenance of body weight less than 85% of that expected; or failure to make expected weight gain during period of growth, leading to body weight less than 85% of that expected.)

B. Intense fear of gaining weight of becoming fat, even though underweight.

C. Disturbance in the way in which one's body weight or shape is experienced, undue influence of body weight or shape on self-evaluation, or denial of the seriousness of the current low body weight.

D. In postmenarcheal females, amenorrhea, i.e., the absence of at last three consecutive menstrual cycles. (A woman is considered to have amenorrhea if her periods occur only following hormone, e.g., estrogen, administration.)

For bulimia nervosa:

A. Recurrent episodes of binge eating. An episode of binge eating is characterized by both of the following:
    (1) eating, in a discrete period of time (e.g., within any 2-hour period), an amount of food that is definitely larger than most people would eat during a similar period of time and under similar circumstances
    (2) a sense of lack of control over eating during the episode (e.g., a feeling that one cannot stop eating or control what or how much one is eating)

B. Recurrent inappropriate compensatory behavior in order to prevent weight gain, such as self-induced vomiting; misuse of laxatives, diuretics, enemas, or other medications; fasting; or excessive exercise.

C. The binge eating and inappropriate compensatory behaviors both occur, on average, at least twice a week for 3 months.

D. Self-evaluation is unduly influenced by body shape and weight.

E. The disturbance does not occur exclusively during episodes of Anorexia Nervosa.

For pica:
A. Persistent eating of nonnutritive substances for a period of at least 1 month.

B. The eating of nonnutritive substances is inappropriate to the developmental level.

C. The eating behavior is not part of a culturally sanctioned practice.

D. If the eating behavior occurs exclusively during the course of another mental disorder (e.g., Mental Retardation, Pervasive Developmental Disorder, Schizophrenia), it is sufficiently severe to warrant independent clinical attention.

Treatment

Treatment is unique per individual. Generally, the more components included in a treatment plan, the faster the recovery.

In general
- Counseling to develop healthy ways of taking control, managing relationships, developing new body images, improving self esteem, finding new ways to find fulfillment.
- Family counseling to change interaction patterns.
- Nutrition counseling to design healthy meals, change eating behavior.
- Changing eating habits to maintain normal body weight.
- Medication and other treatment for depression, anxiety, obsessive behavior.
- Nutritional treatment to correct deficiencies.
- Gynecological treatment.
- Help with addiction to drugs, alcohol or dependence on diet pills.

Anorexia nervosa
- Immediate goal is to prevent starvation, restore a healthier body weight.
- Short hospital stay may be needed to prevent death, suicide.
- Therapy to find the root causes of the problem, correct conditions caused due to the use of unhealthy methods of weight control, learn sensible eating patterns, and decrease preoccupation with weight and food.

Bulimia nervosa
- Dental work to repair damage.

Outcomes
- With treatment 60% recover.
- Even with treatment, about 20% of people with eating disorders make partial recoveries.
- 20% don't improve or die.

Anorexia nervosa
- If handled quickly and properly, 80% recover. After the first year, however, only 50% recover.
- 15-25% are chronically affected by some aspect of their illness, e.g., intestines don't function properly, brain damage.
- Death from medical complications and suicide occurs in 2-10% of sufferers.

Bulimia
- 20% attempt suicide.

Who to Contact
Also refer to "Who Else to Contact." Organizations listed below target their work specifically toward eating disorders.

Academy for Eating Disorders (AED)
6728 Old McLean Village Dr.
McLean, VA 22101
Ph: (703) 556- 9222
Fax: (703) 556 –8729
Web: http://www.acadeatdis.org/
Prevention, education, research on eating disorders.

Association for the Health Enrichment for Large People (AHELP)
P.O. 17743
Blacksurg, VA 27042-1743
Ph.   (540) 951-3527
Fax: (540) 951-3527
E-mail: ahelp@nrv.net
Web: http://www.usit.com/ahelp/
Organization for professionals who serve overweight people to share information.

American Anorexia/Bulimia Association, Inc. (ABBA)
165 West 46th St., Suite 1108
New York, NY 10036
Ph: (212) 575-6200
Web: http://www.aabainc.org
Education, advocacy and research on eating disorders.

Eating Disorders Awareness and Prevention, Inc. (EDAP)
603 Stewart St., Suite 803
Seattle, WA 98101
Ph: (800) 931-2237
       (206) 382-3587
Fax: (206) 829-8501
Web: http://www.edap.org
Prevention, education, referral and support services, advocacy, training, and research on eating disorders.

Anorexia Nervosa and Related Eating Disorders, Inc. (ANRED)
P.O. Box 5102
Eugene, OR 97405
Ph: (800) 931-2237
       (503) 344-1144
E-mail: jarinor@rio.com
Web: http://www.anred.com/
Information on eating and weight loss disorders.

Food Addicts Anonymous
World Service Office
4623 Forest Hill Blvd., Suite #109-4
West Palm Beach, FL 33415-9120
Ph: (561) 967-3871
E-mail: FAAWSO@juno.com
Web: http://www.foodaddictsanonymous.org/
Fellowship of those who are willing to recover from the disease of food addiction. Primary purpose is to stay abstinent and to help other food addicts achieve abstinence.

Family Resources for Education on Eating Disorders (FREED)
9611 Page Ave.
Bethesda, MD 20814-1737
Ph: (301) 493-4568
     (301) 585-0358
E-mail: bigmommary@aol.com
Web: http://cpcug.org/user/rpike/freed.html
Education, resources, support for persons suffering from anorexia, bulimia, and binge eating.

National Association to Advance Fat Acceptance
P.O. Box 188620
Sacramento, CA 95818
Ph: (916) 558-6880
Fax: (916) 558-6881
E-mail: mabnaafa@aol.com
Web: http://www.naafa.org
Works to eliminate discrimination based on body size and provide large people with the tools for self-empowerment through public education, advocacy, and member support.

National Association for Anorexia Nervosa and Associated Disorders, Inc. (ANAD)
P.O. Box 7
Highland Park, IL 60035
Ph: (847) 831-3438
Fax: (847) 433-4632
E-mail: info@anad.org
Web: http://www.anad.org
Education, self-help groups, research promotion, advocay to help eating disordered people and their families.

National Eating Disorders Organization (NEDO)
6655 South Yale Ave.
Tulsa, OK 74136
Ph: (918) 481-4044
Fax: (918) 481-4076
Web: http://www.kidsource.com/NEDO/index.html
Education, consultation, research, and treatment referral services.

Overeaters Anonymous
World Service Office
6075 Zenith Ct. NE
Rio Rancho, NM 87124
Ph: (505) 891-2664
Fax: (505) 891-4320
E-mail: overeatr@technet.nm.org
Web: http://www.overeatersanonymous.org/
Support organization for individuals who are recovering from compulsive overeating.

VITALITY
91 South Main St.
West Hartford, CT 06107
Ph: (860) 521-2515
E-mail: vtlty@tiac.net
Web: http://www.tiac.net/users/vtlty/
Promotes wellness and respect for diverse sizes and shapes.

Recommended Reading

Abstinence: Members of Overeaters Anonymous Share Their Experience, Strength, and Hope
Overeaters Anonymous, Inc., 1994

Afraid to Eat: Children and Teens in Weight Crisis
Frances Berg
Healthy Weight Journal, 1997

After Surviving an Eating Disorder: Strategies for Family and Friends
M. Siegel, J. & M. Weinshel
Harper Collins, 1997

Am I Fat? Helping Young Children Accept Differences in Body Size
Joanne Ikeda, MA, RD; Priscilla Naworski, MS, CHES
ETR Associates, 1992

Am I Thin Enough Yet?: The Cult of Thinness and the Commercialization of Identity
Sharlene Hesse-Biber
Oxford University Press, Inc., 1996

Anatomy of a Food Addiction: The Brain Chemistry of Overeating
Anne Katherine
Gurze Books, 1996

Anorexia and Bulimia
Paul Robbins
Enslow Publishers, 1998

Anorexia and Bulimia
Rita Milios
PPI Publishing, 1994

Anorexia Nervosa: A Guide to Recovery
Lindsey Hall, Monika Ostroff
Gurze Books, 1998

Anorexia Nervosa and Recovery: A Hunger for Meaning
Karen Way, MA
Harrington Park Press, Inc., 1993

The Anorexic Experience, 3rd ed.
Marilyn Lawrence
Trafalgar Square, 1997

Anorexics on Anorexia
Rosemary Shelley
Jessica Kingsley Pub., 1997

Appearance Obsession: Learning to Love the Way You Look
Joni Johnston, Psy. D.
Health Communications, 1994

Appetites
Geneen Roth
NAL/Dutton, 1997

The Art and Science of Rational Eating
Albert Ellis, Michael Abrams, Lidia Dengelegi
Barricade Books, Inc., 1992

Beyond Anorexia: Narrative, Spirituality and Recovery
Catherine Garrett
Cambridge University Press, 1998

Beyond the Food Game: A Spiritual & Psychological Approach to Healing Emotional Eating
Jane Latimer
Living Quest, 1993

The Body Betrayed: A Deeper Understanding of Women, Eating Disorders, and Treatment
Kathryn Zerbe, M.D.
Gurze Books, 1995

The Body Image Trap: Understanding and Rejecting Body Image Myths
Marion Crook, B.Sc.N.
Self Counsel Press, 1991

Body and Soul: A Guide to Lasting Recovery from Compulsive Eating and Bulimia
Susan Meltsner
Fine Communications, 1997

Body Traps: Breaking the Binds that Keep You from Feeling Good About Your Body
Judith Rodin
William Morrow, 1993

Bodylove: Feeling Good About Our Looks – and Ourselves
Rita Freedman
Harper Perennial, 1990

Breaking Free from Compulsive Eating
Geneen Roth
NAL/Dutton, 1993

Breaking Out of Food Jail: How to Free Yourself from Diets and Problem Eating, Once and For All
Jean Antonello
Simon and Schuster Trade, 1996

Bulimarexia: The Binge/Purge Cycle, 2nd ed.
Marlene Boskind-White, William White
W.W. Norton and Co., Inc., 1991

Bulimia: A Guide for Family and Friends
Roberta Trattner Sherman, Ron Thompson
Jossey-Bass Publishers, 1997

Bulimia: A Guide to Recovery: Understanding and Overcoming the Binge-Purge Syndrome, rev. ed.
Lindsey Hall, Leigh Cohn
Gurze Books, 1998

Bulimia: A Guide for Sufferers and Their Families
David Haslam
Butterworth-Heinemann, 1996

Bulimia Nervosa and Binge-Eating: A Guide to Recovery
Peter Cooper
New York University Press, 1995

The Bulimic College Student: Evaluation, Treatment, and Prevention
Leighton Whitaker, Ph.D., William Davis, Ph.D. (Eds.)
Haworth Press, Inc, 1989

Catherine: Story of a Young Girl Who Died of Anorexia
Maureen Dunbar
Penguin, 1997

Certifiably Bulimic
Susan Merkel
Distinctive Publishing, 1992

Chaotic Eating
Helen Bray-Garretson, Ph.D., Kaye Cook, Ph.D.
Zondervan Pub., 1992

Compulsive Exercise and the Eating Disorders: Toward an Integrated Theory of Activity
Alayne Yates
Brunner/Mazel, 1991

Controlling Eating Disorders with Facts, Advice and Resources
Raymond Lemberg, Ph.D.
Oryx Press, 1992

Coping with Eating Disorders, rev. ed.
Barbara Moe
Rosen Publishing Group, 1995

Deadly Diet, 2nd ed.
Camie Ford, Sunny Hale
Paraclete Press, 1995

The Deadly Diet: Recovering from Anorexia and Bulimia, 2nd ed.
Terence Sandbek
New Harbinger Publications, Inc., 1993

Dedication to Hunger: The Anorexic Aesthetic in Modern Culture
Leslie Heywood
University of California Press, 1996

Desperately Seeking Self: A Guidebook for People with Eating Problems
Viola Fodor
Gurze Books, 1997

Diary of an Eating Disorder: A Mother and Daughter Share Their Healing Journey
Chelsea Smith, Beverly Runyon
Taylor Publishing, 1998

Dieting: A Dry Drunk
Becky Jackson
B.L.J. Nautilus Publications, 1991

Disordered Eating Among Athletes: The Athletic Trainer's Role
Human Kenetics Staff, 1997

Don't Diet, Live-It! A Journey Book for Healing Food, Weight and Body Issues
Marsea Marcus, Andre LoBue
Gurze, 1999

Dying to Be Thin: Understanding and Defeating Anorexia Nervosa and Bulimia - A Practical, Lifesaving Guide
Ira Sacker, M.D., Marc Zimmer, Ph.D.
Warner Books, Inc., 1987

Eating, Body Weight, and Performance in Athletes: Disorders of Modern Society
Kelly Brownell, Judith Rodin, Jack Wilmore (Eds.)
Lea & Febiger, 1992

The Eating Disorder Source Book
Carolyn Costin
Lowell House, 1996

Eating Disorders
Elizabeth Sirimarco
Marshall Cavendish Corp., 1993

Eating Disorders
Don Nardo
Lucent Books, 1991

Eating Disorders and Athletes: A Handbook for Coaches
Susan Chappell Holliman (Ed.)
American Alliance for Health, Physical Education, Recreation, 1991

Eating Disorders Among Athletes: Theory, Issues, and Research
David Black (Ed.)
American Alliance for Health, Physical Education, Recreation, 1991

Eating Disorders and Magical Control of the Body: The Treatment of Eating Disorders through Art Therapy
Mary Levens
Routledge, 1995

Eating Disorders: Management of Obesity, Bulimia, and Anorexia Nervosa, 4th ed.
Suzanne Abraham, Derek Llewellyn-Jones
Oxford University Press, 1996

Eating Disorders and Marital Relationships
Stephan van den Broucke, Walter Vandereycken
Routledge, 1998

Eating Disorders: New Directions in Treatment and Recovery
Barbara Kinoy
Columbia University Press, 1994

Eating Disorders and Obesity: A Comprehensive Handbook
Kelly Brownell, Christopher Fairburn (Eds.)
Guilford Publications, 1995

Eating Disorders: A Question and Answer Book About Anorexia Nervosa and Bulimia Nervosa
Ellen Erlanger
Lerner Pub., 1987

Eating Disorders: When Food Turns Against You
Ben Sonder
Franklin Watts, Inc., 1993

Eating and Growth Disorders in Infants and Children
Joseph Woolston
Sage Publications, 1991

Eating Illness Workbook
Joan Ebbitt
Hazelden Foundation, 1987

Eating Our Hearts Out: Personal Accounts of Women's Relationship to Food
Leslea Newman (Ed.)
Crossing Pr., 1993

Eating Without Guilt: Overcoming Compulsive Eating, 2nd ed.
Alice Katz, M.S.
Self Counsel Press, 1991

Element Guide to Anorexia/Bulimia
Julia Buckroyd
Element Books, 1996

Emotional Eating: A Practical Guide to Taking Control
Edward Abramson
Lexington Books, 1993

Emotional Weight: Change Your Relationship With Food by Changing Your Relationship With Yourself
Colleen Sundermeyer
Perigee, 1993

Endorphins, Eating Disorders, and Other Addictive Behaviors
Hans Huebner
W. W. Norton and Co., Inc., 1993

Everybody's Doing It...and Here's How to Quit
Dorie Pass
Golden One Publishing, 1990

Everything You Need to Know About Eating Disorders
Rachel Kubersky
Rosen Publishing Group, 1996

Fasting Girls: The History of Anorexia Nervosa
Joan Jacobs Brumberg
Harvard University Press, 1989

Fat is a Family Affair: A Guide for People with Eating Disorders and Those Who Love Them
Judi Hollis, Ph.D.
Hazelden Foundation, 1989

Fat is a Feminist Issue: The Anti-Diet Guide to Permanent Weight Loss
Susie Orbach
Galahad Books, 1997

Fat and Furious: Women and Food Obsession
Judi Hollis
Fawcett Books, 1995

Father Hunger: Fathers, Daughters and Food
Margo Maine, Ph.D.
Gurze Books, 1991

Feast of Famine: A Physician's Personal Struggle to Overcome Anorexia Nervosa
Joan Johnston, M.D.
Recovery Publications, 1993

Feeding the Empty Heart: Adult Children and Compulsive Eating
Barbara McFarland, Tyeis Baker-Baumann
Harper and Row, 1988

Feeding the Hungry Heart: The Experience of Compulsive Eating
Geneen Roth
NAL/Dutton, 1993

The Five Reasons Why We Overeat: How to Develop a Long-Term Control Plan That's Right for You
Cynthia Last
Carol Publishing Group, 1999

Food Addiction: The Body Knows
Kay Sheppard
Health Communications, Inc., 1993

Food Fight: A Guide to Eating Disorders for Preteens and Their Parents
Janet Bode
Simon and Schuster, 1997

The Food Trap: Breaking its Hidden Control
Pamela Smith
Creation House, 1990

Freeing Someone You Love From Eating Disorders
Mary Dan Eades, M.D.
Body Press/Perigee, 1993

French Toast for Breakfast: Declaring Peace with Emotional Eating
Mary Anne Cohen
Gurze Books, 1995

Full Lives: Women Who Have Freed Themselves from Food and Weight Obsession
Lindsey Hall
Gurze Books, 1993

Good Enough
Cynthia Nappa Bitter
HopeLines, 1998

Good Girls Don't Eat Dessert: Changing Your Relationship to Food and Sex
Rosalyn Meadow, Ph.D., Lillie Weiss, Ph.D.
Harmony Books, 1992

Healing the Hungry Self: The Diet-Free Solution to Lifelong Weight Management
Deirdra Price
Plume, 1998

Helping Athletes with Eating Disorders
Ron Thompson, Roberta Trattner Sherman
Human Kinetics Publishers, 1993

Hope, Help and Healing for Eating Disorders: A New Approach to Treating Anorexia, Bulimia, and Overeating
Gregory Jantz
Harold Shaw Publishers, 1995

Hope and Recovery: A Mother-Daughter Story About Anorexia Nervosa, Bulimia, and Manic Depression
Emma Lou Thayne, Becky Thayne Markosian
Franklin Watts, Inc., 1992

How to Control Your Eating
Carl Arinoldo
Nova Kroshka Books, 1998

How to Get Your Kids to Eat... But Not Too Much
Ellyn Satter
Bull Publishing, 1987

How Schools Can Help Combat Student Eating Disorders
Michael Levine
National Education Assn., 1987

The Hunger Diseases
Raymond Battegay
Jason Aronson, Inc., 1997

Hunger Pains: The Modern Women's Tragic Quest for Thinness
Mary Pipher
Ballantine Books, Inc., 1997

A Hunger So Wide and So Deep: American Women Speak Out on Eating Problems
Becky Thompson
U. of Minn., 1994

The Hunger Within: A Twelve-Week Guided Journey to Recovery from Compulsive Eating
Marilyn Ann Migliore, Philip Ross
Main Street Books, 1998

I Wish I Were Thin - I Wish I Were Fat: The Real Reasons We Overeat and What We Can Do About It
Michelle Joy Levine
Vanderbilt Press, 1997

If You Think You Have an Eating Disorder
John Barnhill, M.D., Nadine Taylor, M.S., R.D.
Dells Books, 1998

Inner Eating
Shirley Billigmeier
Oliver-Nelson Books, 1992

Inner Hunger: A Young Woman's Struggle through Anorexia & Bulimia
Mianne Apostolides
W.W. Norton, 1998

Intuitive Eating: A Recovery Book for the Chronic Dieter: Rediscover the Pleasures of Eating and Rebuild Your Body Image
Evelyn Tribole, Elyse Resch
St. Martin's Mass Market Press, 1996

The Invisible Woman: Confronting Weight Prejudice in American
W. Charisse Goodman
Gurze Books, 1995

Is Your Child Dying to Be Thin? A Workbook for Parents and Family Members on Eating Disorders
Laura Goodman
Dorrance Publishing Co., Inc., 1992

It Ain't the Food: The Emotional Side of Eating Disorders
Barbara Dave
World Comm., 1994

It's Not About Food: Change Your Mind, Change Your Life, End Your Obsessions with Food and Weight
Carol Emery Normandi, Lauralee Roark
Berkeley Publishing, 1999

It's Not Your Fault: Overcoming Anorexia and Bulimia Through Biopsychiatry
Russell Marx, M.D.
Villard Books, 1991

Journeys to Self Acceptance: Fat Women Speak
Carol Wiley (Ed.)
Crossing Press, 1994

Life Isn't Weighed on the Bathroom Scales
Laura Rose
WRS Publishing, 1994

Like Mother, Like Daughter: How Women Are Influenced by Their Mother's Relationship With Food--And How to Break the Pattern
Debra Waterhouse
Hyperion, 1998

Living Beyond Food
Gregory Jantz, Ph.D., N.C.C.
The Center, 1990

Living Binge-Free: A Personal Guide to Victory over Compulsive Eating
Jane Latimer
Living Quest, 1988

Living On Empty – How Intimacy with God and Others Transformed My Relationship with Food
Mary Jane Hamilton
Victor Books, 1994

The Long Road Back: A Survivor's Guide to Anorexia
Judy Tam Sargent, R.N., M.S.N.
North Star Publications, 1999

Losing It: America's Obsession with Weight and the Industry that Feeds on It
Laura Fraser
Dutton, 1997

Losing Your Pounds of Pain: Breaking the Link Between Abuse, Stress, and Overeating
Doreen Virtue
Hay House, Inc., 1994

Love Hunger: Recovery from Food Addiction
Frank Minirth
Fawcett Books, 1991

Making Peace with Food: Freeing Yourself from the Diet/Weight Obsession
Susan Kano
Harper Perennial, 1989

The Monster Within: Overcoming Eating Disorders
Cynthia Rowland McClure
Spirit Press, 1998

My Life as a Male Anorexic
Michael Krasnow
Haworth Press, Inc., 1996

**My Name is Anita and I am a Dyslexic:
An Autobiography**
Anita Griffiths
University Eds., 1991

My Name is Caroline
Caroline Adams Miller
Gurze Books, 1991

**No Fat Chicks: How Big Business Profits
Making Women Hate Their Bodies--How to
Fight Back**
Terry Poulton
Birch Lane Press, 1997

Nobody Overeats
Susan Madden
Sage Creek Press, 1998

**Nothing to Lose: A Guide to Sane Living in a
Larger Body**
Cheri Erdman
Harper San Francisco, 1996

**The Obsession: Reflections on the Tyranny of
Slenderness**
Kim Chernin
Harper Perennial, 1994

One Size Fits All, and Other Fables
Liz Curtis Higgs
Thomas Nelson, 1993

Overcoming Binge Eating
Christopher Fairburn
Guilford Publications, 1995

**Overcoming the Dieting Dilemma: What to Do
When the Diets Don't Do It**
Neva Coyle
Bethany House Publishers, 1991

Overcoming Fear of Fat
Laura Brown, Ph. D., Esther Rothblum, Ph.D. (Eds.)
Harrington Park, 1990

**Overcoming the Legacy of Overeating: How to
Change Your Negative Eating Habits, rev. ed.**
Nan Kathryn Fuchs
Lowell House, 1996

Overcoming Overeating
Jane Hirschmann, Carol Hunter
Fawcett Book Group, 1998

**A Parent's Guide to Anorexia and Bulimia:
Understanding and Helping Self-Starvers and
Binge/Purgers**
Shocken Books, 1987

**A Parent's Guide to Eating Disorders and
Obesity**
Martha Jablow
Doubleday Dell Publishing Group, 1992

**A Parent's Guide to Eating Disorders:
Prevention and Treatment of Anorexia
Nervosa and Bulimia**
Brett Valette
Walker Publishing, 1988

Poor Eaters: Helping Children Who Refuse to Eat
Joel Macht
Plenum Press, 1990

A Practical Guide to the Treatment of Bulimia Nervosa, Vol. 6
Johan Vanderlinden, Ph.D., Jan Norre, M.A., Walter Vandereycken, M.D., Ph.D.
Brunner/Mazel, 1992

Rapha's 12-Step Program for Overcoming Eating Disorders
Robert McGee, Wm. Drew Mountcastle
Search Industries, 1991

Recovery from Compulsive Eating:
A Complete Guide to the Twelve Step Program
Jim A.
Hazelden, 1994

The Secret Language of Eating Disorders:
The Revolutionary New Approach to Curing Anorexia and Bulimia
Peggy Claude-Pierre
Times Books, 1997

Self Esteem Comes in All Sizes: How to Be Happy and Healthy at Your Natural Weight
Carol Johnson
Doubleday, 1996

Self-Starvation: From Individual to Family Therapy in the Treatment of Anorexia Nervosa
Mara Selvini Palazzoli
Jason Aronson, 1996

Shame and Body Image: Culture and the Compulsive Eater
Barbara McFarland, Ed.D., Tyeis Baker-Baumann, M.S.
Health Communications, 1990

Silent Hunger: A Biblical Approach to Overcoming Compulsive Eating and Overweight
Arthur Halliday, Judy Halliday
Fleming H. Revell Co., 1994

So You Think You're Fat?
Dr. Alvin, Virginia Silverstein
Harper Collins Publishers 1991

Somebody to Love: A Guide to Loving the Body You Have
Leslea Newman
Third Side Press, 1992

Starving for Attention
Cherry Boone O'Neill
CompCare Publishers, 1992

Starving to Death in a Sea of Objects:
The Anorexia Nervosa Syndrome
John Sours
Jason Aronson, Inc., 1995

Starving in the Silences: An Exploration of Anorexia Nervosa
Matra Robertson
New York University Press, 1992

Substance Called Food: How to Understand, Control and Recover from Addictive Eating
Gloria Arenson
McGraw-Hill Co., 1989

Surviving an Eating Disorder: New Perspectives and Strategies for Family and Friends
Michele Siegel, Judith Brisman, Margor Weinshel
Harper Collins, 1997

That First Bite: Chance or Choice: A Working Guide Empowering Choice for Those with Eating Disorders
Rose Marie Dunphy, Mary Sullivan
Jeremiah Press, 1992

That First Bite: Journal of a Compulsive Overeater
Karen Rose
New Horizon Press, 1990

Thin Disguise: Understanding and Overcoming Anorexia and Bulimia
Pam Vredevelt, Deborah Newman, Harry Beverly
Thomas Nelson, Inc., 1996

Thinner at Last
Steven Lamm, M.D., Gerald Secor Couzens
Fireside, 1997

Treating and Overcoming Anorexia Nervosa, rev. ed.
Steven Levenkron
Warner Books, 1997

Twelve Steps for Overeaters: An Interpretation of the Twelve Steps of Overeaters Anonymous
Elisabeth L.
Hazelden, 1996

The Twelve Steps and Twelve Traditions of Overeaters Anonymous
Overeaters Anonymous Inc. Staff
Overeaters Anonymous, Inc., 1993

Unbearable Weight: Feminism, Western Culture, and the Body
S. Bordo
University of California Press, 1993

Unlocking the Golden Cage: An Intimate Biography of Hilde Bruch, M.D.
Joanne Hatch Bruch, Stuart Yudofsky
Gurze Books, 1996

Update: Eating Disorders
Deborah Crisfield
Crestwood House, 1995

Wasted: A Memoir of Anorexia and Bulimia
Marya Hornbacher
Harper Collin, 1997

When Food is Love: Exploring the Relationship Between Eating and Intimacy
Geneen Roth
NAL/Dutton, 1992

When Food's a Foe: How to Confront and Conquer Eating Disorders
Nancy Kolodny
Little, Brown and Co., 1992

When Girls Feel Fat: Helping Girls Through Adolescence
Sandra Friedman
Harper Collins Publishers, Ltd., 1998

When Women Stop Hating Their Bodies: Freeing Yourself from Food and Weight Obsession
Jane Hirschmann, Carol Munter
Ballantine Books, 1995

The Withering Child
John Gould
University of Georgia Press, 1993

Women's Conflicts about Eating and Sexuality: The Relationship Between Food and Sex
Rosalyn Meadow, Ph.D., Lillie Weiss, Ph.D.
Harrington Park Press, Inc., 1992

Why Weight? A Guide to Ending Compulsive Eating
Geneen Roth
Plume, 1993

Why Women? Gender Issues and Eating Disorders
Bridget Dolan, Inez Gitzinger
Athlone Press, 1994

Wrinkles on the Heart: A Mother's Journal of One Family's Struggle with Anorexia Nervosa
Mary Fleming Callaghan
Alabaster Press

You are More than What You Weigh
Sharon Sward, LPC
Wholesome Publishers, 1995

You Can't Quit Until You Know What's Eating You: Overcoming Compulsive Eating
Donna Leblanc
Health Communications, 1990

Your Dieting Daughter: Is She Dying for Attention?
Carolyn Costin
Brunner/Mazel, 1996

Books for Youth

About Weight Problems and Eating Disorders
Joy Berry
Children's Press, 1990

Afraid to Eat: Children and Teens in Weight Crisis
Frances Berg
Healthy Weight Journal, 1997

Anorexia Nervosa: Starving for Attention
Dan Harmon, Carol Nadelson
Chelsea House Publishers, 1998

Anorexia Nervosa: When Food is the Enemy
Erica Smith
Hazelden Information Education, 1999

Are You Too Fat, Ginny?
Karin Jasper
Is Five Press, 1988

Belinda's Bouquet
Leslea Newman
Alyson Publications, 1991

Body Blues: Weight and Depression
Laura Weedlreyer
Rosen Publishing Group, 1998

Bulimia Nervosa: The Secret Guide of Bingeing and Purging
Liza Burby
Rosen Publishing Group, 1998

Compulsive Eating: The Struggle to Feed the Hunger Inside
Christie Ward
Rosen Publishing Group, 1998

Coping with Compulsive Eating
Carolyn Simpson
Hazelden Foundation, 1998

Dangers of Diet Drugs and Other Weight-Loss Products
Cece Barrett
Rosen Publishing Group, 1998

Drugs and Eating Disorders
Clifford Sherry
Rosen Group, 1994

Eating Disorders
John Matthews
Facts on File, 1990

Eating Disorders
Charles Patterson
Raintree, 1995

Eating Disorders: A Hot Issue
David Goodnough
Enslow Publishers, 1999

Eating Disorder Survivors Tell Their Stories
Christina Chiu
Rosen Publishing Group, 1998

Eating Habits and Disorders
Rachel Epstein
Chelsea House, 1990

The Encyclopedia of Obesity and Eating Disorders
Dana Cassell, Feleix Larocca, M.D., F.A.P.A.
Facts on File, 1994

Everything You Need to Know About Eating Disorders: Anorexia and Bulimia
Rachel Kuberky
Rosen Publishing Group, 1995

The Facts About Anorexia and Bulimia
Dayna Wolhart
Crestwood House, 1988

Fat Chance
Leslea Newman
Paper Star, 1996

Focus on Eating Disorders: A Reference Handbook (Teenage Perspectives)
M. Sean O'Halloran
A B C-CLIO, Inc., 1993

Food Fight
Janet Bode
Simon & Schuster Childrens, 1998

Food and Love: Dealing with Family Attitudes About Weight
Elizabeth Frankenberger
Rosen Publishing Group, 1998

Inside Eating Disorder Support Groups
Barbara Moe
Rosen Publishing Group, 1998

Perk! The Story of a Teenager with Bulimia
Liza Hall
Gurze Books, 1997

Real Gorgeous: The Truth About Body and Beauty
Kaz Cooke
W.W. Norton & Co., 1995

Starving to Win: Athletes and Eating Disorders
Eileen O'Brien
Rosen Publishing Group, 1998

Straight Talk about Eating Disorders
Michael Maloney, Rachel Kranz
Facts on File, Inc., 1991

What's Real, What's Ideal: Overcoming a Negative Body Image
Brangien Davis
Rosen Publishing Group, 1998

Weight Loss Programs: Weighing the Risks and Realities
Michele Ingber Drohan
Rosen Publishing Group, 1998

Periodicals / Newsletters

Lifeline
Overeaters Anonymous World Service Office
P.O. Box 44020
Rio Rancho, NM 87174-4020
Ph: (505) 891-2664
Fax: (505) 891-4320
E-mail: overeatr@technet.nm.org
Web: http://www.overeatersanonymous.org/

Radiance: The Magazine for Large Women
P.O. Box 30246
Oakland, CA 94604
Ph: (510) 482-0680
Fax: (510) 482-1576
E-mail: info@radiancemagazine.com
Web: http://www.radiancemagazine.com

Vendors

Gurze Books
P.O. Box 2238
Carlsbad, CA 92018
Ph: (800) 756-7533
          (760) 434-7533
Fax: (760) 434-5476
E-mail: gzcatl@aol.com
Web: http://www.gurze.com/
Books, tapes, publications on eating disorders.

National Center for Overcoming Overeating
P.O. Box 1257
Old Chelsea Station
New York, NY 10113-0920
Ph: (212) 875-0442
Web: http://www.OvercomingOvereating.com/
Educational materials on body image and overeating.

Web Sites

Also see "General Web Sites". Many have sections on eating disorders, but they are not listed separately below.

**Close to You Family Resource Network:
The Eating Disorders Site**
Web: http://closetoyou.org/eatingdisorders/
Collection of information.

Indiana University--The Center for Adolescent Studies, Adolescent Mental Health Issues
Web:
http://educ.indiana.edu/cas/tt/v3i2/v3i2toc.html
Eating disorders from a teacher's perspective.

Eating Disorder Network
Web: http://www.rochesteredn.org
Services for family and friends of adolescents with eating disorders.

Something Fishy Website on Eating Disorders
Web: http://www.something-fishy.org
Large collection of information.

Videos

Video tapes can be very useful, but may a challenge to find, especially if they aren't new to the market. Try contacting the producers noted even if the tape isn't listed on their web site, book stores and your library.

Anorexia and Bulimia: The Truth About Eating Disorders
Educational Video Network, 1999
1339 19th St.
Huntsville, TX 77340
Ph: (936) 295-5767
Fax: (936) 294-0233
E-mail: evn@edvidnet.com
Web: http://www.edvidnet.com/default.html
Defines anorexia and bulimia, discusses how and why they occur, consequences, warning signs, recovery.

Bradshaw on Eating Disorders
Bradshaw Cassettes, 1994
P.O. Box 720947
Houston, Texas 77272
Ph: (800) 6-BRADSHAW
Fax: (713) 771-1362
Web: http://www.johnbradshaw.com/
Three-part series on managing food, food addiction and weight obsession, why diets don't work.

Bulimia: The Binge-Purge Obsession
Anita Siegman, Ph.D.
Produced by Eugene Ferraro
Leo Media
110 West Main St.
Urbana, IL, 61801-2715
Ph: (800) 421-6999
      (217) 337-0700
E-mail: info@leomedia.net
Web: http://www.leomed.com/
Explains to high school and college students the chain of events that may lead a young woman into binge-purge behavior.

Dying to be Thin
Produced by Donna Vogt
Dist. by Leo Media
110 West Main St.
Urbana, IL, 61801-2715
Ph: (800) 421-6999
      (217) 337-0700
E-mail: info@leomedia.net
Web: http://www.leomed.com/
Several people who risked death in order to be thin.

Eating Disorders
AGC United Learning, 1996
1560 Sherman Ave., Suite 100
Evanston, IL 60201
Ph: (800) 323-9084
      (847) 328-6700
Fax: (847) 328-6706
E-mail: info@agcunited.com
Web: http://www.agcmedia.com/
Signs to look for in others who may have an eating disorder. Offers hope to sufferers, information on where to turn. Grades 7-12.

Eating Disorders: Profiles of Pain
AGC United Learning, 1997
1560 Sherman Ave., Suite 100
Evanston, IL 60201
Ph: (800) 323-9084
      (847) 328-6700
Fax: (847) 328-6706
E-mail: info@agcunited.com
Web: http://www.agcmedia.com/
Teens share the pressures from the media, parents, peers, that can trigger eating disorders. Psychological isolation and obsession, physical demise, death. Grades 7-12.

Heavy Load
Produced by Video Arts
Dist. By Leo Media
110 West Main St.
Urbana, IL, 61801-2715
Ph: (800) 421-6999
        (217) 337-0700
E-mail: info@leomedia.net
Web: http://www.leomed.com/
Overeating addiction of a young woman, effects on her
family. Idiosyncrasies of the compulsive personality:
denial, procrastination, hiding and sneaking food.

Overeating: An American Obsession
Dist. By Leo Media
110 West Main St.
Urbana, IL, 61801-2715
Ph: (800) 421-6999
        (217) 337-0700
E-mail: info@leomedia.net
Web: http://www.leomed.com/
Web: http://www.leomed.com/catalog/mental.htm
Stories of people struggling to control their weight
problem. Causes of obesity, importance of
comprehensive weight loss programs.

Understanding Anorexia and Bulimia
Educational Video Network, 1993
1339 19th St.
Huntsville, TX 77340
Ph: (936) 295-5767
Fax: (936) 294-0233
E-mail: evn@edvidnet.com
Web: http://www.edvidnet.com/default.html
Causes and cures of eating disorders, seeking
treatment.

---- Fetal Alcohol Syndrome/ Fetal Alcohol Effects Drug-Affected Children

Fetal alcohol syndrome (FAS) is a condition in which a child is born with serious neurological, mental and physical problems because the child's mother drank alcohol while pregnant. FAS is a leading causes of birth defects, developmental disabilities, and mental retardation.

Fetal alcohol effects (FAE) is a similar condition to FAS in that a child has similar intellectual and behavioral problems to those with FAS but without the physical abnormalities.

Drug affected children have problems similar to those with FAS and FAE, but the problem is caused by their mothers using illegal substances during pregnancy.

Frequency
- Affects 1-3 children for every 1,000 live births in the U.S., more than 8,000 annually.
- 44% of women who drink heavily during pregnancy will have a child with FAS.
- 16% of pregnant women drink enough alcohol to be at risk for delivering children with some negative effects.
- Chronic alcoholics have a 30-50% chance of having a child with FAS. Once a woman has had one child with FAS, she has a 75% risk of having a second child with FAS until she stops drinking alcohol.
- FAE is 2-3 times as common as FAS.
- 11% of pregnant women use drugs that could harm their unborn child.

Symptoms and Possible Effects
Alcohol damage to an unborn child can have a wide variety of affects, depending on the volume of alcohol a mother consumes, the point during pregnancy at which consumption begins, genetics and environmental factors. Some of the effects include:

Prebirth
- Miscarriages, premature deliveries and stillbirths.
- Excessive movement.
- High heart rate.
- Brain hemorrhage.
- Decreased oxygen supply.
- Growth retardation.

141

At birth
- ❑ Decreased weight, length, and head circumference.
- ❑ Permanent damage to the brain and central nervous system.
- ❑ Babies exposed to repeated cocaine use during the first trimester of pregnancy can have defects in their hearts, gastrointestinal tracts, genitourinary tracts, skeletal systems and brains.
- ❑ Strokes in babies of mothers who used cocaine within 2-3 days of delivery.
- ❑ Alcohol withdrawal for several days after birth if a newborn's mother drank heavily until birth. Baby will be irritabile, restless, eat poorly, have tremors, vomit, cry in a high pitched tone, not respond well to stimuli.
- ❑ Poor muscle tone, jitteriness.
- ❑ Unable to suck.
- ❑ Seizures.
- ❑ Nerve damage.
- ❑ Cerebral palsy.
- ❑ Heart defects.
- ❑ Immune system problems.
- ❑ Hearing loss.
- ❑ Genital and kidney malformations.
- ❑ Respiratory problems.
- ❑ Death.

Infants
- ❑ Inability to absorb nutrients, fail to thrive.
- ❑ Weight loss after birth.
- ❑ Poor sucking reflects or no desire to eat.
- ❑ Sleep disturbances.
- ❑ Fussiness, unwilling to be held or comforted.
- ❑ Developmental delays.
- ❑ Defects in muscle tone, reflexes and movement.
- ❑ Delays in sitting and walking.
- ❑ Vision difficulties.
- ❑ Excess fluid in the brain.
- ❑ High pain tolerance.
- ❑ Growth deficiencies.

Young children
- ❑ Neurological problems.
- ❑ Poor language development.
- ❑ Behavior problems, short attention span, distractibility, impulsivity, low frustration tolerance.
- ❑ Slow toilet training.
- ❑ Slow motor development.
- ❑ Hyperactivity, impulsiveness, attention deficit disorder.
- ❑ Behavioral problems.
- ❑ Loss of some intellectual functioning.
- ❑ By age 2 cocaine-exposed infants may catch up up in their weight and height, but their heads may still be too small. Intelligence may be within normal range, however.

School age children
- ❑ Learning disabilities.
- ❑ Organizational problems.

Adolescents
- ❑ Oppositional defiance.
- ❑ During early childhood, they remain thin and short, but by late adolescence they may have attained normal height and weight.

Physical characteristics
- ❑ Head has a small circumference and a flattened midface.
- ❑ Dental deformities.
- ❑ Eyes are widely spaced with narrow eyelids. Short eye openings with folds of skin on the inner and upper part of the eye. Poor eye muscle development leads to drooping eyelids, crossed eyes, and nearsightedness. Eyes can't focus together.
- ❑ Short upturned nose, sunken or low nasal bridge, fat face, small midface, thin upper lip.
- ❑ Ears are large and low-set. Frequent ear infections.
- ❑ Groove in the midline of the lip is short or smooth. Cleft palate.
- ❑ Heart defects.
- ❑ Limb abnormalities in joints, hands, feet, fingers and toes. Weak grasp. Curvature of the spine.
- ❑ Simian crease.
- ❑ In some cases, major structural abnormalities have been described, such as absence of the corpus callosum, the portion of the brain that connects the left and right cerebral hemispheres.
- ❑ Birthmarks.
- ❑ Orthopedic problems.
- ❑ Infants born to cocaine-abusing mother have difficulty with attention, muscle tone, reflexes, and movement that may last for months after birth. These babies shut off the environment by either sleeping or crying. Experience rapid respiration, disorganized motor activity.

Behavioral symptoms
- ❑ Lack of ability to give and receive affection and maintain friendships.
- ❑ Trouble recognizing and expressing feelings.
- ❑ Self-destructive.
- ❑ Cruel to others.
- ❑ Steal, hoard.
- ❑ Preoccuped with fire, blood, gore.
- ❑ Lack internal controls.
- ❑ Poor eye contact.
- ❑ Superficial social skills only.
- ❑ May not show normal anxiety or guilt.
- ❑ Lie, blame others.
- ❑ Children tend to be over-friendly and outgoing, use little caution.
- ❑ Easily manipulated by others, have poor judgment, low self esteem, depression.
- ❑ At risk for drug and alcohol abuse.
- ❑ Change is difficult.
- ❑ May dislike being touched.
- ❑ Rarely laugh.
- ❑ Sleep disturbances.
- ❑ Body rocking.
- ❑ Poor eye-hand coordination.
- ❑ Similar behaviors with autism and behavior problems typical of ADHD.

Cognitive symptoms
- ❑ Low IQ, in the mildly retarded range. FAE IQs tend to be in the borderline range.
- ❑ Language disorders, nonverbal language, baby talk, meaningless speech.
- ❑ Low attention span.

Learning disabilities
Experience difficulty with:
- ❑ Generalizing information.
- ❑ Matching words and behavior.
- ❑ Mastering new skills or remembering something they recently learned.
- ❑ Short-term memory.
- ❑ Flexibility of thought; may understand a concept only if expressed one way.
- ❑ Predicting outcomes.
- ❑ Distinguishing fact from fantasy.
- ❑ Learning from experience.
- ❑ Cause and effect.
- ❑ Distinguishing friends from strangers.
- ❑ Acquiring new words, understanding semantics.
- ❑ Spontaneous vocalizations.
- ❑ Comprehension.
- ❑ Keeping behavior consistent with verbal communication.
- ❑ Talking about relationships.
- ❑ Referring to prior or future events (everything is in the present.)
- ❑ Generalizing from one task to another.
- ❑ Performing consistently; they are unpredictable and only sporadically master skills.
- ❑ Receiving, processing, storing, and retrieving information.
- ❑ Reasoning abstractly.
- ❑ Concentrating on a single task for an extended period of time.
- ❑ Handling money.
- ❑ Conceptualizing and dealing with time.
- ❑ Keeping thoughts straight.

Causes

- ▪ Seen in children of women who have been heavy drinkers throughout pregnancy. Alcohol levels in fetuses of mothers who drink are as least as high as those in the mother. An unborn baby has very limited ability to metabolize alcohol independently and is dependent on the mother's liver tissue to detoxify alcohol.
- ▪ FAS will not occur if the father was drinking heavily or if the pregnant woman was drinking a very small amount of alcohol on rare occasions, though FAE have been observed in infants whose mothers ingested relatively small amounts of alcohol during pregnancy. Abstinence is best.
- ▪ The risk of FAS/FAE increases with mother's age.
- ▪ Drinking alcohol while breast feeding retards brain growth in a child even if the child is healthy at birth.

Diagnostic Processes

Diagnostic processes measure symptoms described above.

Treatment
- Prevention. Mother must stop consuming alcohol and using substances in anticipation of and during pregnancy.
- Treatment of children is based on symptoms.

Outcomes
- No cure for FAS/FAE/drug affected children. Can merely compensate to overcome problems.
- Facial deformities may fade over time.
- Though not an outcome of FAS, if a mother doesn't stop drinking after her child is born, she's at risk for neglecting or abusing her child. Only 10-30% of children with FAS live with a biological parent.
- Independent living is challenging for FAS/FAE sufferers. Some end up homeless, on the streets.
- Abnormally high number of adults with FAS in prisons.

Who to Contact
Also refer to "Who Else to Contact." Organizations listed below target their work specifically toward fetal alcohol syndrome. Organizations listed below target their work specifically toward drug and substance abuse.

Fetal Alcohol Syndrome Family Resource Institute
P.O. Box 2525
Lynnwood, WA 98036
Ph: (800) 999-3429
       (253) 531-2878
E-mail: delindam@accessone.com
Web: http://www.accessone.com/~delindam/
Education, information, support, referrals.

National Organization on Fetal Alcohol Syndrome
216 G. St. NE
Washington, DC 20002
Ph: (202) 785-4585
Fax: (202) 466-6456
E-mail: information@nofas.org
Web: http://www.nofas.org/
Develops medical school curriculum, disseminates information, conferences.

Recommended Reading

Alcohol, Tobacco and Other Drugs May Harm the Unborn
Paddy Cook
Diane Publishing Co., 1993

The Broken Cord
Michael Dorris
Harper Perennial, 1990

The Challenge of Fetal Alcohol Syndrome: Overcoming Secondary Disabilities
Ann Pytkowicz Streissguth, Jonathan Kanter (Eds.)
University of Washington Press, 1997

The Challenging Child
Stanley Greenspan
Addison-Wesley, 1995

Children with Prenatal Drug Exposure
Lynette Chandler, Ph.D., P.T., Shelly Lane, Ph.D., ORT/L, FAOTA (Eds.)
Haworth Press, Inc., 1997

Children of Prenatal Substance Abuse
Shirley Sparks, M.S.
Singular Publishing Group, Inc., 1993

The Child with Special Needs: Encouraging Intellectual and Emotional Growth
Stanley Greenspan
Addison-Wesley, 1998

Children with Prenatal Alcohol and/or Other Drug Exposure: Weighing the Risks of Adoption
Susan Edelstein, Judy Howard
Child Welfare LA Press, 1995

Cocaine-Exposed Infants: Social, Legal and Public Health Issues
James Inciardi, Hilary Surratt, Christine Saum
Sage Publications, Inc., 1997

Crack-Affected Children: A Teacher's Guide
Mary Bllis Waller
Corwin Press, 1993

Crack Babies: An Escalating Problem Facing Society
Jane Scherer
PPI Publishing, 1991

Crack Babies: A National Epidemic
Publishing Company Diane (Ed.)
Diane Publishing Co., 1991

Dangerous Legacy: The Babies of Drug-Taking Parents
Ben Sonder
Franklin Watts, Inc., 1994

Developmental Problems of Drug-Exposed Infants
Louis Rossetti, Ph.D. (Ed.)
Singular Publishing Group, Inc., 1992

Educating Young Children Prenatally Exposed to Drugs and at Risk: Report and Resource Compendium
Shirley Jackson
Diane Publishing Co., 1993

Enduring Effects of Prenatal Alcohol Exposure on Child Development: Birth through Seven Years
Ann Pytkowicz Streissguth, Fred Bookstein, Helen Barr, Paul Sampson
University of Michigan Press, 1993

Fantastic Antone Succeeds! Experiences in Educating Children with Fetal Alcohol Syndrome
Judith Kleinfield, Siobhan Wescott
U. of Alaska Press, 1993

Fetal Alcohol Syndrome
Amy Nevitt
Rosen Publishing Group, Inc., 1996

Fetal Alcohol Syndrome: Diagnosis, Epidemiology, Prevention, and Treatment
Institute of Medicine, Frederick Battaglia ,Cynthia Howe, Kathleen Stratton
National Academy of Social Insurance, 1995

Fetal Alcohol Syndrome: A Guide for Families & Communities
Ann Pytkowicz Streissguth
Paul H. Brookes, 1997

Grandmothers as Caregivers: Raising Children of the Crack Cocaine Epidemic
Meredith Minkler, Kathleen Roe
Sage Publications, Inc., 1993

Handle with Care: Helping Children Prenatally Exposed to Drugs and Alcohol
Sylvia Fernandez Villarreal, Lora-Ellen McKinney, Marcia Quackenbush
ETR Associates, 1992

Infants and Children with Prenatal Alcohol and Drug Exposure: A Guide to Identification and Intervention
Keeta DeStefano Lewis, R.N., P.H.N., M.S.N.
Hazelden, 1995

Kids, Crack, and the Community: Reclaiming Drug-Exposed Infants and Children
Barbara Hicks
National Educational Service, 1993

Maternal Substance Abuse and the Developing Nervous System
Ian Zagon, Theodore Slotkin (Eds.)
Academic Press, Inc., 1992

Modern Concepts in Fetal Alcohol Syndrome and Fetal Alcohol Affects
Cheryl Schroeder, Ed. D.
Creative Consultants, 1994

Mother's Survival Guide to Recovery: All About Alcohol, Drugs and Babies
Laurie Tanner
New Harbinger Publications, 1996

Perinatal Substance Abuse: Research Findings and Clinical Implications
Theo Sonderegger (Ed.)
Johns Hopkins University Press, 1992

Prenatal Cocaine Exposures
Richard Konkol
CRC Press, Inc., 1996

Prenatal Exposure to Drugs/Alcohol: Characteristics and Educational Implications of Fetal Alcohol Syndrome and Cocaine/Polydrug Effects
Jeanette Soby
Charles C. Thomas Pub., 1994

Reaching Out to Children With FAS/FAE: A Handbook for Teachers, Counselors, and Parents Who Live and Work With Children Affected by Fetal Alcohol Syndrome
Diane Davis
Center for Applied Research in Education, 1995

Recent Developments in Alcoholism, Vol. 9: Children of Alcoholics: Genetic Predisposition, Fetal Alcohol Syndrome, Vulnerability to Disease, Social and Environmental
Marc Galanter (Ed.)
Plenum Press, 1991

Recognizing and Managing Children with Fetal Alcohol Syndrome/Fetal Alcohol Effects: A Guidebook
Brenda McCreight
Child Welfare League of America, 1997

Understanding the Drug-Exposed Child: Approaches to Behavior and Learning
Ira Chasnoff
Imprint Publications, 1998

Understanding Fetal Alcohol Syndrome: A Guide for Families and Communities
Ann Streissguth, Ph.D.
Paul H. Brookes, 1997

What You Can Do to Prevent Fetal Alcohol Syndrome
Sheila Blume, M.D.
Johnson Institute-QVS, Inc., 1992

Books for Youth

Drugs and Birth Defects
Nancy Nielson, Sue Hurwitz
Rosen Publishing Group, 1993

Videos

Video tapes can be very useful, but may a challenge to find, especially if they aren't new to the market. Try contacting the producers noted even if the tape isn't listed on their web site, book stores and your library.

Fetal Alcohol Syndrome: The Early Years
AGC United Learning, 1997
1560 Sherman Ave., Suite 100
Evanston, IL 60201
Ph: (800) 323-9084
        (847) 328-6700
Fax: (847) 328-6706
E-mail: info@agcunited.com
Web: http://www.agcmedia.com/
Importance of early intervention with a child with F.A.S./F.A.E. Grades 10-up.

Fetal Alcohol Syndrome and Effect: Stories of Help and Hope
Hazelden, 1993
P. O. Box 176
Center City, Minn. 55012
Ph: (800) 323-9000
E-mail: bookstore@hazelden.org
Web: http://www.hazelden.org/
Defines fetal alcohol syndrome and effect, how children are diagnosed, positive prognosis possible for fetal alcohol children.

The School Years
AGC United Learning, 1997
1560 Sherman Ave., Suite 100
Evanston, IL 60201
Ph: (800) 323-9084
        (847) 328-6700
Fax: (847) 328-6706
E-mail: info@agcunited.com
Web: http://www.agcmedia.com/
Meeting the needs of FAS/FAE children in the classroom, and at the school and district levels.

A Focus on Prevention
AGC United Learning, 1997
1560 Sherman Ave., Suite 100
Evanston, IL 60201
Ph: (800) 323-9084
        (847) 328-6700
Fax: (847) 328-6706
E-mail: info@agcunited.com
Web: http://www.agcmedia.com/
Facts and advice on the prevention of F.A.S., F.A.E. Grades 10-up.

Fetal Development and Birth
AGC United Learning, 1997
1560 Sherman Ave., Suite 100
Evanston, IL 60201
Ph: (800) 323-9084
        (847) 328-6700
Fax: (847) 328-6706
E-mail: info@agcunited.com
Web: http://www.agcmedia.com/
Describes FAS and its impact on the developing child. Grades 9-12.

Worth the Trip: Raising and Teaching Children with Fetal Alcohol Syndrome
Vida Health Communications, 1996
6 Bigelow St.
Cambridge, MA 02139
Ph: (800) 550-7047
        (617) 864-4334
E-mail: info@vida-health.com
Web: http://www.vida-health.com
Strategies for meeting the developmental and behavioral challenges faced by children with FAS.

Web Sites

Also see "General Web Sites". Many have sections on fetal alcoholic syndrome, but they are not listed separately below.

Fetal Alcohol Syndrome Community Resource Center

Web: http://www.azstarnet.com/~tjk/fashome.htm
Large collection of information.

Reservoir

Web:
http://www.coolware.com/health/medical_reporter/fas.html
Description, sources of help.

Vendors

Creative Consultants, Inc.

P.O. Box 6023
Laramie, Wyoming 82070
Ph: (307) 745-3435
Fax: (307) 745-3415
E-mail: CreaConInc@aol.com
Web: http://members.aol.com/creaconinc/index.html
Information on FAS and FAE on web site.

---- Learning Disorders

A group of cognitive disorders in which a child has difficulty learning in spite of his or her intelligence level. (Learning disabled children may actually be gifted.) These problems occur because of the way in which the child's brain receives, retains, organizes, recalls, or expresses information, in areas such as:

- Reading
- Math
- Writing
- Language
- Motor skills, coordination.

Because the nervous system of a learning disabled child lags in development, he may become overwhelmed at the amount of information and sensations bombarding him and respond by tuning out or behaving inappropriately.

Symptoms
Learning Disorders in General

☐ Developmental milestones lagging behind those of other children.
☐ Poor performance on group tests.
☐ Confusion with instructions.
☐ Disorganized thinking, obsession around an idea.
☐ Difficulty in discriminating sizes, shapes, colors.
☐ Difficulty understanding time concepts, inability to plan free time, arriving late to class, lingering afterward.
☐ Difficulty with problem solving, abstract reasoning, decision making.
☐ Poor organizational and sequencing skills.
☐ Poor memory.
☐ Poor visual-motor coordination, general awkwardness.
☐ No hand dominance (left, right).
☐ Distorted concept of his body.
☐ Work completed slowly.

❏ Accurate copying of a model is difficult.
❏ Poor study skills.
❏ Homework that is misplaced, forgotten, turned in late, sloppy, misunderstood.
❏ Shyness, inattention, fatigue, day dreaminess, short attention span, distractibility.
❏ Disinhibition (lack of self-control; unaware of how others view him).
❏ Inability to stop a task or behavior when asked.
❏ Inability to perform on demand.
❏ Poor adjustment to environmental changes.
❏ Impulsive behavior, hyperactivity, low tolerance for frustration, excessive variation in mood and response, failure to see consequences of actions, inappropriate reactions, gullibility, disruptiveness.
❏ Poor peer relationships and social judgment.
❏ Negative attitude, depression, anxiety, phobias, poor self image.

Dyslexia

A special type of learning disorder in which a child has impaired language processing skills. Problem exists between the ability to learn and the ability to achieve in school. However, children with dyslexia often show special talent in areas that require visual, spatial, and motor integration.

❏ Difficulty understanding phonics, recalling letters, digits, words, phrases in the correct sequence.
❏ Lack of awareness of sounds in words and syllables. Difficulty identifying or spelling words.
❏ Confusion with numbers and letters (e.g., b-d, broad-board, 23-32, M-3).
❏ Difficulty with reading comprehension.
❏ Difficulty conveying thoughts in written form.
❏ Difficulty with handwriting, reading, writing, spelling, math.
❏ Misunderstanding of relationships between numbers and words that represent them (e.g., halves).
❏ Confusion over math process signs (e.g., +, -).
❏ Problems with verbal short-term memory.
❏ Difficulty with orientation, direction, organization, instructions.
❏ Difficulty with pronunciation, oral and written expression.
❏ Difficulty with opposites.
❏ Difficulty with timed tests.
❏ Speech delay.
❏ Missing key words, asking for things by their use rather than by name. Uses words that are "close to right", forgets names of people, places, things and dates.
❏ Difficulty expressing himself and understanding others.
❏ Headaches while reading.
❏ Uncertainty about which hand to use.
❏ Confusion about directions and time, forgetting where he is or is going. Stays in "present tense", making sequencing difficult, affecting reading comprehension, writing and planning.
❏ Daydreaming.
❏ Difficulty with maintaining eye contact.
❏ Clumsiness.
❏ Difficulty sitting still, paying attention.
❏ Lateness in learning to talk, preferring action to words.
❏ Giftedness in math, science, music, art, engineering, athletics and people skills.

Learning/Communications Model

Learning disorders are more easily understood in terms of their affect on learning /communications. These models describes how a child receives, integrates, remembers, and returns information.

Receptive (Input) disorders

Information is received through a child's senses, (e.g., visual, auditory, tactile.) When one of these senses is not operating correctly, the child is said to experience "perceptual disorders." The child may not consistently understand what is said to him; he may mispronounce words, misunderstand the significance of comments such as polite phrasing. He tends to compensate with his other senses. He may have difficulty with syntax or the ordering of his words, emphasizing the wrong aspect of a topic, modulating his voice and pitch.

Integration disorders

Once information is received, the child has to interpret it through sequencing, abstraction, and organization. Sequencing puts information in the correct order. Abstraction helps the child derive meaning from symbols that are seen, heard, and felt (i.e., words and sounds). If a child has difficulties in sequencing, abstraction, or organizing the information, he will mislearn information.

Sequencing disorders

A child may know the steps involved in a task, but do them in the wrong order. For example, he may know all the days of the weeks in order, but can't tell you what day comes after Tuesday without starting at Sunday and going through the sequence. He may put on his shoes before his socks.

Abstraction disorders

A child with a learning disorder may have difficulty deriving the correct general meaning from a symbol or word. She may have trouble going from specific or literal thinking to abstract thinking. (An example of abstract thinking is the seemingly unrelated connections that need to be made to understand puns and jokes.)

Organization disorders

Once information is recorded in memory, sequenced, and understood, it must be integrated with what's already been learned and what continues to be received. Children challenged with organizational disorders have difficulty putting multiple pieces of information together to form a new concept. They may learn a set of facts, for example, but have difficulty determining general information from the fact set. Their materials and workspace may also be disorganized, work not taken home or not returned to school. Poor time management.

Memory disorders

Once integrated, information is stored in short-term and finally long-term memory. A child with a memory disorder will have trouble retaining information, possibly primarily from a particular input mode, such as hearing. As a result, a child may not remember what she saw a few minutes ago, not remember what she heard last week, or not remember the correct sequence of letters needed to spell a word. Most children with a memory disorder experience problems with *short-term* memory.

Output disorders

Stored information can be recalled and used by the child in language skills. Written and spoken words and numbers are symbols that allow a child to communicate. If he has difficulties using these symbols, communication will be a challenge.

Language disorders

There are two forms of language communication that a child can use - spontaneous language and demand language. In spontaneous language, the child himself initiates the communication. In demand language, someone attempts to engage the child in communication. A child with a demand language learning disorder may be very articulate spontaneously but struggle to answer a question (demand language.)

Motor disorders

A child may struggle with gross motor disorder, which causes clumsiness, stumbling, difficulty with physical activities such as running and riding a bike. Fine motor disorders most frequently appear in writing; a child may hold a pencil awkwardly, experience hand fatigue, misshape or misplace letters. Many children with a fine motor disorder also are challenged with a written language disorder in which they have difficulty getting thoughts to flow while also collecting information needed for spelling, grammar, and punctuation. Getting all the information to come together and then be written on paper is a challenge.

Frequency, Other Helpful Stats

- Learning disorders: 5-10% of the school population. Reading disorders are the most common form.
- 5-10% of learning disordered children also have ADHD.
- By adolescence, one in three learning disabled children will have been retained in a grade and most are at least one year behind in basic academic work.
- 50-65% have at last one psychiatric disorder. It common for these children to receive multiple diagnoses.
- 15-20% of the population has dyslexia. Four times more prevalent in males than females.

Causes of Learning Disorders

This is a partial list of potential causes. Determining the exact cause of a learning disorder for a child may be difficult, if not impossible.

- Heredity (25-40% of disordered children).
- Prebirth problems, e.g., maternal malnutrition, bleeding during pregnancy, poor placental attachment in the uterus, toxemia, infectious disease of mother, mother's use of certain drugs or alcohol during pregnancy, RH incompatibility.
- Birthing problems, e.g., long or difficult delivery, too rapid delivery (change in air pressure too quickly), insufficient oxygen, prematurity, breech delivery, cord around neck, poor position in the uterus, dry birth, forceps delivery that caused intracranial pressure, a narrow pelvic arch in the mother.
- Post-birth problems, e.g., delay in breathing after birth, high fever at an early age, sharp blow to the head, meningitis, encephalitis, oxygen deprivation, respiratory distress, or breath holding.

Diagnostic Processes

For learning disorders in general:

- A child should have medical, vision, hearing and neurological exams to determine if any biological problems exist. Other things to watch for include mental retardation, communication disorders, seizures, chronic illness.
- Neuropsychological testing may be useful to help identify which functions of the brain are stronger or weaker than others.
- Psychological and educational testing can point out cognitive and visual-perceptual strengths and weaknesses, psychiatric disorders, and problems with self image. Testing may be done to determine the child's current level of academic skills, intellectual potential, learning style, and his specific learning disorder.
- Classroom observation.
- Evaluation of the school environment to determine if there are problems that may amplify a problem.
- Evaluation of a child's social history, watching for things such as problems at home, lack of opportunity, cultural factors, family attitudes towards learning.
- Don't overlook the basics, such as hunger during the day and normal variations in academic attainment.
- Evaluations to help confirm dyslexia to determine directional orientation, e.g., does the child confuse left/right, up/down? Which hand and eye does he prefer?

DSM IV Diagnostic Criteria

Reprinted with permission from the *Diagnostic and Statistical Manual of Mental Disorders, Fourth Edition, Text Revision.* Copyright 2000 American Psychiatric Association.

Reading Disorder:
A. Reading achievement, as measured by individually administered standardized tests of reading accuracy or comprehension, is substantially below that expected given the person's chronological age, measured intelligence and age-appropriate education.

B. The disturbance in Criterion A significantly interferes with academic achievement or activities of daily living that require reading skills.

C. If a sensory deficit is present, the reading difficulties are in excess of those usually associated with it.

Mathematics Disorder:
A. Mathematically ability, as measured by individually administered standardized tests, is substantially below that expected given the person's chronological age, measured intelligence, and age-appropriate education.

B. The disturbance in Criterion A significantly interferes with academic achievement or activities of daily living that require mathematical ability.

C. If a sensory deficit is present, the difficulties in mathematical ability are in excess of those usually associated with it.

Disorder of Written Expression:

A. Writing skills, as measured by individually administered standardized tests (or functional assessments of writing skills), are substantially below those expected given the person's chronological age, measured intelligence, and age-appropriate education.

B. The disturbance in Criterion A significantly interferes with academic achievements or activities of daily living that require the composition of written texts (e.g., writing grammatically correct sentences and organized paragraphs.)

C. If a sensory deficit is present, the difficulties in writing skills are in excess of those usually associated with it.

Treatment

Learning disorders generally are not cured, but compensated for. Early detection is important so that the child receives help before falling too far behind in school, experiencing social problems, or becoming discouraged about his abilities. Treatment options include:

- Special education to teach a child how to compensate for learning challenges.
- Direct and intensive training/tutoring by someone who understands how to help learning disabled children.
- Use of teaching techniques that match a child's learning style, that break down activities into small steps and are then taught in sequence to help the child organize information.
- Peer tutoring.
- Technology-based tutoring.
- Speech therapy.
- Specialized physical therapy that helps acclimate the child's body in space, that teaches such things as right, left, and midline orientation.
- Multi-sensory training, which joins visual, auditory, verbal, and writing in one unified approach to reading and writing.

Who to Contact

Also refer to "Who Else to Contact" section for broader-based organizations. Organizations listed below target their work specifically toward learning disorders.

American Council on Rural Special Education (ACRES)
Kansas State University
2323 Anderson Ave, Suite 226
Manhattan, KS 66502-2912
Ph: (785) 532-2737
Fax: (785) 532-7732
E-mail: acres@ksu.edu
Web: http://www.ksu.edu/acres
Focuses on special education issues for those in rural areas.

Association of Educational Therapists
1804 W. Burbank Blvd.
Burbank, CA 91506
Ph: (818) 843-1183
Fax: (818) 843-7423
E-mail: aetla@aol.com
Web: http://www.aetonline.org/
Professional membership organization for education therapists. Educational material.

Center for Research on Learning
University of Kansas
521 Joseph R. Pearson Hall
1122 West Campus Road
Lawrence, KS 66045
Ph: (785) 864-4780
E-mail: crl@ukans.edu
Web: http://www.ku-crl.org/htmlfiles/core.html
Information related to teaching students who are at risk for school failure.

Council for Exceptional Children (CEC)
1110 North Glebe Road, Suite 300
Arlington, VA 22201-5704
Ph: (888) CEC-SPED
TTY: (703) 264-9446
Fax: (703) 264-9494
E-mail: service@cec.sped.org
Web: http://www.cec.sped.org
Resources for improving educational outcomes for those with disabilities and giftedness.

Council for Learning Disabilities
P.O. Box 40303
Overland Park, KS 66204-4303
Ph: (913) 492-8755
Fax: (913) 492-2546
E-mail: eversr@winthrop.edu
Web: http://www.cldinternational.org
Organization of professionals who promote effective teaching and research related to learning disabilities.

Davis Research Foundation
3755 Omec Circle
Rancho Cordova, CA 95742
Ph: (888) 484-5563
Fax: (916) 631-4336
Web: http://www.help-kids-read.org/
Counseling and teaching methods to resolve learning disorders.

Dyslexia Research Institute
5746 Centerville Road
Tallahassee, FL 32308
Ph: (850) 893-2216
Fax: (850) 893-2440
E-mail: dri@dyslexia-add.org
Web: http://www.dyslexia-add.org
Provides parenting information, adult education, advocacy and consultation, research and development resources.

Independent Educational Consultants Association
3251 Old Lee Highway, Suite 510
Fairfax, VA 22030-1504
Ph: (703) 591-4850
Fax: (703) 591-4860
E-mail: Requests@IECAonline.com
Web: http://www.educationalconsulting.org/
Professional association of educational consultants. Works with parents, children on school selection.

International Reading Association
800 Barksdale Road
P.O. Box 8139
Newark, DE 19714-8139
Ph: (302) 731-1600
Fax: (302) 731-1057
E-mail: pubinfo@reading.org
Web: http://www.reading.org/
Works to improve reading instruction. Conferences, journal. Special interest group for disabled readers.

Laubach Literacy
1320 Jamesville Ave.
Syracuse, NY 13210
Ph: (888) 528-2224
      (315) 422-9121
E-mail: info@laubach.org
Web: http://www.laubach.org/
Educational group dedicated to helping adults improve their reading, writing, math and problem-solving skills.

Learning Disabilities Association of America (LDAA)
4156 Library Road
Pittsburgh, PA 15234-1349
Ph: (412) 341-1515
       (412) 341-8077
Fax: (412) 344-0224
E-mail: ldanatl@usaor.net
Web: http://www.ldanatl.org/
Advocacy, education, research, services to relieve affects of learning disabilities.

Marin Puzzle People
199 Greenfield Ave.
San Rafael, CA 94901
Ph: (415) 459-0870
E-mail: dyslexia@hooked.net
Web: http://www.hooked.net/users/dyslexia/
Assists adults through educational, vocational and social programs.

National Adult Literacy and Learning Disabilities (ALLD) Center
Academy for Educational Development
1875 Connecticut Ave. NW
Washington, DC 20009-1202
Ph: (800) 953-2553
       (202) 884-8185
Fax: (202) 884-8422
       (202) 884-8429
E-mail: info@nalldc.aed.org
Web: http://novel.nifl.gov/nalldtop.htm
Information exchange, training, technical assistance.

National Association of Private School for Exceptional Students
1522 K St., NW Suite 1032
Washington, DC 20005
Ph: (202) 408-3338
Fax: (202) 408-3340
E-mail: napsec@aol.com
Web: http://www.spedschools.com/napsec.html
Association of private special education schools that serve publicly, privately placed children with disabilities.

National Center for Learning Disabilities
381 Park Ave. South, Suite 1401
New York, NY 10016
Ph: (888) 575-7373
       (212) 545-7510
Fax: (212) 545-9665
Web: http://209.190.217.242/index.html
Information, resources, referral, education programs, advocacy.

National Institute for Literacy
1775 I Street NW, Suite 730
Washington, DC 20006-2401
Ph: (202) 233-2025
Fax: (202) 233-2050
Web: http://www.nifl.gov
Works to ensure high literacy among adults.

Parents of Gifted/Learning Disabled Children
2420 Eccleston St.
Silver Spring, MD 20902
Ph: (301) 986-1422
Fax: (301) 929-9304
E-mail: Jilmeyers@aol.com
Web:
http://www.geocities.com/Athens/1105/gtld.html#special
Supports parents, students, educators on LD, giftedness.

Recording for the Blind and Dyslexic
20 Roszel Road
Princeton, NJ 08540
Ph: (609) 452-0606
E-mail: rfbd@lafn.org
Web: http://www.rfbd.org/
Produces recordings of textbooks, reference and professional materials for those who can't read standard print.

Schwab Foundation for Learning
1650 South Amphlett Blvd., Suite 300
San Mateo, CA 94402
Ph: (800) 230-0988
       (650) 655-2410
Fax: (650) 655-2411
E-mail: infodesk@schwablearning.org
Web: http://www.schwablearning.org
Education and resouces to help LD students.

Talking Book Program
National Library Service for the Blind and Physically Handicapped, Library of Congress
Washington, D.C. 20542
Ph: (202) 707-5100
TDD: (202) 707-0744
Fax: (202) 707-0712
E-mail: nls@loc.gov
Web: http://www.loc.gov/nls/
Library of recorded materials for those with learning disabilities.

Recommended Reading

The ABCs of Learning Disabilities
Bernice Wong
Academic Press Inc., 1996

BOSC Directory: Facilities for Learning Disabilities, 1999-2000
Irene Slovak
Books on Special Children Publishers, 1997

About Dyslexia: Unraveling the Myth
Priscilla Vail
Modern Learning Press/Programs for Education, 1990

Bridges to Literacy: Learning from Reading Recovery
Diane DeFord, Gay Su Pinnell, Carol Lyons
Heinemann, 1991

Academic Skills Problems: Direct Assessment and Intervention
Edward Shapiro, Ph.D.
Guilford Publications, 1989

Brilliant Idiot: An Autobiography of a Dyslexic
Abraham Schmitt
Good Books, 1992

Another Door to Learning: True Stories of Learning Disabled Children and Adults, and the Keys to Their Success
Judy Schwarz
Crossroad Publishing, 1992

Career Development & Transition Education for Adolescents with Disabilities, 2nd ed.
Gary Clark, Oliver Kolstoe
Allyn and Bacon, 1994

Assessment of Exceptional Students: Educational and Psychological Procedures
Ronald Taylor
Allyn and Bacon, 1997

Career Ladders for Challenged Youths in Transition from School to Adult Life
Shepherd Siegel, Matt Robert, Karen Greener, Gary Meyer, William Halloran, Robert Gaylord-Ross
PRO-ED, 1993

Beyond the Rainbow: A Guide for Parents of Children with Dyslexia and Other Learning Disabilities, 2nd ed.
Patricia Dodds, Ed. D., Nancy Robeson, M.Ed., Paula Rosteet
Educational Interventions, 1993

Children and Adults with Learning Disabilities
Tom Smith, Edward Polloway, Carol Dowdy
Allyn and Bacon, 1997

Children's Difficulties in Reading, Spelling and Writing: Challenges and Responses
David Pumfrey, Colin Elliott
Farmer Press, 1990

Classroom Success for the LD and ADHD Child, rev. ed.
Suzanne Stevens
John F. Blair Publishing, 1997

College and Career Success for Students with Learning Disabilities
Roslyn Dolber
VGN Career Horizons, 1996

College Guide for Students with Learning Disabilities
Annette Sclafani, Michael Lynch
Laurel Publishing Corp., 1993

College Students with Learning Disabilities: A Handbook
Susan Vogel
Learning Disabilities Association Bookstore, 1997

Common Sense About Dyslexia
Anne Marshall Huston
Madison Books, 1987

Complete Learning Disabilities Directory, 1998
Laura Mars (Ed.)
Grey House Publishing Inc., 1997

Complete Learning Disabilities Handbook: Ready-to-Use Techniques for Teaching Learning-Handicapped Students
Joan Harwell
Center for Applied Research in Education, 1989

Complete Learning Disabilities Resource Library: Ready-to-Use Tools and Materials for Remediating Specific Learning Disabilities, Vol. II
Joan Harwell
Center for Applied Research in Education, 1995

Coping with Learning Disability, rev. ed.
Lawrence Clayton, Jaydene Morrison
Rosen Publishing Group, 1995

Crossover Children: A Source Book for Helping Children Who are Gifted and Learning Disabled
Marlene Bireley
Council for Exceptional Children, 1995

Curriculum Adaptations for Students with Learning and Behavior Problems: Principles and Practices, 2nd ed.
John Hoover, James Patton
PRO-ED, 1997

Dancing in the Rain: Stories of Exceptional Progress by Parents of Children with Special Needs
Annabel Stehli
Georgiana Organization, 1995

Day-to-Day Dyslexia in the Classroom
Joy Pollock, Elisabeth Waller
Routledge, 1994

Developing Independent Readers: Strategy-Oriented Reading Activities for Children with Special Needs
Cynthia Conway Waring
Prentice Hall, 1994

Developmental Variation and Learning Disorders
Melvin Levine
Educators Publishing Service, 1987

Directory of Facilities and Services for the Learning Disabled, 1997-98
Academic Therapy Publications, 1998

Dissimilar Learners
Carolyn Cooper, Ph.D., MaryAnn Lingg, Ph.D., Angelo Puricelli, Ph.D., George Yard, Ph. D.
Pegasus Publications, Ltd., 1995

Dysgraphia: Why Johnny Can't Write: A Handbook for Teachers and Parents
Diane Cavey
PRO-ED, 1993

Dyslexia
Wendy Moragne
Millbrook Press, 1997

Dyslexia in Adults: Taking Charge of Your Life
Kathleen Nosek
Taylor Publishing Co., 1997

Dyslexia in Children: Multidisciplinary Perspectives
Angela Fawcett, Rod Nicolson
Harvester Wheatsheaf, 1994

Dyslexia and Hyperlexia: Diagnosis and Management of Developmental Reading Disabilities
P. G. Aaron
Kluwer Academic Publishers, 1989

Dyslexia and Mathematics
T. R. Miles, Elaine Miles
Routledge, 1992

Dyslexia My Life: One Man's Story of His Life with a Learning Disability
Girard Sagmiller, Gigi Lane
G&R Publications, 1995

Dyslexia: Research and Resource Guide
Carol Sullivan Spafford, George Grosser
Allyn and Bacon, 1996

Dyslexia Theory and Practice of Remedial Instruction, 2nd ed.
Diana Brewster Clark
York Press, 1995

The Dyslexic Scholar: Helping Your Child Succeed in the School System
Kathleen Nosek
Taylor Publishing Co., 1995

Education of Children and Adolescents with Learning Disabilities
Abraham Ariel
Macmillan Publishing Co., 1992

Educational Care: A System for Understanding and Helping Children with Learning Problems at Home and in School
Melvin Levine
Educators Publishing Service, 1994

Educational Technology and Learning Disabilities: A Resource Directory of Software and Hardware Products
Learning Disabilities Association of America, 1992

Enhancing Self-Concepts and Achievement of Mildly Handicapped Students
Carroll Jones
Charles C. Thomas Publisher, 1992

Faking It: A Look into the Mind of a Creative Learner
Christopher Lee, Rosemary Jackson
Boynton/Cook Publishers, 1992

From High School to College: Keys to Success for Students with Learning Disabilities
Craig Michaels
National Center on Employment and Disability
Human Resources Center, 1988

The Gift of Dyslexia: Why Some of the Smartest People Can't Read and How They Can Learn, rev. ed.
Ronald Davis
Berkley Publishing Group, 1997

Guide to Colleges with Programs and Services for Students with Learning Disabilities
Midge Lipkin
Schoolsearch Press, 1993

Guide to Private Schools for Students with Learning Disabilities
Midge Lipkin, Ph.D.
Schoolsearch Press, 1989

Handbook of Learning Disabilities: A Multisystem Approach
Jack Westman
Allyn and Bacon, 1990

Help for the Learning Disabled Child
Lou Stewart, M.A.T./L.D.
Slosson Educational Publications, 1991

Help Me to Help My Child: A Sourcebook for Parents of Learning Disabled Children
Jill Bloom
Little, Brown and Co., 1990

Help! My Child Isn't Learning: Turning Frustration into Understanding and Hope
Grant Martin, M.D.
Focus on the Family, 1995

Helping Children Overcome Learning Difficulties, 3rd ed.
Jerome Rosner
Walker and Co., 1993

Helping Your Dyslexic Child: A Step-by-Step Program for Helping Your Child Improve Reading, Writing, Spelling, Comprehension, and Self Esteem
Eileen Cronin
Prima Publishing, 1994

How to Succeed in College with Dyslexia
James Woods
Sem-Co Books, 1989

How to Teach Your Dyslexic Child to Read: A Proven Method for Parents and Teachers
Bernice Baumer
Carol Publishing Group, 1996

A Human Development View of Learning Disabilities: From Theory to Practice
Corrine Kass, Ph.D., Cleborne Maddux, Ph. D.
Charles C. Thomas Publisher, 1993

Human Exceptionality: Society, School, and Family
Michael Hardman, Clifford Drew, M. Winston Egan
Allyn and Bacon, 1996

I Have a Friend with Learning Disabilities
Hannah Carlson, M.Ed., CRC, Dale Carlson
Bick Publishing House, 1997

The IEP Primer and the Individualized Program: Preschool through Postsecondary Transition, 4th ed.
Beverly School
Academic Therapy Publications, 1997

If They Can Do It, We Can Too! Kids Write about Famous People Who Overcame Learning Differences Similar to Theirs
Margo Holen Dinneen, Learning Lab Students at Deephaven Elementary
Deaconess Press, 1992

In the Mind's Eye: Visual Thinkers, Gifted People with Learning Difficulties, Computer Images and the Ironies of Creativity
Thomas West
Prometheus Books, 1991

Inclusion: A Practical Guide for Parents
Lorraine Moore
Peytral Publications, 1996

Independent Strategies for Efficient Study, rev. ed.
Karen Rooney, Ph.D.
J.R. Enterprises, 1990

An Introduction to the Nature and Needs of Students with Mild Disabilities: Mild Mental Retardation, Behavior Disorders, and Learning Disabilities
Carroll Jones, Ph. D.
Charles C. Thomas Publisher, 1996

Introduction to Special Education
Deborah Deutsch Smith
Prentice Hall, 1997

Introduction to Special Education: The Inclusive Classroom
Karen Waldron, Ph.D.
Delmar Publications, 1998

The K&W Guide to Colleges for the Learning Disabled, 1998 Ed.
Marybeth Kravets, Imy Wax
Random House, 1997

Keys to Parenting a Child with a Learning Disability
Barry McNamara, Francine McNamara
Barron's Educational Series, 1995

LD Child and the ADHD Child: Ways Parents and Professionals Can Help
Suzanne Stevens
John F. Blair Publisher, 1996

Learning About Learning Disabilities
Bernice Wong
Academic Press, 1991

Learning Denied
Denny Taylor
Heinemann, 1991

The Learning Differences Source Book
Nancy Boyles, Darlene Contadino
Lowell House, 1997

Learning Disabilities
Jean McBee Knox
Chelsea House, 1989

Learning Disabilities A to Z: A Parent's Complete Guide to Learning Disabilities from Preschool to Adulthood
Corrine Smith, Ph.D., Lisa Strick
Free Press, 1997

Learning Disabilities and ADHD: A Family Guide to Living and Learning Together
Betty Osman, Ph.D.
John Wiley and Sons, 1997

Learning Disabilities in Adulthood
Paul Gerber, Ph.D., Henry Reiff, Ph.D. (Eds.)
Butterworth-Heinemann, 1993

Learning Disabilities: Characteristics, Identification, and Teaching Strategies
William Bender
Allyn and Bacon, 1992

Learning Disability: The Imaginary Disease
Thomas Finlan
Bergin and Garvey, 1994

Learning Disabilities: From Theory toward Practice
Lawrence O'Shea, Dorothy O'Shea, Robert Algozzine
Merrill, 1998

Learning Disability Intervention Manual, rev. ed.
Stephen McCarney (Ed.)
Hawthorne, 1995

Learning Disabilities: The Interaction of Learner, Task, and Setting, 4th ed.
Corinne Roth Smith
Allyn and Bacon, 1998

The Learning Disabled Child
Sylvia Farnham-Diggory
Harvard University Press, 1992

Learning Disabilities: Lifelong Issues
William Ellis, Shirley Cramer
Paul H. Brookes, 1996

The Learning Disabled Child: A School and Family Concern, 2nd ed.
Jeffries McWhirter
University Press of America, 1988

Learning Disabilities, Medicine and Myth: A Guide to Understanding the Child and the Physician
Robert Johnston
College Hill, 1987

Learning Re-Abled: The Learning Disability Controversy and Composition Studies
Patricia Dunn
Boynton/Cook Publishers, 1995

Learning Disabilities: A Review of Available Treatments
William Feldman
Charles C. Thomas, Publisher, 1990

Learning in Spite of Labels: Practical Teaching Tips and a Christian Perspective of Education
Joyce Herzog
Greenleaf Press, 1994

Learning Disabilities: Theories, Diagnosis, and Teaching Strategies, 7th ed.
Janet Lerner
Houghton Mifflin Co., 1997

Lessons Learned: Students with Learning Disabilities Share What They've Discovered about Life and Learning
Dave Fullen
Mountain Books, 1993

The Learning Disabilities Trap: How to Save Your Child from the Perils of Special Education
Harlow Unger
Contemporary Books, 1998

Literacy Programs for Adults with Developmental Disabilities
Gerard Giordano, Ph.D.
Singular Publishing Group, 1996

Living with Dyslexia
Barbara Riddick
Routledge, 1995

Living with a Learning Disability, rev.
Barbara Cordoni
Southern Illinois University Press, 1990

Making the Grade: Reflections on Being Learning Disabled
Dayle Upham, Virginia Trumbull
Heinemann, 1997

Math and Students with Learning Disabilities: A Practical Guide to Course Substitutions
Paul Nolting, Ph.D.
Academic Success Press, 1993

The Misunderstood Child: A Guide for Parents of Children with Learning Disabilities, 3rd ed.
Larry Silver, M.D.
Random House, 1998

My Name is Anita and I am a Dyslexic: An Autobiography
Anita Griffiths
University Eds., 1991

National Directory of Four Year Colleges, Two Year Colleges, and Post High School Training Programs for Young People with Learning Disabilities, 7th ed.
P.M. Fielding, John Ross
Partners in Publishing, 1993

Nature of Learning Disabilities: Critical Elements of Diagnosis & Classification
Kenneth Kavale, Steven Forness
L. Erlbaum, 1995

Neuropsychological Treatments of Dyslexia
Dirk Bakker
Oxford University Press, 1990

No Easy Answers: The Learning Disabled Child at Home and at School, rev. ed.
Sally Smith
Bantam Books, 1995

No One to Play With: The Social Side of Learning Disabilities, rev. ed.
Betty Osman, Henriette Blinder
Academic Therapy Publications, 1995

Off Track: When Poor Readers Become "Learning Disabled"
Louise Spear-Swerling, Robert Sternberg
Westview Press, 1996

On Being L. D.: Perspectives and Strategies of Young Adults
Stephen Murphy
Teachers College Press, 1992

Optimizing Special Education: How Parents Can Make a Difference
Nancy Wilson
Insight Books, 1992

The Other Route into College: Alternative Admission
Stacy Needle
Random House, 1991

Overcoming Dyslexia in Children, Adolescents, and Adults
Dale Jordan
PRO-ED, 1989

Parenting a Child with a Learning Disability: A Practical, Empathetic Guide
Cheryl Gerson Tuttle, M.ED., Penny Paquette
Lowell House, 1993

Parent's Guide to Learning Disabilities
Stephen McCarney, Angela Bauer
Hawthorne Educational Services, 1995

Performance Breakthroughs for Adolescents with Learning Disabilities or ADD: How to Help Students Succeed in the Regular Education Classroom
Geraldine Markel, Judith Greenbaum
Research Press, 1996

Peterson's Guide to Colleges with Programs for Learning-Disabled Students, 5th ed.
Charles Mangrum, Stephen Strichart (Eds.)
Peterson's Guides, 1997

A Practical Parent's Handbook on Teaching Children with Learning Disabilities
Shelby Holley
Charles C. Thomas Publisher, 1994

Prescriptions for Children with Learning and Adjustment Problems: A Consultant's Desk Reference, 3rd ed.
Ralph Blanco, Ph.D., David Bogacki, Ph.D.
Charles C. Thomas Publisher, 1988

Promoting Postsecondary Education for Students with Learning Disabilities: A Handbook for Practitioners
Loring Brinckerhoff, Stan Shaw, Joan McGuire
PRO-ED, 1993

Questions and Answers about Learning Disabilities: The Learning Disabled, Their Parents and Professionals Speak Out
Sally Shearer Swenson, M.A., Phyllis Gilman Weisberg, Ph.D.
PRO-ED, 1988

Reading Disability: A Human Approach to Evaluation and Treatment of Reading and Writing Difficulties, 4th ed.
Florence Roswell, Gladys Natchez
Basic Books, 1989

Reading and Learning Disabilities: Research and Practice
Joyce French, Nancy Ellsworth, Marie Amoruso
Garland Publishing, 1995

Reading - Learning Disability: An Ecological Approach
Jill Bartoli, Morton Botel
Teachers College Press, 1988

Ready-To-Use Learning Disabilities Activity Kit
Joan Harwell
Center for Applied Research in Education, 1993

The Reality of Dyslexia, 2nd ed.
John Osmond
Brookline Books, 1995

The Resource Room: A Guide for Special Educators
B. E. McNamara
State University of New York Press, 1989

Reversals: A Personal Account of Victory Over Dyslexia
Eileen Simpson
Noonday Press, 1991

Roads to Reading Disability: When Poor Readers Become "Learning Disabled"
Louise Spear-Swerling, Robert Sternberg
Westview Press, 1996

The Runaway Learning Machine: Growing Up Dyslexic
James Bauer
Educational Media Corporation, 1992

Scientific Watergate -- Dyslexia
Harold Levinson, M.D.
Stonebridge, 1994

Second Chance: A Guide to Post-Secondary Options for Young Adults with Severe Learning Disabilities
Donald Levitan, Dennis Mahoney, Diana Ellis Sorrento, Rob Spongberg (Eds.)
Riverview School, 1993

Smart But Feeling Dumb: The Challenging New Research on Dyslexia - And How It May Help You, rev. ed.
Harold Levinson
Warner Books

Smart Kids with School Problems: Things to Know and Ways to Help
Priscilla Vail
E.P. Dutton, 1987

So Your Child Has a Learning Problem: Now What? 2nd ed.
Fred Wallbrown, Ph.D., Jane Wallbrown, Ph. D.
Clinical Psychology Publishing Co., 1990

Something's Not Right: One Family's Struggle with Learning Disabilities
Nancy Lelewer
VanderWyk and Burnham, 1994

Special Education: A Practical Approach for Teachers, 3ʳᵈ ed.
James Ysseldyke, Bob Algozzine
Houghton Mifflin Co., 1994

Special Kids Problem Solver: Ready-to-Use Interventions for Helping All Students with Academic, Behavioral and Physical Problems
Kenneth Shore
Prentice Hall, 1999

Strategies for Success: Classroom Teaching Techniques for Students with Learning Problems
Lynn Metlzer, Bethany Roditi, Donna Haynes, Kathleen Biddle, Michelle Paster, Susan Taber
PRO-ED, 1996

Strategies for Teaching Students with Learning and Behavior Problems
Ruth Lyn Mees
Brooks/Cole, 1996

Succeeding Against the Odds: Strategies and Insights from the Learning Disabled
Sally Smith
Jeremy P. Tarcher, 1991

Succeeding in the Workplace: Attention Deficit Disorder and Learning Disabilities in the WorkPlace
Kathleen Nadeau, Patricia Quinn, Dale Brown, Peter Latham, Patricia Latham
JKL Commun., 1994

Success for College Students with Learning Disabilities
Susan Vogel, Janet Lerner, Pamela Adelman
Springer-Verlag, 1992

Survival Guide for College Students with ADD or LD
Kathleen Nadeau
American Psychological Press, 1994

The Survival Guide for Teenagers with LD
Rhoda Cummings, Gary Fisher
Free Spirit Publishing, 1993

Swimming Upstream: A Complete Guide to the College Application Process for the Learning Disabled Student
Diane Wilder Howard
Hunt House Publishing, 1988

Teaching Adolescents with Learning Disabilities: Strategies and Methods
Donald Deshler, B. Keith Lenz, Edwin Ellis
Love Publishing Co., 1996

Teaching Adults with Learning Disabilities
Dale Jordan
Krieger Publishing Co., 1996

Teaching Kids with Learning Difficulties in the Regular Classroom: Strategies and Techniques Every Teacher Can Use to Challenge and Motivate Struggling Students
Susan Winebrenner
Free Spirit, 1996

Teaching Learning Strategies to Adolescents and Adults with Learning Disabilities, 3rd ed.
B. Keith Lenz, David Scanlon, Edwin Ellis
PRO-ED, 1996

Teaching Mathematics to Students With Learning Disabilities, 3rd ed.
Nancy Bley, Carol Thornton
PRO-ED, 1995

Teaching Reading to Disabled and Handicapped Learners
Harold Love, Freddie Litton
Charles C. Thomas Publisher, 1994

Teaching Secondary Students with Mild Learning and Behavior Problems: Methods, Materials, Strategies, 3rd ed.
Lowell Masters, Barbara Mori, Allen Mori
PRO-ED, 1999

Teaching Students with Learning and Behavior Problems: Managing Mild-to-Moderate Difficulties in Resource and Inclusive Settings, 6th ed.
Donald Hammill, Nettie Bartel
PRO-ED, 1995

Teaching Students with Learning Disabilities: Strategies for Success
Karen Waldron
Singular Publishing Group, 1992

Teaching Students with Learning Problems, 5th ed.
Cecil Mercer, Ann Mercer
Prentice Hall, 1997

Teaching Students with Moderate/Severe Disabilities, Including Autism: Strategies for Second Language Learners in Inclusive Settings, 2nd ed.
Elva Duran
Charles C. Thomas Publisher, 1996

Teaching Study Skills and Strategies to Students with Learning Disabilities, Attention Deficit Disorders, or Special Needs, 2nd ed.
Stephen Strichart, Charles Mangrum II, Patricia Iannuzzi
Allyn and Bacon, 1998

To be Gifted and Learning Disabled: From Identification to Practical Intervention Strategies
Susan Baum, Steve Owen, John Dixon
Creative Learning Press, 1991

To Teach a Dyslexic
Don McCabe
AVKO Educational Research Foundation, 1995

Transition Strategies for Persons with Learning Disabilities
Craig Michaels, Ph.D. (Ed.)
Singular Publishing Group, 1994

The Tuned-In, Turned-On Book About Learning Problems
Marnell Hayes, Ed.D.
Academic Therapy Publications, 1994

Turnabout Children: Overcoming Dyslexia and Other Learning Disabilities
Mary MacCracken
New American Library, 1987

Understanding Dyslexia: A Practical Approach for Parents and Teachers
Anne Marshall Huston
Madison Books, 1992

Understanding LD (Learning Differences): A Curriculum to Promote LD Awareness, Self Esteem and Coping Skills in Students Ages 8-13
Susan McMurchie
Free Spirit Publishing, 1994

Understanding the Learning Disabled Athlete: A Guide for Parents, Coaches and Professionals
Andrew Yellen, Ph.D., Heidi Yellen, M.A., C.E.T.
Charles C. Thomas Publisher, 1987

For Youth

Adam Zigzag
Barbara Barrie
Bantam Doubleday Dell Publishing Group, 1994

All Kinds of Minds: A Young Student's Book about Learning Abilities and Learning Disorders
Mel Levine, M.D.
Educators Publishing Service, 1993

Best Fight
Anne Schlieper
Albert Whitman and Co., 1994

When Learning is Tough: Kids Talk About Their Learning Disabilities
Cynthia Roby
Albert Whitman and Co., 1994

Why Are You Calling Me LD? 2nd ed.
Holly Parzych
Peekan Publications, 1995

Why is My Child Having Trouble at School?
Barbara Novick, Maureen Arnold
Villard Books, 1991

You, Your Child, and "Special" Education: A Guide to Making the System Work
Barbara Coyne Cutler, Ed. D
Paul H. Brookes, 1993

Different is Not Bad, Different is the World -- A Book About Learning and Physical Disabilities
Sally Smith
Sopris West, 1994

The Don't-Give-Up Kid and Learning Differences, 2nd ed.
Jeanne Gehret
Verbal Images Press, 1996

Dyslexia
Elaine Landau
Franklin Watts, 1991

The Facts About Learning Disabilities
Paul Almonte, Theresa Desmond
Crestwood House, 1992

Probably Still Nick Swansen
Virginia Euwer Wolff
Henry Holt and Co., 1988

The Hard Life of Seymour E. Newton
Ann Herold
Herald Press, 1990

Reach for the Moon
Samantha Abeel
Pfeifer-Hamilton Publishers, 1994

How Dyslexic Benny Became a Star
Joe Griffith
Yorktown Press, 1998

The School Survival Guide for Kids with LD
Rhoda Woods Cummings, Ed.D., Gary Fisher, Ph.D.
Free Spirit Publishing, 1991

Josh: A Boy With Dyslexia
Caroline Janover
Waterfront Books, 1988

Secrets Aren't Always for Keeps
Barbara Aiello
Twenty-First Century Books, 1988

Keeping a Head in School: A Student's Book about Learning Abilities and Learning Disorders
Mel Levine
Educators Publishing Services, 1990

Tall Enough to Own the World
Berniece Rabe
Franklin Watts, 1989

Learning Disorders
Jacquelyn Harris
Twenty-First Century Books, 1993

Trouble with School: A Family Story About Learning Disabilities
Kathryn Boesel Dunn
Woodbine House, Inc. 1993

Living with Learning Disabilities: A Guide for Students
David Hall
Lerner Publications Co., 1993

The Tuned-In, Turned-On Book About Learning Problems
Marnell Hayes
Academic Therapy Publications, 1994

Many Ways to Learn: Young People's Guide to Learning Disabilities
Judith Stern, Uzi Ben-Ami
Magination Press, 1996

Turning Around the Upside-Down Kids: Helping Dyslexic Kids Overcome Their Disorder
Harold Levies, M.D., Addle Sanders
Evens, 1992

My Name is Brain-Brian
Jeanne Betancourt
Scholastic, 1993

Unjust Cause
Tehila Peterseil
Pitspopany Press, 1997

What Do You Mean I Have a Learning Disability?
Katherine Marie Dryer
Walker, 1991

When Learning is Tough: Kids Talk About Their Learning Disabilities
Scything Robe
Concept Books, 1994

The Worst Speller in Jr. High
Caroline Garner
Free Spirit Publishing, 1995

You Don't Have to Be Dyslexic, 2nd ed.
Joan Smith
Learning Time Products, 1996

You Don't Outgrow It: Living with Learning Disabilities
Marnell Hayes
Academic Therapy Publications, 1993

Your Plan for Success: A College Preparation Manual for Students with Learning Disabilities
Kristine Wiest Webb
Peekan Publications, 1995

Yours Truly, Shirley
Ann Martin
Holiday House, 1988

Videos

Video tapes can be very useful, but may a challenge to find, especially if they aren't new to the market. Try contacting the producers noted even if the tape isn't listed on their web site, book stores and your library.

All Children Learn Differently
Learning Disabilities Association of America
4156 Library Road
Pittsburgh, PA 15234-1349
Ph: (412) 341-1515
Fax: (412) 344-0224
E-mail: ldanatl@usaor.net
Web: http://www.ldanatl.org/
Specialists in medicine, perception, language and education talk about taking a nutritional/educational approach to the remediation of learning disabilities.

How Difficult Can This Be?
Richard Lavoie
WETA Videos, 1989
22-D Hollywood Ave.
Ho-Ho-Kus, NJ 07423
Ph: (800) 343-5540
Fax: (201) 652-1973
E-mail: ldonline@weta.org
Web: http://www.ldonline.org
Classroom through an LD child's eyes.

Last One Picked ...First One Picked On: Learning Disabilities and Social Skills
Richard Lavoie
WETA Videos, 1994
22-D Hollywood Ave.
Ho-Ho-Kus, NJ 07423
Ph: (800) 343-5540
Fax: (201) 652-1973
E-mail: ldonline@weta.org
Web: http://www.ldonline.org
Social problems that LD children face with practical solutions for teachers.

L.D. Stories I and I / On the Edge
Lab School of Washington
Products and Services Division
4759 Reservoir Road, NW
Washington, DC 20007
Ph: (202) 944-3083
Web: http://www.labschool.org/

A Leader's Guide for Youth with Learning Disabilities
Learning Disabilities Association of America
4156 Library Road
Pittsburgh, PA 15234-1349
Ph: (412) 341-1515
Fax: (412) 344-0224
E-mail: ldanatl@usaor.net
Web: http://www.ldanatl.org/
Shows how leaders of groups can integrate individuals with learning disabilities into regular programs, similar to scouts. Uses scouting as an example.

Learning Disabilities: Dyslexia
AGC United Learning, 1996
1560 Sherman Ave., Suite 100
Evanston, Il 60201
Ph: (800) 323-9084
         (847) 328-6700
Fax: (847) 328-6706
E-mail: info@agcunited.com
Web: http://www.agcmedia.com
Causes and ways to overcome dyslexia. Grades 6-12.

Look What You've Done! Stories of Hope and Resilience
Robert Brooks
WETA Videos, 1997
22-D Hollywood Ave.
Ho-Ho-Kus, NJ 07423
Washington, D.C.
Ph: (800) 343-5540
Fax: (201) 652-1973
E-mail: ldonline@weta.org
Web: http://www.ldonline.org/
Finding "islands of competence" to help build confidence.

Picture of Success
Pat Buckley Moss, Dr. Larry Silver
Learning Disabilities Association of America
4156 Library Road
Pittsburgh, PA 15234-1349
Ph: (412) 341-1515
Fax: (412) 344-0224
E-mail: ldanatl@usaor.net
Web: http://www.ldanatl.org/
Tells the story of a successful dyslexic.

When the Chips Are Down
Richard Lavoie
WETA Video, 1997
22-D Hollywood Ave.
Ho-Ho-Kus, NJ 07423
Ph: (800) 343-5540
Fax: (201) 652-1973
E-mail: ldonline@weta.org
Web: http://www.ldonline.org
How to deal with behavioral problems, preventive discipline, create a stable, predictable environment in which LD children can flourish.

Periodicals / Newsletters

Exceptional Children

Council for Exceptional Children
1110 North Glebe Road, Suite 300
Arlington, VA 22201-5704
Ph: (888) CEC-SPED
       (703) 620-3660
TTY: (703) 264-9446
Fax: (703) 264-9494
E-mail: service@cec.sped.org
Web: http://www.cec.sped.org/bk/ec-jour.htm
Research, topical issues, perspectives on education and development of children with exceptionalities.

Intervention in School and Clinic

PRO-ED Journals
8700 Shoal Blvd.
Austin, TX 78758-6897
Ph: (800) 897-3202
Fax: (800) 397-7633
Web: http://www.proedinc.com/
Practitioner-oriented journal designed to provide practical, research-based ideas to those who work with students with learning disabilities and emotional / behavioral problems for whom minor curriculum and environmental modifications are ineffective.

Journal of Early Intervention

Council for Exceptional Children
1110 North Glebe Road, Suite 300
Arlington, VA 22201-5704
Ph: (888) CEC-SPED
       (703) 620-3660
TTY: (703) 264-9446
Fax: (703) 264-9494
E-mail: service@cec.sped.org
Web: http://www.cec.sped.org/bk/catalog/17.htm

Learning Disabilities: A Multidisciplinary Journal

Learning Disabilities Association
4156 Library Road
Pittsburgh, PA 15234-1349
Ph: (412) 341-1515
Fax: (412) 344-0224
E-mail: ldanatl@usaor.net
Web: http://www.ldanatl.org/Pubs.html
Oriented toward professionals in the field of learning disabilities. Advocacy, assessment, college programs, cultural differences, law, public policy.

Perspectives

International Dyslexia Association
Chester Bldg.
8600 La Salle Road, Suite 382
Baltimore, MD 21286-2044
Ph: (800) ABCD123
       (410) 296-0232
Fax: (410) 321-5069
E-mail: info@interdys.org
Web: http://www.interdys.org/

Postsecondary LD Report

Block Educational Consulting
4218 Olentangy Blvd.
Columbus, OH 43214-3034
Ph: (614) 263-0938
E-mail: lsblock@aol.com
Web: http://www.ldreport.com/
Information on issues crucial to the transition of students with learning disabilities, ADD, and head injury from high school to postsecondary education.

Reaching Beyond

Marin Puzzle People
199 Greenfield Ave
San Rafael, CA 94901
Ph: (415) 459-0870
Web: http://www.hooked.net/users/dyslexia/

Remedial and Special Education

PRO-ED Journals
8700 Shoal Blvd.
Austin, TX 78758-6897
Ph: (800) 897-3202
Fax: (800) 397-7633
Web: http://www.proedinc.com/
Professional journal devoted to issues involving the education of persons for whom typical instruction is not effective.

Teaching Exceptional Children

Council for Exceptional Children
1110 North Glebe Road, Suite 300
Arlington, VA 22201-5704
Ph: (888) CEC-SPED
          (703) 620-3660
TTY: (703) 264-9446
Fax: (703) 264-9494
E-mail: service@cec.sped.org
Web: http://www.cec.sped.org/bk/catalog/16.htm
For teachers and administrators of children with
disabilities and children who are gifted. Methods,
materials for classroom, current issues.

Topics in Early Childhood Special Education

PRO-ED Journals
8700 Shoal Blvd.
Austin, TX 78758
Ph: (800) 897-3202
Fax: (800) 397-7633
Web: http://www.proedinc.com/

Web Sites

Also see "General Web Sites". Many have sections on learning disabilities, but they are not listed
separately below.

All Kinds of Minds

E-mail: AKOMinds@aol.com
Web: http://www.allkindsofminds.org/index.html
Education, training for parents, educators on L.D.

LD Resources

Web: http://www.ldresources.com/
Large source of information on learning disabilites.

LD Online

Web: http://www.ldonline.org/
Large source of information on learning disabilities.

Teens Helping Teens

Ph: (212) 961-1930
E-mail: ldteens@taconic.net
Web: http://www.ldteens.org
Teens helping teens deal with learning disabilities.

Vendors

AB-CD Rom USA, Inc.

9856 Lemonwood Dr.
Boynton Beach, FL 33437
Ph: (800) 974-6642
Fax: (561) 732-4692
E-mail: info@ab-cdrom.com
Web: http://www.ab-cdrom.com/
"Climbing with Phonics" CD teaches basic to advanced
reading, writing, spelling, phonics. Features Orton-
Gillingham approach.

American Guidance Service (AGS)

4201 Woodland Road
Circles Pines, MN 55014
Ph: (800) 328-2560
          (763) 786-4343
Fax: (800) 471-8457
          (763) 786-9077
E-mail: agsmail@agsnet.com
Web: http://www.agsnet.com
Publisher of assessments, textbooks, instructional
materials for students with a wide ability range.

Child Development Institute
17853 Santiago Blvd, Suite 107-328
Villa Park, CA 92861
Ph: (714) 998-8617
Fax: (714) 637-6957
E-mail: webmaster@childdevelopmentinfo.com
Web: http://www.cdipage.com
Information and materials for children with learning disabilities, ADD/ADHD, dyslexia.

Davis Dyslexia Association International
Ph: (650) 692-7141
      (888) 999-3324
Fax: (650) 692-7075
E-mail: ddai@dyslexia.com
Web: http://www.dyslexia.com
Materials and training for helping others to overcome learning problems.

Different Roads to Learning
12 W. 18th St., Suite 3E
New York, NY 10011
Ph: (800) 853-1057
      (212) 604-9637
Fax: (800) 317-9146
E-mail: julie@difflearn.com
Web: http://www.difflearn.com/
On-line catalog specializing in learning materials and playthings for children with developmental delays.

Dr. Giler: Attention Deficit Disorder (ADD or ADHD) With or Without Learning Disabilities (LD)
549 N. Hope St.
Santa Barbara, CA 93110
Ph: (805) 563-2325
Fax: (805) 687-1204
E-mail: jzgiler@earthlink.net
Web: http://ld-add.com/index.htm
Materials and assistance with ADD, LD.

Edu-Kinesthetics, Inc.
P.O. Box 3395
Ventura, CA 93006-
Ph: (888) 388-9898
      (805) 650-3303
E-mail: educbooks@aol.com
Web: http://www.braingym.com/
Materials for kinesthetic (movement) learners.

Great Ideas for Teaching
P.O. Box 444
Wrightsville Beach, NC 28480
Ph: (800) 839-8339
      (910) 256-4494
Fax: (800) 839-8498
      (910) 256-4493
E-mail: gift@gift-inc.com
Web: http://www.gift-inc.com
Speech, language, auditory processing materials.

IntelliTools Inc.
1720 Corporate Circle
Petaluma, CA 94954
Ph: (800) 899-6687
      (707) 773-2000
Fax: (707) 773-2001
E-mail: info@intellitools.com
Web: http://www.intellitools.com/
Software and adaptive computer devices for elementary students with special needs.

Laureate Learning Systems, Inc.
110 East Spring St.
Winooski, VT 05404-1898
Ph: (800) 562-6801
      (802) 655-4755
Fax: (802) 655-4757
E-mail: customer-service@laureatelearning.com
Web: http://www.laureatelearning.com/
Software for people with special needs.

Library Reproduction Service
14214 S. Figueroa St.
Los Angeles, CA 90061
Ph: (800) 255-5002
        (310) 354-2610
Fax: (310) 354-2601
E-mail: lrsprint@aol.com
Web: http://www.lrs-largeprint.com/
Large print reproductions of educational materials.

LinguiSystems
3100 4th Ave.
P.O. Box 747
East Moline, IL 61244-9700
Ph: (800) 776-4332
        (309) 755-2300
E-mail: service@linguisystems.com
Web: http://www.linguisystems.com/
Speech, language arts materials.

MINDPLAY
160 W. Ft. Lowell Rd.
Tucson, AZ 85705
Ph: (520) 888-1800
Fax: (520) 888-7904
E-mail: mail@mindplay.com
Web: http://mindplay.com/index.html
Software for children with special needs.

Power Learning Center Computer Assisted Instruction
3510 NE Flanders St.
Portland, OR 97232
Ph: (503) 232-0221
Fax: (503) 235-3552
E-mail: plnwebmaster@powerlearningnetwork.com
Web: http://www.powerlearningnetwork.com
Internet-based training for adolescents and young
adults who have difficulty learning in traditional ways.

Scientific Learning Corporation
1995 University Ave. Suite 400
Berkeley, CA 94704
Ph: (888) 665-9707
Fax: (510) 665-1717
E-mail: info@scilearn.com
Web: http://www.scilearn.com/
Software to help with speech and language problems,
assessment tool.

SofDesign International, Inc.
301 South Sherman, Suite 202
Richardson , TX 75081
Ph: (800) 755-7344
        (972) 644-0098
Fax: (972) 644-4286
E-mail: dyslexia@sofdesign.com
Web: http://www.sofdesign.com/dyslexia/
Instructional materials for students with dyslexia.

Special Kids
Ph: (800) 543-7153
E-mail: info@specialkids.com
Web: http://www.specialkids1.com/
Learning videotapes and educational materials for youth
with learning disabilities.

---- *Mental Retardation*

A brain disorder in which a person's intellectual functioning is significantly below average resulting in challenges in communication and life skills.

Associated Conditions
These conditions are some which carry the symptoms of mental retardation:

- Fragile X syndrome
- Prader-Willi syndrome
- Angelman syndrome
- Rett's syndrome
- Williams syndrome
- Lesch-Hyhan syndrome
- Down syndrome.

.

Frequency
- 0.8 - 1.2% of the population .

Symptoms and Possible Effects
- IQ is below normal. IQ scores are used to determine the level of severity of mental retardation:

Severity	IQ Range	% of Those with Retardation
Mild	IQ 50 to 70	85%
Moderate	IQ 40 to 50	10%
Severe	IQ 25 to 40	3%
Profound	IQ below 25	2%

Other symptoms are associated with severity.

Mild
- Social and communication skills develop by age 5.
- Slight impact in sensorimotor skills.
- May look like other children until a later age.
- May develop academically through the sixth grade level, though it may take much longer.
- As adults, they can typically learn social and vocational skills, though guidance may be needed.
- May also be successful in a community living setting.

Moderate
- Communication skills develop during childhood.
- Able to handle personal care with supervision.
- May benefit from vocational training and doing semi- or unskilled work with supervision.
- May peak out academically at the second grade level.
- Difficulty recognizing social conventions.
- Tend to do well living in a supervised setting.

Severe
- Little communication skills as a young child, though this may develop at school age.
- Can be trained to do self care.
- May be able to learn alphabet, simple counting, sight read a few words.
- As an adult, may be able to perform simple tasks with supervision.
- May be able to adapt to living in a group home.

Profound
- Communication possible with training.
- Considerable problems with sensorimotor functions, but can improve with training.
- Self care is possible with appropriate training.
- Most have a neurological condition that causes mental retardation.
- Learning is possible in an individualized setting.
- Simple tasks can be done with close supervision.

Below is a description of the symptoms of various syndromes that can cause mental retardation:

Fragile X syndrome
- Inherited by men with family histories of the syndrome (male siblings or maternal uncles.)
- Caused by damage of the X chromosome.
- Hyperactivity, attention deficit, disciplinary problems.
- Children with severe retardation demonstrate developmental delays at very young ages. Those with mild retardation may not have significant developmental delays until preschool age.
- Elongated faces, prominent jaws, long ears.
- Enlarged testicles, prolapse of the mitral heart valve.
- High and arched palates, narrow nasal bridges, epicanthal folds and simian creases.
- Hypotonia and clumsiness.
- Echolalia, perseveration, and non-fluent speech.
- Auditory perception and memory problems.
- Difficulty processing new, sequential information.
- Difficulty solve problems.

- IQ scores tend to decrease over time.
- May experience seizures.
- Self-stimulatory behavior, such as hand flapping; self-injurious behavior, such as head banging.

Prader-Willi syndrome

- Caused by a defect in chromosome pair #15, inherited from the father's side of the family.
- Decreased muscle tone, short stature, obesity, mild mental retardation, undeveloped gonads, almond-shaped, upslanting eyes, narrow forehead.
- Behavioral symptoms relate to their striking obesity – demanding, stealing, and even foraging for food. This is a result of an abnormality in the hypothalamus, which makes them feel empty.
- Impulsiveness, obstinancy, and disinhibition.
- Delays in language and motor development, learning disabilities, feeding problems in infancy, sleep disturbances, skin picking, temper tantrums, and a high pain threshold.
- Approximately 1 in 10,000 people affected.
- Treated with behavior modification.

Angelman syndrome

- Caused by a defect in chromosome pair #15, interited from the mother's side of the family.
- Hand-flapping, little or no speech, attention deficit, hyperactivity, feeding and sleeping problems, delays in motor development, biting and hair pulling. Many have a stiff-legged gait and jerky body movements.
- Very sociable, affectionate, and laugh frequently.
- Most have abnormal EEGs and epilepsy.
- Most have severe mental retardation.
- Wide smiling mouth, thin upper lip, and deep set eyes.
- More than half have low levels of pigmentation in their eyes, hair, and skin.
- Approximately 1 in 25,000 individuals affected.
- Treated with behavior modification, speech therapy, and occupational therapy.

Rett's syndrome

- Progressive neurological disorder that occurs in girls, related to the X chromosome.
- Tend to have normal development during the first year of life, but then begin losing motor and mental skills.
- Head growth stops, spasticity and epilepsy may occur. By later childhood, these girls are typically nonambulatory and nonverbal.
- Often exhibit autistic-like behaviors, such as repetitive hand movements, toe walking, body rocking, sleep problems.
- Shakiness of the torso and sometimes the limbs. Unsteady, stiff gait.
- Breathing difficulties (hyperventilation, apnea, air swallowing).
- Teeth grinding and chewing difficulties.
- Mental retardation is between the levels of severe and profound.
- Hypoactivity.

Williams syndrome
- Genetic disorder characterized by mild mental retardation.
- Caused by abnormality in chromosome pair #7.
- Delays in development and language, problems in gross motor skills, sensitivity to sound.
- Fussy eating.
- Perseveration.
- Cardiovascular abnormalities, high blood pressure, high calcium levels.
- Almond-shaped eyes, oval ears, full lips, small chins, narrow faces, and broad mouths.
- Highly social.
- Approximately 1 out of 20,000 - 50,000 births.

Lesch-Hyhan syndrome
- Inherited through the X chromosome.
- Caused by a disorder in how purines, building blocks of DNA, are metabolized.
- Mental retardation and progressive neurological problems.
- Compulsive lip and finger biting.
- Aggressive behavior.
- Pica is seen in those with severe and profound mental retardation.

Causes
- Over 350 causes of mental retardation, yet in 75% of the cases the specific cause is unknown.
- Various syndromes, as outlined above.
- Fragile X syndrome is responsible for a good share of the severe mental retardation seen in men.
- Can be caused by prebirth influences such as trauma, environmental toxins, infections, congenital anomalies.

Diagnostic Processes
- Psychological testing to determine IQ and to help determine the degree of severity.
- Assessment of other skills.

DSM IV Diagnostic Criteria
Reprinted with permission from the *Diagnostic and Statistical Manual of Mental Disorders, Fourth Edition, Text Revision.* Copyright 2000 American Psychiatric Association.

A. Significantly subaverage intellectual functioning: an IQ of approximately 70 or below on an individual administered IQ test (for infants, a clinical judgment of significantly subaverage intellectual functioning.)

B. Concurrent deficits or impairments in present adaptive functioning (i.e., the person's effectiveness in meeting the standards expected for his or her age by his or her cultural group) in at least two of the following areas: communication, self-care, home living, social/interpersonal skills, use of community resources, self-direction, functional academic skills, work, leisure, health, and safety.

C. The onset is before age 18 years.

Treatment
Concurrent efforts in the areas of education, social skills, recreational activities, behavior management.

Outcomes

Not curable, but can be compensated for. Development of other disorders (e.g., bipolarity, ADHD, schizophrenia, depression, anxiety, obsessive-compulsive disorder) are more common among persons with mental retardation.

Who to Contact

Also refer to "Who Else to Contact." Organizations listed below target their work specifically toward mental retardation.

American Association on Mental Retardation (AAMR)
444 N. Capitol St. NW, Suite 846
Washington, DC 20001-1512
Ph: (800) 424-3688
     (202) 387-1968
Fax: (202) 387-2193
Web: http://www.aamr.org/
Information, programming on mental retardation.

Angelman Syndrome Foundation
414 Plaza Dr., Suite 209
Westmont, IL 60559
Ph: (800) IF-ANGEL
     (630) 734-9267
Fax: (630) 655-0391
E-mail: info@angelman.org
Web: http://www.angelman.org
Education, information exchange, research.

The ARC of the United States
1010 Wayne Ave., Suite 650
Silver Spring, MD 20910
Ph: (301) 565-3842
Fax: (301) 565-5342
E-mail: info@thearc.org
Web: http://TheArc.org
Education, research, advocacy for those with mental retardation.

Best Buddies International
100 Southeast 2nd St., Suite 1990
Miami, FL 33131
Ph: (305) 374-2233
Fax: (305) 374-5305
E-mail: info@bestbuddies.org
Web: http://www.bestbuddies.org
Provides opportunities for individuals with mental retardation to become friends.

Foundation for Exceptional Children
Division on Mental Retardation
1110 North Glebe Road, Suite 300
Arlington, VA 22201-5704
Ph: (888) CEC-SPED
     (703) 620-3660
TTY (text only): (703) 264-9446
Fax: (703) 264-9494
E-mail: service@cec.sped.org
Web: http://www.cec.sped.org
Helps those with mental retardation.

International Rett Syndrome Association
9121 Piscataway Road
Clinton, MD 20735
Ph: (800) 818-RETT
     (301) 856-3334
Fax: (301) 856-3336
E-mail: irsa@rettsyndrome.org
Web: http://www.rettsyndrome.org
Education, research.

Joseph P. Kennedy, Jr., Foundation
1325 G St. NW, Suite 500
Washington, DC 20005-4709
Ph: (202) 393-1250
Fax: (202) 824-0351
E-mail: maggiemclaughlin@aol.com
Web: http://familyvillage.wisc.edu/jpkf/index.html
Works to improve the way society deals with those with mental retardation, education on causes.

The Prader-Willi Syndrome Association
5700 Midnight Pass Road
Sarasota, FL 34242
Ph: (800) 926-4797
     (941) 312-0400
Fax: (941) 312-0142
E-mail: pwsausa@aol.com
Web: http://www.pwsausa.org/
Information, support services, research.

President's Committee on Mental Retardation
352 G Hubert Humphrey Building
200 Independence Ave.
Washington, D.C. 20201
Ph: (202) 619-0634
Fax: (202) 205-9519
E-mail: pcmr@acf.dhhs.gov
Web: http://www.acf.dhhs.gov/programs/pcmr/
Advises the President of the U.S., Secretary of Health
and Human Services on mental retardation.

Special Olympics, Inc.
1325 G St., NW, Suite 500
Washington, DC 20005
Ph: (202) 628-3630
Fax: (202) 824-0200
Web: http://www.specialolympics.org/
International program of year-round sports training and
athletic competition for children and adults with mental
retardation.

Voice of the Retarded, Inc.
5005 Newport Dr. , Suite 108
Rolling Meadows, IL 60008
Ph: (847) 253-6020
Fax: (847) 253-6054
E-mail: vor@compuserve.com
Web: http://www.vor.net/
Works with those with mental retardation to access
quality residential services and support options.

Recommended Reading

**Advances in Mental Retardation and
Developmental Disabilities, Vol. 5: Strategies
for Teaching Students with Mild Mental
Retardation**
Robert Gable (Ed.)
Taylor and Francis, Inc., 1993

**Beyond Gentle Teaching: A Nonaversive
Approach to Helping Those in Need**
John McGee, F. Menolascino
Plenum Press, 1991

**Community Living for People with
Developmental and Psychiatric Disabilities**
John Jacobson, Sara Burchard
Johns Hopkins University Press, 1992

**Community Occupational Therapy with
Mentally Handicapped Adults: (Therapy in
Practice Series, 16)**
Debbie Isaac
Chapman and Hall, 1990

**Counseling and Psychotherapy with Persons
with Mental Retardation and Borderline
Intelligence**
Douglas Strohmer, H. Thompson Prout (Eds.)
John Wiley and Sons, Inc., 1996

**Directory of Residential Centers for Adults with
Developmental Disabilities**
Oryx Press
2214 North Central at Encanto
Phoenix, AZ 85004-1483
Web: http://www.oryxpress.com/about.htm

**Don't Accept Me as I Am: Helping Retarded
Performers Excel**
Plenum Press, 1988

**Ethical Dilemmas in Caregiving: A Guide for
Staff Serving Adults with Mental Retardation**
Mary Howell, M.D., Ph.D.,Richard Pitch
Greenwood Publishing Group, Inc., 1989

Families and Mental Retardation: New Directions in Professional Practice
Diane Marsh
Praeger Pub., 1992

Handbook of Behavior Modification with the Mentally Retarded, 2nd ed.
Johnny Matson (Ed.)
Plenum Press, 1990

Handbook of Mental Deficiency, Psychological Theory and Research
William MacLean (Ed.)
Lawrence Erlbaum Assocs., Inc., 1996

Issues in the Developmental Approach to Mental Retardation
Edward Zigler, Jacob Burack, Robert Hodapp (Eds.)
Cambridge University Press, 1994

Language and Communication in Mental Retardation: Development, Processes, and Intervention
Sheldon Rosenberg, Leonard Abbeduto
Lawrence Erlbaum Assocs., Inc., 1993

Language in Mental Retardation
Jean Rondal
Singular Publishing Group, Inc., 1996

Leslie's Story: A Book about a Girl with Mental Retardation
Martha McNey, Leslie Fish
Lerner Pub., 1996

Mental Health in Mental Retardation: Recent Advances and Practices
Nick Bouras (Ed.)
Cambridge University Press, 1996

Mental Retardation, 5th ed.
Mary Beirne-Smith, James Patton, Richard Ittenbach
Prentice Hall, 1998

Mental Retardation
Robert Dunbar
Franklin Watts, 1991

Mental Retardation: Developing Pharmacotherapies
John Ratey, M.D. (Ed.)
American Psychiatric Press, 1991

Mental Retardation (Encyclopedia of Health)
Laura Dolce
Chelsea House, 1993

Mental Retardation: Foundations of Educational Programming
Linda Hickson, Leonard Blackman, Elizabeth Reis
Allyn and Bacon, 1994

Mental Retardation: A Life Style Approach, 6ᵗʰ ed.
Clifford Drew, Michael Hardman, Don Logan
Prentice Hall, 1995

Mental Retardation in Social Context
Duane Stroman
University Press of America, 1989

Movement Differences and Diversity in Autism-Mental Retardation: Appreciating and Accommodating People with Communications and Behavior Challenges
Anne Donnellan, Martha Leary
D R I Press, 1994

Musical Savants: Exceptional Skill in Mentally Retarded
Leon Miller
Lawrence Erlbaum Assocs., Inc., 1989

One of Them
Norene Pavlik
Our Sunday Visitor, 1988

Pieces of Purgatory: Mental Retardation In and Out of Institutions
J. David Smith
Brooks/Cole, 1995

Retarded Isn't Stupid, Mom!
Sandra Kaufman
Paul H. Brookes, 1988

Stasia's Gift
Brian Kelley, Mark Littleton, Alsie Kelley
Crossway Books, 1993

Strategies for Teaching Students with Mild to Severe Mental Retardation
Robert Gable, Ph.D., Steven Warren, Ph.D. (Eds.)
Paul H. Brookes, 1993

Teaching Students with Mental Retardation: A Life Goal Curriculum Planning Approach
Glen Thomas
Prentice Hall, 1996

Teaching Students with Mental Retardation: A Life Goal Curriculum Planning Approach
Glen Thomas
Prentice Hall, 1996

"We're People First": The Social and Emotional Lives of Individuals with Mental Retardation
Elaine Castles
Praeger Pub. Text, 1996

When Slow Is Fast Enough: Educating the Delayed Preschool Child
Joan Goodman
Guilford Publications, 1993

Books for Youth

Don't Call Me Marda
Sheila Kelly Welch
Our Child Press, 1993

Emily in Love
Susan Goldman Rubin
Harcourt and Brace, 1997

Know About Mental Illness
Margaret Hyde, Elizabeth Forsyth
Walker & Co., 1996

Leslie's Story: A Book About a Girl With Mental Retardation
Leslie Fish
Lerner Publications Co., 1996

Risk n' Roses
Jan Slepian
Philomel Books, 1990

Somebody Called Me a Retard Today and My Heart Felt Sad
Ellen O'Shaughnessy
Walker & Co., 1992

Wish on a Unicorn
Karen Hesse
Henry Holt & Co., 1991

Periodicals / Newsletters

News and Notes
American Association on Mental Retardation
AAMR Subscription Center
49 Sheridan Avenue
Albany NY 12210
Ph: (518) 436-9689
Fax: (518) 436-7433
Email: qcorp@compuserve.com
Web: http://www.aamr.org

Vendors

Love and Learning
P.O. Box 4088
Dearnborn, MI 48126
Ph: (313) 581-8436
E-mail: Lovlearn@concentric.net
Web: http://www.loveandlearning.com/
Reading system, workshops.

---- *Post Traumatic Stress Disorder*

Disabling psychological condition resulting from witnessing or being involved in a traumatic event such as natural disaster, car or plane crash, rape, assault, other violent crimes against oneself or a member of one's family. Can occur in anyone in the wake of severe trauma outside the normal range of experience. The traumatic event produces intense fear and feelings of helplessness. A child goes through significant distress, interfering with functioning socially, in school, and other important areas of life.

Also called
- Anxiety
- Gross stress reaction
- Shell shock
- Transient situational disturbance.

Frequency
- Seen in about one third of women who have been raped.
- 2.5 - 5 million Americans affected.

Symptoms and Possible Effects
PTSD symptoms in children may go through 3 phases:

Acute/protest phase
- ❑ Lasts until some order is restored and fear is lessened.
- ❑ Experience chronic anxiety, continuing distressing thoughts, difficulty sleeping, difficulty concentrating.
- ❑ Fear, frantic feelings, startles easily.
- ❑ Victim's life has become fully disorganized by the event.
- ❑ General feeling of apprehensiveness.
- ❑ Anger, rage.
- ❑ Immediate attempts to restore control, attachments, and purposeful meaning in life. To gain control, one might seek legal remedies, file insurance claims, return to the scene of the crime to review what happened, replay the event in one's mind for the same reason.
- ❑ Seek out others for solace, comfort and help in sharing painful feelings.
- ❑ Preoccupied with staying alert and safe.

Chronic/numbing phase
- ❑ Because one's body can't sustain indefinite anger and protest, it moves into this phase to be able to limit its capacity to respond.
- ❑ Withdrawal, isolation. Emotional numbness; feelings of detachment from others.
- ❑ Depression.
- ❑ Previously enjoyed activities are abandoned. Less motivated to engage in something new.
- ❑ Thinking becomes narrow and uncreative. Focus is on survival.
- ❑ Views the world as a dangerous place.
- ❑ Recurring, distressing memories, attempting to understand what happened. May relive the event.
- ❑ Grief. May feel guilty that he/she has survived if others did not.
- ❑ Avoids specific thoughts, feelings, activities, situations.
- ❑ Dissociation, helplessness.
- ❑ Remain uninvolved with and uninterested in normal activities.
- ❑ Disrupted and unplanned daily routines. Doesn't eat regular meals nor sleep at regular intervals.
- ❑ Work may become sporadic.
- ❑ Social isolation, apprehensive towards others.

Dissociation phase
- ❑ The brain places the traumatic act out of consciousness by creating a separate "place" for it with its own feelings, thoughts, physical body movements. The dissociated event is stored there.
- ❑ Event continues to resurface as the victim works to avoid or assimilate it.
- ❑ Children tend not to relive the trauma consciously but reenact it in play or nightmares.
- ❑ Flashbacks, which can occur weeks or years after the event, may be so intense as to feel real. Internal and external cues can trigger flashbacks.

Other symptoms seen at any phase
- ❑ Chronic nightmares, dreams of death.
- ❑ Difficulty with concentration or memory.
- ❑ Impulsive actions.
- ❑ Pessimism about the future, expectation of early death, belief in omens.
- ❑ Stomaches, headaches.
- ❑ Feeling of having no control.
- ❑ Attachments to others are damaged.
- ❑ Inability to make sense of what's happened.
- ❑ Damaged self esteem.
- ❑ School activities and performance decrease.
- ❑ Emotional development slowed down.
- ❑ Substance abuse.

What Can Be Going On at the Same Time?
- ▪ Substance abuse.
- ▪ Attention-deficit hyperactivity behavior.
- ▪ Eating disorders.
- ▪ Oppositional defiant behavior.
- ▪ Phobias.
- ▪ Separation anxiety.
- ▪ Amnesia.

Causes

Not everyone who experiences a traumatic event will develop PTSD, but when many symptoms persist for weeks or months, or when they are extreme, professional help is needed. The types of events that can cause PTSD include experiencing or witnessing:

- Sexual or physical abuse.
- Combat and terrorism.
- Violence, crime.
- Serious accidents, disasters.
- Family alcoholism or other addition.
- Sudden life-threatening illness or death.

What Else Could it Be?

Children with post traumatic stress disorder have symptoms that may mimic those of other conditions, such as those noted below. To properly diagnose the problem, these may need to be ruled out as causes for the problem.

- ✓ Acute stress disorder
- ✓ Adjustment disorder
- ✓ ADD / ADHD
- ✓ Bipolar depression
- ✓ Malingering

- ✓ Obsessive compulsive disorder
- ✓ Overanxious disorder
- ✓ Psychotic disorders due to a general medical condition
- ✓ Schizophrenia
- ✓ Substance-induced disorder

DSM IV Diagnostic Criteria

Reprinted with permission from the *Diagnostic and Statistical Manual of Mental Disorders, Fourth Edition, Text Revision.* Copyright 2000 American Psychiatric Association.

A. The person has been exposed to a traumatic event in which both of the following were present:

> (1) the person experienced, witnessed, or was confronted with an event or events that involved actual or threatened death or serious injury, or a threat to a physical integrity of self or others
> (2) the person's response involved intense fear, helplessness, or horror. Note: In children, this may be expressed instead by disorganized or agitated behavior

B. The traumatic event is persistently reexperienced in one (or more) of the following ways:

> (1) recurrent and intrusive distressing recollections of the event, including images, thoughts, or perceptions. Note: In young children, repetitive play may occur in which themes or aspects of the trauma are expressed.
> (2) recurrent distressing dreams of the event. Note: In children, there may be frightening dreams without recognizable content.
> (3) acting or feeling as if the traumatic event were recurring (includes a sense of reliving the experience, illusions, hallucinations, and dissociative flashback episodes, including those that occur on awakening or when intoxicated.) Note: In your children, trauma-specific reenactment may occur.
> (4) intense psychological distress at exposure to internal or external cues that symbolize or resemble an aspect of the traumatic event
> (5) physiological reactivity on exposure to internal or external cues that symbolize or resemble an aspect of the traumatic event

C. Persistent avoidance of stimuli associated with the trauma and numbing of general responsiveness (not present before the trauma), as indicated by three (or more) of the following:

   (1) efforts to avoid thoughts, feelings, or conversations associated with the trauma
   (2) efforts to avoid activities, places, or people that arouse recollections of the trauma
   (3) inability to recall an important aspect of the trauma
   (4) markedly diminished interest or participation in significant activities
   (5) feeling of detachment of estrangement from others
   (6) restricted range of affect (e.g., unable to have loving feelings)
   (7) sense of a foreshortened future (e.g., does not expect to have a career, marriage, children, or a normal life span)

D. Persistent symptoms of increased arousal (not present before the trauma), as indicated by two (or more) of the following:

   (1) difficulty falling or staying asleep
   (2) irritability or outbursts of anger
   (3) difficulty concentrating
   (4) hypervigilance
   (5) exaggerated startle response

E. Duration of the disturbance (symptoms in Criteria B,C, and D) is more than 1 month.

F. The disturbance causes clinically significant distress or impairment in social, occupational, or other important areas of functioning.

Treatment

- Identification of the major trauma in the client's history, using diagnostic instruments.
- Monitor suicide risk.
- Work to increase stability of thoughts and feelings. May be done through support networks.
- Sometimes an individual needs help to stabilize all of the crises in his or her life before actually beginning to work on the trauma experience itself.
- Hypnosis may help in going back and walking through the original trauma.
- Learning coping skills, relaxation techniques.
- Learning mastery of the situation, attachment to others or other involvement, developing a meaningful life.
- Eye movement desensitization and reprocessing (EMDR) involves using eye movements to help in the review and reprocessing of troublesome memories.
- Talk therapy.
- Medication.

Outcomes

- Symptoms are more intense and longer lasting when trauma is personal vs. seeing it occur to others.
- Damage to social and psychological processes is more widespread when the trauma occurs in childhood. There seems to be a particularly damaging effect on children when the injury or abuse occurs before they are capable of using words and thought to understand what happened.
- If trauma comes from abusive parents or caregivers, overwhelming feeling of betrayal during a dependent period of a child's life. Young children are actually more damaged by their subsequent inability to trust, anticipate and predict others' behavior than by the actual abuse. Their psychological trauma, because it occurs at such a basic level, damages their ability to keep their thinking organized, or to feel what is going on around them in an appropriate way.

Who to Contact

Also refer to "Who Else to Contact." Organizations listed below target their work specifically toward post traumatic stress syndrome.

EMDR Institute (Eye Movement Desensitization and Reprocessing)
P.O. Box 51010
Pacific Grove, CA 93950-6010
Ph: (831) 372-3900
Fax: (831) 647-9881
E-mail: inst@emdr.com
Web: http://www.emdr.org/
Information and training on EMDR therapy.

International Society of Traumatic Stress Studies
60 Revere Dr, Suite 500
Northbrook, IL 60062
Ph: (847) 480-9028
Fax: (847) 480-9282
E-mail: istss@istss.org
Web: http://www.istss.org
Professionals who share information on the affects of trauma to advance research, clinical strategy development, and public policy.

National Center for PTSD
VA Medical Center
White River Junction, VT 05009
Ph: (802) 296-5132
Fax: (802) 296-5135
E-mail: ncptsd@ncptsd.org
Web: http://www.dartmouth.edu/dms/ptsd/
Research, education, consultation programs on PTSD and other psychological and medical consequences of traumatic stress.

Sidran Traumatic Stress Foundation
200 E. Joppa Road, Suite 207
Towson, MD 21286
Ph: (410) 825-8888
E-mail: sidran@sidran.org
Web: http://www.sidran.org/
Education, advocacy, research related to the early recognition and treatment of those suffering from injuries of traumatic stress.

Recommended Reading

Aftermath: Survive and Overcome Trauma
Mariann Hybels-Steer
Simon and Schuster Trade, 1994

Allies in Healing: When the Person You Love Was Sexually Abused as a Child
Laura Davis
Harper Perennial, 1991

Back from the Brink: A Family Guide to Overcoming Traumatic Stress
Don Catherall, Ph.D.
Bantam Books, 1992

Children and Disasters
Conway Saylor (Ed.)
Plenum Press, 1993

Children of Trauma: Rediscovering Your Discarded Self
Jane Middleton-Moz
Health Communications, 1989

Children of Trauma: Stressful Life Events and Their Effects on Children and Adolescents
Thomas Miller (Ed.)
International Universities Press, 1996

Coping with Trauma: A Guide to Self-Understanding
Jon Allen, Ph.D.
American Psychiatric Press, 1995

The Courage to Heal
Ellen Bass, Laura Davis
Harper & Row, 1988

Developmental Perspectives on Trauma: Theory, Research, and Intervention
Dante Cicchetti, Sheree Toth (Eds.)
Univ. Roche, 1997

Disasters: Mental Health Interventions
John Weaver
Professional Resource Press, 1995

EMDR: The Breakthrough Therapy for Overcoming Anxiety, Stress, and Trauma
Francine Shapiro, Ph.D., Margot Silk Forrest
Basic Books, 1998

From Pain to Violence: The Traumatic Roots of Destructiveness
Felicity de Zulueta
Jason Aronson, Inc., 1994

Healing the Incest Wound: Adult Survivors in Therapy
Christine Courtois
W. W. Norton and Co., Inc., 1996

I Can't Get Over It: A Handbook for Trauma Survivors, 2nd ed.
Aphrodite Matsakis, Ph.D.
New Harbinger Publications, 1996

Managing Traumatic Stress Through Art: Drawing From the Center
Barry Cohen, Mary-Michola Barnes, Anita Rankin
Sidran Press, 1995

Memory and Abuse: Remembering and Healing the Wounds of Trauma
Charles Whitfield, M.D.
Health Communications, 1995

Mending Ourselves: Expressions of Healing and Self-Integration
Lynn Wasnak (Ed.)
Many Voices Press, 1993

Outgrowing the Pain Together: A Book for Spouses and Partners of Adults Abused as Children
Eliana Gil, Ph.D.
DTP, 1992

Post-Traumatic Stress Disorder: The Victim's Guide to Healing and Recovery
Raymond Flannery, Jr.
Crossroad, 1992

PTSD/Borderlines in Therapy: Finding the Balance
Jerome Kroll
W.W. Norton and Co., Inc., 1993

Recovered Memories of Abuse: Assessment, Therapy, Forensics
Kenneth Pope, Laura Brown
American Psychological Association, 1996

Rediscovering Childhood Trauma: Historical Casebook and Clinical Applications
Jean Goodwin, M.D., M.P.H. (Ed.)
American Psychiatric Press, Inc., 1993

Remembering, Repeating, and Working Through Childhood Trauma: The Psychodynamics of Recovered Memories, Multiple Personality, Ritual Abuse, Incest...
Lawrence Hedges
Jason Aronson, Inc., 1994

The Scared Child: Helping Kids Overcome Traumatic Events
Barbara Brooks, Paula Siegel
John Wiley and Sons, Inc., 1996

Searching for Memory: The Brain, the Mind, and the Past
Daniel Schacter
Harper Collins, 1997

Shattered Assumptions: Towards a New Psychology of Trauma
Ronnie Janoff-Bulman
Free Press, 1992

Something Bad Happened: A Series of Six Creative Books for Healing Post-Traumatic Stress
Debra Whiting Alexander, Ph.D.
Bureau for At Risk Youth, 1992

Stress in Psychiatric Disorders
Robert Paul Liberman, Joel Yager (Eds.)
Springer Publishing Co., Inc., 1994

Strong at the Broken Places: Overcoming the Trauma of Childhood Abuse
Linda Sanford
Random House, 1990

Survivor Prayers: Talking with God about Childhood Sexual Abuse
Catherine Foote
Westminster John Knox Press, 1994

Too Scared To Cry: Psychic Trauma in Childhood
Lenore Terr
Harper Collins, 1992

Trauma and Dreams
Deirdre Barrett
Harvard University Press, 1996

Trauma in the Lives of Children: Crisis and Stress Management Techniques for Counselors and Other Professionals
Kendall Johnson, Ph.D.
Hunter House, Inc., 1989

Trauma: The Pain That Stays
Robert Hicks
Fleming H. Revell Co., 1996

The Trauma Response: Treatment for Emotional Injury
Diana Sullivan Everstine, Louis Everstine
W. W. Norton and Co., Inc., 1992

Trauma and Survival: Post-Traumatic and Dissociative Disorders in Women
Elizabeth Waites
W. W. Norton and Co., Inc., 1992

Treating Traumatized Children: New Insights and Creative Interventions
Beverly James
The Free Press, 1989

Unchained Memories: True Stories of Traumatic Memories Lost and Found
Lenore Terr
Basic Books, 1994

Undaunted Spirits: Portraits of Recovery from Trauma
Mary Baures, Ph.D.
The Charles Press, 1994

Unspeakable Truths and Happy Endings: Human Cruelty and the New Trauma Therapy
Rebecca Coffey
Sidran Press, 1998

Victims No Longer: Men Recovering from Incest and Other Sexual Child Abuse
Mike Lew, Ellen Bass
Harper & Row, 1990

Women Who Hurt Themselves: A Book of Hope and Understanding
Dusty Miller
Basic Books, 1995

Waking the Tiger – Healing Trauma: The Innate Capacity to Transform Overwhelming Experiences
Peter Levine
North Atlantic Books, 1997

Working with Traumatized Children: A Handbook for Healing
Kathryn Brohl
Child Welfare League of America, 1996

When Nothing Makes Sense: Disaster, Crisis, and Their Effects on Children
Gerald Deskin, Greg Steckler
Fairview Press, 1996

Books for Youth

Coping with Post-Traumatic Stress Disorder
Carolyn Simpson, Dwain Simpson
Rosen Group, 1997

Straight Talk About Post-Trauma Stress: Coping with the Aftermath of Trauma
Kay Porterfield
Facts on File, Inc., 1996

Videos

Video tapes can be very useful, but may a challenge to find, especially if they aren't new to the market. Try contacting the producers noted even if the tape isn't listed on their web site, book stores and your library.

Cavalcade Productions
P.O. Box 2480
Nevada City, CA 95959
Ph: (800) 345-5530
E-mail: cavpro@nccn.net
Web: http://www.pacific.net/~cavideo/
Carries a wide selection of trauma-related videos.

Play Therapy for Abused Children (several videos on this topic)
Child Developmental Media
5632 Van Nuys Blvd., Suite 286
Van Nuys, CA 91401
Ph: (800) 405-8942
Fax: (818) 994-6549
E-mail: info@childdevelopmentmedia.com
Web: http://www.childdevmedia.com/

Periodicals / Newsletters

The Post-Traumatic Gazette
Patience Press
P.O. Box 2757
High Springs, FL 32655
Ph: (877) PATIENCE
     (904) 454-1651
E-mail: ptg@patiencepress.com
Web: http://www.patiencepress.com/
New ideas, treatments, resources.

Web Sites

Also see "General Web Sites". Many have sections on post traumatic stress syndrome, but they are not listed separately below.

Children, Stress, and Natural Disasters:
School Activities for Children
University of Illinois Extension Disaster Resources
Web:
http://www.ag.uiuc.edu/~disaster/teacher/csndactx.html
Classroom and curriculum guides to help students.

Vendors

Cavalcade Productions
PO Box 2480
Nevada City, CA 95959
Ph: (800) 345-5530
E-mail: cavpro@nccn.net
Web: http://www.pacific.net/~cavideo/
Training videos for mental health professionals,
focusing on trauma issues.

Veritas Programming Ltd.
111 Main Street
Brattleboro, VT 05301
Ph: (802) 257-1054
E-mail: Veritas@sover.net
Web: http://www.sover.net/%7Eschwcof
Publisher of anxiety disorder and PTSD materials.

Patience Press
P.O. Box 2757
High Springs, FL 32655
Ph: (877) PATIENCE
     (904) 454-1651
Web: http://www.patiencepress.com/
Publish books and literature about PTSD.

---- *Schizophrenia*

A serious psychiatric illness that causes strange thinking and feelings as well as unusual behavior. Uncommon before the teenager years, schizophrenia is difficult to recognize in its early stages. Marked by hallucinations and delusions.

Also called
- Nervous breakdown
- Dementia praecox

Frequency
- 1 in 100 people.
- Typical age of onset for men is age 16 to 20, for women 20 to 30. Onset after age 40 is rare.
- In the 16-25 year age group, schizophrenia affects more men than women. In the 25-30 year age group, it affects more women than men.
- Although rare, there is a childhood form of the illness can occur in children as young as age 5. It occurs in about 1 in 10,000 children and is 5 times more common in boys than girls.
- More common in those genetically predisposed to the disease. The probability of developing schizophrenia:
    - as the child of two parents, neither of whom has the disease, is 1%.
    - as the child of one parent with the disease is 13%.
    - as the child of both parents with the disease is 35-40%.
    - as a grandchild, niece, nephew of someone who is ill is 3%.
    - as a sibling of someone who is ill is 10%.
    - as an identical twin of someone who is ill is 35-50%.
- 30% of homeless people suffer from schizophrenia.
- There are as many people with schizophrenia in jails and prisons as there are in all hospitals.

Symptoms and Possible Effects
Symptoms are progressive. Personality change is the first noticeable symptom, though it may begin with a psychotic episode.

Types of Schizophrenia

Disorganized type
❑ Poor concentration, moodiness, confusion, strange ideas.
❑ Incoherent, rambling speech.
❑ Delusions.
❑ Inappropriate or non-displayed emotion.

Paranoid type
❑ Delusions and/or hallucinations about persecution.
❑ Exaggerated ego.
❑ Unexplained anxiety, anger, jealousy, violence.

Catatonic type
❑ Few reactions, no speech.
❑ Resists movement or displays excited, though purposeless, physical activity.
❑ Maintains a rigid or bizarre posture.

Residual type
❑ After a recognizable episode of schizophrenia occurs, there are no remaining overt symptoms.
❑ Less intense symptoms may remain, however, such as social withdrawal, eccentric behavior, inappropriate emotions, illogical thinking.

Undifferentiated type
❑ Symptoms can't be classified solely into one category.

Categories of symptoms within the above types are:

Psychotic
❑ Talks to self or objects.
❑ Belief that one's thoughts have been removed and replaced with those of someone else. Belief that one's thoughts are being broadcast over radio or TV.
❑ Magical thinking.
❑ Delusions of grandeur such as thinking one can do anything, is invulnerable to danger, and able to right injustices.
❑ Delusions, hallucinations. Hears voices, which may be threatening or condemning; they may also give direct orders such as, "Kill yourself".

Cognitive impairment
❑ Lack of concentration.
❑ Unable to think logically and causally, abstractly. Jumps from topic to topic.
❑ Unable to make decisions.
❑ Blocking of thoughts. Focuses on inner thoughts rather than the outside world. Overstimulated by one's own internal chaos and confusion.
❑ Speech may become incoherent.

❑ Withdrawal because communication is difficult. Confused and overwhelmed while with other people.
❑ Feeling of living in a dream.
❑ High sensitivity to stimuli (noise, light, colors, textures). Inability to sort and interpret sensations and respond appropriately. Overtime, the sensitivity dulls.
❑ Conflicting thoughts and feelings.
❑ Difficulty focusing thoughts and speech.
❑ Difficulty in learning.
❑ Perceptual problems.
❑ Limited or inappropriate emotional expression.
❑ Increased ability to recall childhood events.
❑ Flooding of thoughts.
❑ Loss of sense of time.
❑ Not able to empathize with others.
❑ Depressed.
❑ When an acute episode is subsiding, may withdraw from others, have personality changes, such as being angry, suspicious or evasive.
❑ Unable to resolve contradictory thoughts and feelings.
❑ Hostile.
❑ General loss of interest in life, even in important situations. Unable to express joy.
❑ Forgets things.
❑ Withdrawn, quiet, moody.
❑ Sudden personality change with exaggerated feelings. Experiences guilt, fear, rapidly changing emotions, especially in early stages. In later stages, emotions flatten.
❑ Hyperactivity or inactivity.
❑ Inability to cope with minor problems. Extreme reactions to criticism.
❑ Inability to cry or excessive crying.
❑ Thoughts may be slow to form, come extra fast, or not at all.
❑ Belief that they are being persecuted, spied on, plotted against.
❑ Intense misperceptions that trigger dread, panic, fear, anxiety.
❑ Intense psychological distress.
❑ Adoption of strange posture and mannerisms.

Other symptoms
❑ Altered sense of self, feeling out of sync timewise, free floating, non-existent.
❑ Poor muscle tone and coordination.
❑ Increased focus on religion or the occult.
❑ Feeling that all one's actions are under the control of others.
❑ Vulnerable to stressful events.
❑ Strange behavior such as saving trash, stealing food.
❑ Lack of energy.
❑ Personal hygiene is abandoned.
❑ Overactive, frenzied behavior.
❑ Change in sleep habits, e.g., reversing night and day.
❑ Deteriorating performance at school, athletics and work. Drops out of activities.
❑ Slowness of movement, underactivity, lack of drive.
❑ Involvement in car accidents.
❑ Drug or alcohol abuse.
❑ Losing things.
❑ Rapid weight loss.

❑ Attempts to escape through frequent moves or hitchhiking trips.
❑ Excessive writing (or childlike printing) with no apparent meaning.
❑ Migraine headaches. Fainting.
❑ Inappropriate laughter.
❑ Refusal to touch people or things without wearing gloves.
❑ Shaving head or body hair.
❑ Self-mutilation or threats of it.
❑ Staring, flat gaze.
❑ Stubbornness.
❑ Peculiar use of words.
❑ Highly sensitivity to touch.
❑ May not be able to tell where their bodies end and the rest of the world starts.

Early warning signs in children
❑ Mistaking dreams for reality.
❑ Visual and auditory hallucinations.
❑ Confused thinking.
❑ Vivid and strange thoughts and ideas.
❑ Moodiness.
❑ Odd behavior.
❑ Believe that people are "out to get them".
❑ Revert to the behavior of a younger child.
❑ Anxiety and fearfulness.
❑ Belief that television is real.
❑ Problems in making and keeping friends.
❑ Behavior may change slowly over time. Shyness or new fears and ideas may set in.
❑ May cling to parents or talk non-sensically.

Delusions
❑ False or bizarre beliefs. Common themes are persecution, grandiose ideas, religion, having a special talent, involvement with aliens or the CIA, being the target of attempted murder.
❑ May be convinced that events are all related to oneself.
❑ Belief that one is someone else, or has a relationship with someone famous.
❑ Belief that one can broadcast thoughts to others and vice versa. Remarks they hear have secret meaning for them alone.

Causes
Unknown, however, recent research points to the possibility of:
▪ A viral infection in the second trimester of pregnancy.
▪ A developmental disorder.
▪ Malfunctioning of the limbic system, which filters sensory input.
▪ Stress which can trigger psychotic episodes.

What Else Could it Be?

Children with schizophrenia have symptoms that may mimic those of other conditions, such as those noted below. To properly diagnose the problem, these may need to be first ruled out.

- ✓ Delirium
- ✓ Dementia
- ✓ Dissociative states
- ✓ Manic depression
- ✓ Psychotic disorder due to a medication condition.

- ✓ Substance-induced psychotic disorder
- ✓ Mood disorder with psychotic features
- ✓ Schizoaffective disorder
- ✓ Schizophreniform disorder
- ✓ Schizotypal, schizoid or paranoid personality disorder

Diagnostic Process

Review of symptoms over time.

DSM IV Diagnostic Criteria

Reprinted with permission from the *Diagnostic and Statistical Manual of Mental Disorders, Fourth Edition, Text Revision.* Copyright 2000 American Psychiatric Association.

A. *Characteristic symptoms:* Two (or more) of the following, each present for a significant portion of time during a 1-month period (or less if successfully treated):
  (1) delusions
  (2) hallucinations
  (3) disorganized speech (e.g., frequent derailment or incoherence)
  (4) grossly disorganized or catatonic behavior
  (5) negative symptoms, i.e., affective flattening, alogia, or avolition

NOTE: Only one Criterion A symptom is required if delusions are bizarre or hallucinations consist of a voice keeping up a running commentary on the person's behavior or thoughts, or two or more voices conversing with each other.

B. *Social/occupational dysfunction:* For a significant portion of the time since the onset of the disturbance, one or more major areas of functioning such as work, interpersonal relations, or self-care are markedly below the level achieved prior to the onset (or when the onset is in childhood or adolescence, failure to achieve expected level of interpersonal, academic, or occupational achievement.)

C. *Duration*: Continuous signs of the disturbance persist for at least 6 months. This 6-month period must include at least 1 month of symptoms (or less if successfully treated) that meet Criterion A (i.e., active-phase symptoms) and may include periods of prodromal or residual symptoms. During these prodromal or residual periods, the signs of the disturbance may be manifested by only negative symptoms or two or more symptoms listed in Criterion A present in an attenuated form (e.g., odd beliefs, unusual perceptual experiences).

D. *Schizoaffective and Mood Disorder exclusion:* Schizoaffective Disorder and Mood Disorder With Psychotic Features have been ruled out because either (1) no Major Depressive, Manic, or Mixed Episodes have occurred concurrently with the active-phase symptoms; or (2) if mood episodes have occurred during active-phase symptoms, their total duration has been brief relative to the duration of the active and residual periods.

E. *Substance/general medical condition exclusion:* The disturbance is not due to the direct physiological effects of a substance (e.g., a drug of abuse, a medication) or a general medical condition.

F. *Relationship to a Pervasive Developmental Disorder:* If there is a history of Autistic Disorder or another Pervasive Development Disorder, the additional diagnosis of Schizophrenia is made only if prominent delusions or hallucinations are also present for at least a month (or less if successfully treated.)

Treatment
- Early and continual treatment is essential to prevent more severe symptoms from occurring and to shorten the length of time needed to respond to treatment.
- Neuroleptic and other medication, hospitalization.
- Individual, family, group therapy.
- Specialized programs.
- Electroshock therapy.

Outcomes
- Not curable, but treatable.
- 25% of people who suffer from schizophrenia suffer only one episode in their lifetime with recovery coming within 2 years. 25% may improve greatly and live without continued treatment. Another 25% may improve but need a good deal of support. The rest remain hospitalized, not improve, or die, often by suicide.
- Continuing problems throughout life, with periods of near-normal functioning.
- The main reason for relapse is failure to take prescribed medication. Antipsychotic medications are very strong and often have unpleasant side effects.
- Most of those with schizophrenia respond to drug therapy, and many are able to lead productive and fulfilling lives.
- The severity of the psychosis may level off later in life.

Who to Contact
Also refer to "Who Else to Contact" section for broad-based organizations. Organizations listed below target their work specifically toward schizophrenia.

The National Alliance for Research on Schizophrenia and Depression
60 Cutter Mill Road, Suite #404
Great Neck, NY 11021
Ph: (516) 829-0091
Fax: (516) 487-6930
E-mail: info@narsad.org
Web: http://www.mhsource.com/narsad.html
Supports scientific research on brain disorders, publishes information.

National Schizophrenics Foundation
15920 West Twelve Mile Road
Southfield, MI 48076
Ph: (800) 482-9534
     (248) 557-6777
Fax: (248) 557-5995
E-mail: mhamich@aol.com
Web: http://www.sanonymous.org/
Education. Sponsors Schizophrenics Anonymous, a self-help support group for people with schizophrenia.

Schizophrenia Help
Ph: (323) 226-1411
E-mail: jarosberg@aol.com
Web: http://www.schizophrenia-help.com
Shares information, exposes those who are considered treatment resistant to an atmosphere of hope and a treatment model that considers the healthy parts of the individual as the important focus.

Recommended Reading

Cognitive-Behavioral Therapy of Schizophrenia
David Kingdon, Douglas Turkington
Guilford Publications, 1993

Conquering Schizophrenia: A Father, His Son and a Medical Breakthrough
Peter Wyden
Knopf, 1998

Contemporary Issues in the Treatment of Schizophrenia
Christian Shriqui, M.D., Henry Nasrallah, M.D. (Eds.)
American Psychiatric Press, 1995

Coping With Schizophrenia: A Guide for Families
Kim Mueser, Ph.D., Susan Gingerich, M.S.W.
New Harbinger Publications, 1994

Dialogue with Sammy: A Psychoanalytic Contribution to the Understanding of Child Psychosis
Serge Lebovici
Columbia University Press, 1990

The Family Face of Schizophrenia: True Stories of Mental Illness with Practical Counsel from America's Leading Experts
Patricia Backlar
J.P. Tarcher, 1995

The Four of Us: The Story of a Family
Elizabeth Swados
Farrar, Straus and Giroux, 1991

How to Live with Schizophrenia, rev. ed.
Abram Hoffer Ph. D., Humphry Osmond
Citadel Publishing, 1997

Imagining Robert: Brothers, Madness, and Survival: A Memoir
Jay Neugeboren
Henry Holt and Co., 1998

Living and Working with Schizophrenia, rev. ed.
J.J. Jeffries, E. Plummer, M.V. Seeman, J.F. Thornton
University of Toronto Press, 1990

Managing Depression
Frederic Flach, Rickie Flach
Hatherleigh, 1996

My Sister's Keeper
Margaret Moorman
W.W. Norton, 1992

Psychosocial Approaches to Deeply Disturbed Persons
Peter Breggin, M.D., E. Mark Stern, Ed.D. (Eds.)
Haworth Press, Inc., 1996

Psychotherapy of Schizophrenia: Effective Clinical Approaches -- Controversies, Critiques and Recommendations
Gaetano Benedetti, Pier Furlan
Hogrefe & Huber, 1993

The Quiet Room: A Journey Out of the Torment of Madness
Lori Schiller, Amanda Bennett
Warner Books, 1996

Reconstructing Schizophrenia
Richard Bentall (Ed.)
Routledge, 1992

Sampling Normal and Schizophrenic Inner Experience
Russell Hurlburt
Plenum Press, 1990

Schizophrenia
Patrick Young
Chelsea House, 1988

Schizophrenia: The Facts, 2nd ed.
Ming Tsuang, Stephen Farraone
Oxford University Press, Inc., 1997

Schizophrenia Genesis: The Origins of Madness
Irving Gottesman, Ph.D., FRCPsych.
W. H. Freeman, 1991

Schizophrenia: From Mind to Molecule
Nancy Andreasen, M.D, Ph.D. (Ed.)
American Psychiatric Press, 1995

Schizophrenia and Human Value: Chronic Schizophrenia, Science, and Society
Peter Barham
Columbia University Press, 1993

Schizophrenia and Manic-Depressive Disorder: The Biological Roots of Mental Illness as Revealed by the Landmark Study of Identical Twins
E. Fuller Torrey, Ann Bowler
Basic Books, 1995

Schizophrenia: The Positive Perspective, in Search of Dignity for Schizophrenic People
Peter Chadwick
Routledge, 1997

Schizophrenia and Primitive Mental States: Structural Collapse and Creativity
Peter Giovacchini, M.D.
Jason Aronson, Inc., 1997

Schizophrenia: A Scientific Delusion
Mary Boyle
Routledge, 1993

Schizophrenic Disorders: Sense and Nonsense in Conceptualization, Assessment, and Treatment
Leighton Whitaker
Plenum Press, 1992

Schizophrenic Disorders: Theory and Treatment from a Psychodynamic Point of View
Ping-Nie Pao
International Universities Press, 1993

Social Skills Training for Schizophrenia: A Step by Step Guide
Alan Bellack, Kim Mueser, Susan Gingerich, Julie Agresta
Guilford Publications, 1997

Surviving Mental Illness: Stress, Coping and Adaptation
Agnes Hatfield, Harriet Lefley
Guilford Publications, 1993

Surviving Schizophrenia: A Manual for Families, Consumers and Survivors, 3rd ed.
E. Fuller Torrey, M.D.
Harper and Row, 1995

Understanding Schizophrenia: A Guide to the New Research on Causes and Treatment
Richard Keefe, Philip Harvey
The Free Press, 1994

Vitamin B-3 and Schizophrenia: Discovery, Recovery, Controversy
Abram Hoffer, M.D.
Quarry Press, 1997

The Voices of Robby Wilde
Elizabeth Kytle, Robert Coles
University of Georgia Press, 1995

Welcome, Silence: My Triumph Over Schizophrenia
Carol North, M.D.
Simon and Schuster, 1987

Working with the Person with Schizophrenia: The Treatment Alliance
Michael Selzer, Timothy Sullivan, Monica Carsky, Kenneth Terkelsen
New York University Press, 1989

Working with Schizophrenia: A Needs Based Approach
Gwen Howe
Taylor and Francis, Inc., 1995

Books for Youth

The Encyclopedia of Schizophrenia and the Psychotic Disorders
Richard Noll, M.A.
Facts on File, Inc., 1991

The Girl with the Crazy Brother
Betty Hyland
Franklin Watts, 1987

Humming Whispers
Angela Johnson
Orchard Books, 1995

My Sister Then and Now
Virginia Knoll
Lerner Publications, 1992

Web Sites

Also see "General Web Sites". Many have sections on schizophrenia, but they are not listed separately below.

The Schizophrenia Home Page
Web: http://www.schizophrenia.com
Information, support on schizophrenia.

Videos

Video tapes can be very useful, but may a challenge to find, especially if they aren't new to the market. Try contacting the producers noted even if the tape isn't listed on their web site, book stores and your library.

I'm Still Here: The Truth About Schizophrenia
Wheeler Communications Group, Inc.
266 West Lake Road
Honeoye, NY 14471
Ph: (716) 229-4210
Web: http://www.wheelercom.com/
People with schizophrenia describe their lives.

Schizophrenia: The Treatment Spectrum
Wheeler Communications Group, Inc.
266 West Lake Road
Honeoye, NY 14471
Ph: (716) 229-4210
Web: http://www.wheelercom.com/
Medication, training in social and daily living skills, housing facilities, employment, financial, approaches to dual diagnosis, advocacy.

Schizophrenia: The Role of Medication
Wheeler Communications Group, Inc.
266 West Lake Road
Honeoye, NY 14471
Ph: (716) 229-4210
Web: http://www.wheelercom.com/
Medications used for schizophrenia, control of side effects, relapse. Enables patients to participate in their rehabilitation programs.

Serious Mental Illness: Recognition and Intervention
Wheeler Communications Group, Inc.
266 West Lake Road
Honeoye, NY 14471
Ph: (716) 229-4210
Web: http://www.wheelercom.com/
Concept of serious mental illness as a biological problem. Symptoms focus on schizophrenia. Health care experts and the mother of a young man with schizophrenia discuss intervention, crises, choices in care.

Schizophrenia: The Role of Psychosocial Rehabilitation
Wheeler Communications Group, Inc.
266 West Lake Road
Honeoye, NY 14471
Ph: (716) 229-4210
Web: http://www.wheelercom.com/
Nature of psychosocial rehabilitation as a means of recovery of the person rather than recovery from the illness. Resources available to help acquire skills in the areas of social relationships, work, self care.

Understanding and Communicating With a Person Who Has Delusions
Nurseminars, Inc.
12204 W. Sunridge Dr.
Nine Mile Falls, WA 99026
Ph: (509)-468-9848
Fax: (509) 466-6586
E-mail: marymoller@psychiatricwellness.com
Web:
http://www.psychiatricwellness.com/nurseminars.html

Understanding and Communicating with a Person Who is Hallucinating
Nurseminars, Inc.
12204 W. Sunridge Dr.
Nine Mile Falls, WA 99026
Ph: (509) 468-9848
Fax: (509) 466-6586
E-mail: marymoller@psychiatricwellness.com
Web:
http://www.psychiatricwellness.com/nurseminars.html

Understanding Relapse: Managing the Symptoms of Schizophrenia
Nurseminars, Inc.
12204 W. Sunridge Dr.13154
Nine Mile Falls, WA 99026
Ph: (509) 468-9848
Fax: (509) 466-6586
E-mail: marymoller@psychiatricwellness.com
Web:
http://www.psychiatricwellness.com/nurseminars.html

---- Tourette's Syndrome

Neurological problem characterized by habitual motor and vocal tics that begin between the ages of 2 and 15, and continue for more than a year. A tic is a sudden, rapid, recurring motor movement or vocalization. A child may suppress the tics for a short while, but eventually must release them. The intensity of the tics may vary. Tourette's syndrome (T.S.) frequently occurs with other conditions, such as ADHD and obsessive/compulsive behavior.

Also called
- Gilles de la tourette syndrome
- Maladie des tics

Frequency
- 100,000-200,000 people in the U.S.
- 1 in 100 boys, 1 in 600 girls.
- 1 in 2000 school children.
- 20% experience onset before kindergarten, 65% between ages 5-9, 15% between ages 10-15.
- The average age of diagnosis is 7-10. Symptoms are apparent in almost all cases by age 11.
- 25-35% have aggressive behavior with T.S.

Symptoms and Possible Effects
- ❑ Facial tics, such as eye blinking, grimacing, squinting, nose picking.
- ❑ Vocal tics, such as guttural throat noises, throat clearing, coughing, grunting, barking, high-pitched cries, belching, hiccuping, vulgar or obscene words (15% of cases).
- ❑ Head or neck jerking.
- ❑ Tics can build in intensity to rapid, purposeless, involuntary movements.
- ❑ Frequency of tics may range from many times a day to intermittently, varying in intensity.
- ❑ Tics may move to different parts of the body.
- ❑ Tics can be suppressed for seconds or even hours, depending on their severity and the current situation. Excessive control, however, can result in an "build-up" which must be released, possibly explosively.

❑ Over half the cases include coprolalia (foul language, obscene gestures), echolalia (word repetition), palilalia (rapid and driven repetition of words), compulsive touching, obsessive doubting.
❑ Irritability, distractibility, motor restlessness, impulsivity, depression.
❑ Giving large importance to unusual things, such as the shape of an object, or feeling that one is living in a movie. These feelings may wax and wane suddenly.
❑ Anxiety, anger, excitement, fatigue, illness and stress intensify symptoms.
❑ The behavior of children with T.S. is easily misunderstood, with tics being thought to be psychological.
❑ Behavior problems, such as quick temper, intense reactions, mood changes, impulsivity, oppositional or defiant behavior.
❑ Negative academic and social symptoms, such as lack of organization, inability to play quietly, excessive talking with interruptions, failure to listen, losing things, acting dangerously without considering the consequences.

What Else Could it Be?

Children with Tourette's syndrome have symptoms that are also seen with other conditions, such as those noted below. To properly diagnose a problem, these may need to be ruled out as causes for the problem.

✓ Abnormal movements as a result of other conditions (e.g., Huntington's disease, stroke, Lesch-Hyhan syndrome, Wilson's disease, Sydenham's chorea, multiple sclerosis, post-viral encephalitis, head injury).

✓ Hemifacial spasms (irregular, repetitive, unilateral jerks of facial muscles)

✓ Athetoid movements (slow, irregular, writhing movements, frequently in the fingers and toes, but may be seen in the face and neck).

✓ Synkinesis (involuntary movement accompanying a voluntary one, e.g., movement of the mouth when the person is closing an eye)

✓ Choreiform movements (random, nonrepetitive "dancing" movements)

✓ Myoclonic movements (brief, sudden muscle contractions that may affect muscles.)

✓ Chronic motor or vocal tic disorder. May last many years with few changes.

✓ Muscle spasms

✓ Compulsions

✓ Schizophrenia

✓ Dystonic movements (alternating between slow, twisting movements and muscular tension)

✓ Stereotypic movement disorder

✓ Hemiballismic movements (occasional large, unilateral movements of arms and legs)

✓ Transient tics. Disappear spontaneously in less than 1 year. May occur several times over the years, however. Occur in 15% of children, 3-4 times more boys than girls are affected. Often begin in early school years.

What Can Be Going On at the Same Time?
- At least 2/3 of these children also have obsessive-compulsive symptoms, half severe enough to interfere with daily living.
- 50-70% have ADD/ADHD.
- Sensory integration problems.
- Difficulties with impulse control.
- 25-33% have learning disorders.
- Sleep disorders.

Causes
- Genetic. 50% chance of passing the gene to the next generation. Girls with the gene have a 70% chance of displaying symptoms; boys with the gene have a 99% chance of displaying symptoms.
- The neurochemical basis for T.S. has not yet been determined, though an oversensitivity to dopamine may be involved. Imbalances in other neurotransmitter systems such as serotonin and norepinephrine may play a role. (Neurotransmitters are chemicals in the brain that carry signals from one nerve cell to another.)
- T. S. is not the result of any direct effects of substance use or a general medical condition.

Diagnostic Process
- Diagnosis is made through evaluation of symptoms and family history. No definitive tests.
- Neuroimaging studies, such as magnetic resonance imaging (MRI), computerized tomography (CT), and electroencephalogram (EEG) scans, or certain blood tests may rule out other conditions that might be confused with T.S.

Correct diagnosis of T.S. frequently takes a while because not all physicians are familiar with it. Because tics can wax and wane in severity and can also be suppressed, they may not be apparent during doctor visits.

DSM IV Diagnostic Criteria
Reprinted with permission from the *Diagnostic and Statistical Manual of Mental Disorders, Fourth Edition, Text Revision.* Copyright 2000 American Psychiatric Association.

A. Both multiple motor and one of more vocal tics have been present at some time during the illness, although not necessarily concurrently. (A *tic* is a sudden, rapid, recurrent, nonrhythmic, stereotyped motor movement or vocalization.)

B. The tics occur many times a day (usually in bouts) nearly every day or intermittently throughout a period of more than 1 year, and during this period there was never a tic-free period of more than 3 consecutive months.

C. The onset is before age 18 years.

D. The disturbance is not due to the direct physiological effects of a substance (e.g., stimulants) or a general medical condition (e.g., Huntington's disease or postviral encephalitis.)

Treatment

- Depending on the severity of symptoms, a child may not need treatment; 20% of those with the disorder don't need medication.
- Medication may be used to help suppress tics, reduce drive, relieve compulsive behavior, relieve depression, help the child to focus and pay attention. There is no one medication helpful to everyone with T.S., nor does any medication completely eliminate symptoms. Some stimulants may make tics worse.
- Supportive interventions at school, social skills training, family therapy to create a positive home environment, group therapy for the child to meet others with similar problems, parenting support to deal with situations and feelings and to learn to be affective advocates.
- Relaxation techniques and biofeedback may help reduce stress and thus reduce ticcing, though it will not suppress tics altogether.

Outcomes

- There is no cure for T.S. However, many children improve as they mature, enabling some to stop taking medication.
- Not degenerative, no effect on life span.
- 30-50% have fewer symptoms by late adolescence.
- In a few cases, complete remission occurs after adolescence.
- As T.S. symptoms wane, neuropsychiatric disorders such as depression, panic attacks, mood swings, and antisocial behavior may increase.
- Long-term use of neuroleptic drugs may cause various side affects, one of which is an involuntary movement disorder called tardive dyskinesia. This condition usually disappears when medication is discontinued. Rarely affects children, but it is found in young adults.

Who to Contact

Also refer to "Who Else to Contact." Organizations listed below target their work specifically toward Tourette's syndrome.

Tourette Syndrome Association, Inc.
42-40 Bell Blvd.
Bayside, NY 11361-2820
Ph: (718) 224-2999
Fax: (718) 279-9596
E-mail: ts@tsa-usa.org
Web: http://www.tsa-usa.org
Education, support services, research funding.

Recommended Reading

Children with Tourette Syndrome: A Parents' Guide
Tracy Haerle (Ed.)
Woodbine House, 1992

Gilles de la Tourette Syndrome
Arthur Shapiro, Elaine Shapiro, J. Gerald Young, Todd Feinberg
Lippincott-Raven, 1988

Guide to the Diagnosis and Treatment of Tourette Syndrome, 3rd ed.
Ruth Dowling Bruun, M.D., Donald Cohen, M.D., James Leckman, M.D.
Tourette Syndrome Assn., 1995

Handbook of Tourette's Syndrome and Related Tic and Behavioral Disorders
Roger Kurlan (Ed.)
Marcel Dekker, Inc., 1992

Living With Tourette Syndrome
Elaine Shimberg
Simon and Schuster Trade, 1995

A Mind of Its Own: Tourette's Syndrome: A Story and a Guide
Ruth Dowling Bruun, Bertel Bruun
Oxford University Press, 1994

Ryan: A Mother's Story of Her Hyperactive-Tourette Syndrome Child
Susan Hughes
Hope Press, 1990

Search for the Tourette Syndrome and Human Behavior Genes
David Comings, M.D.
Hope Press, 1996

Tourette Syndrome
Elaine Landau
Franklin Watts, Inc., 1998

Tourette Syndrome and Human Behavior
David Comings, M.D.
Hope Press, 1990

Tourette's and Attention Deficit Hyperactivity Disorder: Toughing it Out at Home and at School
Joan Murphy, M. Ed., LPC (Ed.)
Baton Rouge TS Support Group, 1995

Tourette's Syndrome and Tic Disorders: Clinical Understanding and Treatment
Donald Cohen, Ruth Bruun, James Leckman (Eds.)
John Wiley and Sons, 1988

Tourette's Syndrome: Tics, Obsessions, Compulsions, Developmental Psychopathology and Clinical Care, 2nd ed.
James Leckman, Donald Cohen
John Wiley and Sons, 1998

Twitch and Shout: A Touretter's Tale
Lowell Handler
E.P. Dutton, 1998

Understanding Tourette Syndrome, Obsessive Compulsive Disorder and Related Problems : A Developmental and Catastrophe Theory Perspective
John Michael Berecz
Springer Pub., 1992

The Unwelcome Companion: An Insider's View of Tourette Syndrome, rev. ed.
Rick Fowler
Silver Run Publications, 1996

---- Who Else to Contact

The following organizations help parents, teachers, home schoolers, and health care providers on a range of topics related to children's mental health and neurological challenges. Refer to chapters on special challenges to find challenge-specific organizations. When contacting an organization, be sure to enclose a large, self-addressed and stamped envelope with your request. Also consider enclosing a donation.

ABLEDATA National Rehabilitation Information Center
8630 Fenton Street, Suite 930
Silver Spring, MD 20910
Ph: (800) 227-0216
Fax: (301) 608-8958
Ph: (301) 589-3563
E-mail: adaigle@macroint.com
Web: http://www.abledata.com
National database of information on assistive technology and rehabilitation equipment.

Administration on Developmental Disabilities
Administration on Developmental Disabilities
U.S. Department of Health and Human Services
Mail Stop: HHH 300-F, 370 L'Enfant Promenade, SW
Washington, D.C. 20447
Ph: (202) 690-6590
E-mail: add@acf.dhhs.gov
Web: http://www.acf.dhhs.gov/programs/add/
Works with states, communities, private sector to assist those with developmental disabilities.

Alliance of Genetic Support Groups
4301 Connecticut Ave. NW, #404
Washington, DC 20008-2304
Ph: (202) 966-5557
Fax: (202) 966-8553
Helpline: (800) 336-GENE
E-mail: info@geneticalliance.org
Web: http://www.geneticalliance.org/
Individuals, professionals, organizations working to enhance lives of those impacted by genetic conditions.

American Academy of Child and Adolescent Psychiatry
3615 Wisconsin Ave., N.W.
Washington, D.C. 20016-3007
Ph: (202) 966-7300
Fax: (202) 966-2891
Web: http://www.aacap.org
Assists families in understanding developmental, behavioral, emotional and mental disorders.

American Association of Children's Residential Centers
440 First St, NW, 3rd Floor
Washington, DC 20001
Ph: (202) 628-1816
E-mail: aacrc@dc.net
Web: http://aacrc-dc.org/
Advances knowledge of therapeutic living environments for children and adolescents with behavioral disorders.

American Association of People with Disabilities
1819 H St., NW, Suite 330
Washington, DC 20006
Ph: (800) 840-8844
        (202) 457-0046
Fax: (202) 457-0473
E-mail: aapd@aol.com
Web: http://www.aapd.com/
Leverages the numbers of people with disabilities, their families, friends to access economic and other benefits.

American Psychological Association (APA)
750 First St., NE
Washington, DC 20002-4242
Ph: (800) 374-2721
        (202) 336-5500
Web: http://www.apa.org/
Offers information on disabilities.

ARCH National Resource Center for Respite and Crisis Care
Chapel Hill Training-Outreach Project
800 Eastowne Dr., Suite 105
Chapel Hill, NC 27514
Ph: (800) 671-2594
        (919) 490-5577
Fax: (919) 490-4905
E-mail: Ylayden@intrex.net
Web: http://www.chtop.com/archbroc.htm
Has a national respite locator service.

Association of Jewish Family and Children's Agencies
557 Cranbury Road, Suite 2
East Brunswick, NJ 08816-5419
Ph: (800) 634-7346
Fax: (732) 432-7127
E-mail: AJFCA@ajfca.org
Web: http://www.ajfca.org
Specialized human service agencies, including services for developmentally disabled adults and children.

Association for Persons in Supported Employment
1627 Monument Ave.
Richmond, VA 23220
Ph: (804) 278-9187
Fax: (804) 278-9377
E-mail: apse@apse.org
Web: http://www.apse.org/home.html
Improves integrated employment opportunities, services and outcomes for people with disabilities.

Birth Defect Research for Children, Inc.
930 Woodcock Road, Suite 225
Orlando, FL 32803
Ph: (407) 895-0802
Web: http://www.birthdefects.org/
Information for parents about birth defects, support services. Studies links between birth defects and environmental toxins. Matching program that links families that have children with similar birth defects.

Beach Center on Families and Disability
University of Kansas
Haworth Hall, Room 3136
1200 Sunnyside Ave.
Lawrence, KS 66045-7534
Ph: (785) 864-7600
Fax: (785) 864-7605
E-mail: beach@dole.lsi.ukans.edu
Web: http://www.beachcenter.org
Researches disability policy, its affect on families with children with disabilities.

Boundless Playgrounds, Inc.
One Regency Dr.
Bloomfield, CT 06002-2310
Ph: (860) 243-8315
Web: http://www.boundlessplaygrounds.org
Helps communities create universally accessible
playgrounds.

**CARF – Rehabilitation Accreditation
Commission**
4891 E. Grant Road
Tucson, AZ 85712
Ph/TDD: (520) 325-1044
Fax: (520) 318-1129
Web: http://www.carf.org/index.html
Accredits programs and services for assisted living,
behavioral health care, medical rehabilitation, etc.

The Center for Mental Health Services
5600 Fishers Lane, Room 17-99
Rockville, MD 20857
Ph: (800) 798-2647 (KEN)
Fax: (301) 984-8796 (KEN)
E-mail: ken@mentalhealth.org
Web: http://www.mentalhealth.org/cmhs/
Leads federal efforts to treat mental illness by
promoting mental health. KEN (Knowledge Exhange
Network) provides mental health information.

Children Awaiting Parents
700 Exchange St.
Rochester, NY 14608
Ph: (716) 232-5110
Fax: (716) 232-2634
E-mail: patb@eznet.net
Web: http://www.ggw.org/cap/
Helps America's children who have special challenges
to find adoptive families.

Children's Defense Fund
25 E. Street NW
Washington, DC 20001
Ph: (202) 628-8787
E-mail: cdfinfo@childrensdefense.org
Web: http://www.childrensdefense.org
Advocates for children, including those with
disabilities.

Children's Hospice International
2202 Mt. Vernon Ave., Suite 3C
Alexandria, VA 22301
Ph: (800) 2-4- CHILD
         (703) 684-0330
Fax: (703) 684-0226
E-mail: chiorg@aol.com
Web: http://www.chionline.org/
Provides a network of support and care for children
with life-threatening conditions and their families.

Christian Council on Persons with Disabilities
7120 W. Dove Ct.
Milwaukee, WI 53223
Ph: (414) 357-6672
E-mail: info@ccpd.org
Web: http://www.ccpd.org/
Christian organizations working in disability ministry.

Confident Kids Support Groups
330 Stanton St.
Arroyo Grande, CA 93420
Ph: (805) 473-7945
Fax: (805) 473-7948
E-mail: confidentkids@juno.com
Web: http://www.confidentkids.com
Bible-based support group with life skills curriculum
that helps families with children deal with life stresses.

The Consortium for Citizens with Disabilities
1730 K St., NW, Suite 1212
Washington, DC 20006
Ph: (202) 785-3388
Fax: (202) 467-4179
E-mail: Info@c-c-d.org
Web: http://www.c-c-d.org/
National organizations advocating public policy that
ensures self-determination, independence, inclusion.

Courage Center
3915 Golden Valley Road
Golden Valley, MN 55422
Ph: (763) 520-0520
Fax: (763) 520-0577
E-mail: jenim@courage.org
Web: http://www.courage.org/
Vocational services, camp, residence.

The Dana Alliance for Brain Initiatives
745 Fifth Ave., Suite 700
New York, NY 10151
E-mail: dabiinfo@dana.org
Web: http://www.dana.org
Promotes research and education on the brain.

Developmental Delay Registry (DDR)
4401 East West Highway, Suite 207
Bethesda, MD 20814
E-mail: devdelay@mindspring.com
Web: http://www.devdelay.org/
Information and networking for parents and
professionals working with children who have delays
in motor, sensory-motor, language, social, emotional
areas.

Disabled Sports USA
451 Hungerford Dr. #100
Rockville, MD 20850
Voice: (301) 217-0960
Fax: (301) 217-0968
TDD: (301) 217-0963
E-mail: Information@dsusa.org
Web: http://www.dsusa.org
Offers nationwide sports rehabilitation programs to
those with permanent physical disabilities.

**DREAMMS for Kids, Inc. (Developmental
Research for the Effective Advancement of
Memory and Motor Skills)**
273 Ringwood Road
Freeville, NY 13068-9618
Ph: (607) 539-3027
Fax: (607) 539-9930
E-mail: janet@dreamms.org
Web: http://www.dreamms.org/
Assistive technology-related research, development,
and information dissemination.

Elwyn, Inc.
111 Elwyn Road
Elwyn, PA 19063
Ph: (610) 891-2000
Fax: (610) 891-2458
Web: http://www.elwyn.org/
A human services organization serving all ages,
various challenges.

Emotional Health Anonymous (EHA)
P.O. Box 2081
San Gabriel, CA 91778
Ph: (626) 287-6260
E-mail: sgveha@flash.net
Web: http://www.flash.net/~sgveha/
Network of mutual-support self-help groups for people
who are recovering from emotional illness not related
to substance abuse.

Emotions Anonymous International
P.O. Box 4245
St. Paul, MN 55104-0245
Ph: (651) 647-9712
Fax: (651) 647-1593
E-mail: info@EmotionsAnonymous.org
Web: http://www.emotionsanonymous.org/
Twelve-step program for people recovering from
emotional difficulties.

Family Voices
P.O. Box 769
Algodones, NM 87001
Ph: (505) 867-2368
Fax: (505) 867-6517
E-mail: kidshealth@familyvoices.org
Web: http://www.familyvoices.org
Information, education on children's health care needs.

Federal Consumer Information Center
Pueblo, CO 81009
Ph: (888) 878-3256
E-mail: catalog.pueblo@gsa.gov
Web: http://www.pueblo.gsa.gov/
Health and parenting information, a few publications
on special-needs topics.

Federal Resource Center for Special Education
Academy for Educational Development
1825 Connecticut Ave. NW
Washington, DC 20009
Ph: (202) 884-8215
TTY: (202) 884-8200
Fax: (202) 884-8443
E-mail: frc@aed.org
Web: http://www.dssc.org/frc/frc.htm
Technical assistance network to respond to needs of
students with disabilities, especially those from
under-represented populations.

Federation for Children with Special Needs
1135 Tremont St., Suite 420
Boston, MA 02120
Ph: (617) 236-7210
Fax: (800) 331-0688
        (617) 572-2094
E-mail: fcsninfo@fcsn.org
Web: http://www.fcsn.org
Supports parents, organizations working on behalf of
children with special needs and their families.

**Federation of Families for Children's Mental
Health**
1101 King St., Suite 420
Alexandria, VA 22314
Ph: (703) 684-7710
Fax: (703) 684-1040
E-mail: ffcmh@crosslink.net
Web: http://www.ffcmh.org/
Works with professionals, policy makers, organizations
on needs of children with emotional problems.

Feingold Association of the United States
127 East Main St., Suite 106
Riverhead, NY 11901
Ph: (631) 369-9340
Fax: (631) 369-2988
E-mail: Help@feingold.org
Web: http://www.feingold.org
Dietary techniques for better behavior, learning and
health. Program is based on elimination diet.

**Georgetown University Child Development
Center**
3307 M St. NW
Washington, DC 20007
Ph: (202) 687-6835
TTY: (202) 687-5503
Fax: (202) 687-8899
E-mail: gucdc@gunet.georgetown.edu
Web:
http://www.dml.georgetown.edu/depts/pediatrics/gucdc
Serves vulnerable children , families. Works to influence
local, national, international programs and policy.

**Global Alliance of Mental Illness Advocacy
Networks**
308 Seaview Ave.
Staten Island, NY 10305
Ph: (718) 351-1717
Fax: (718) 667-8893
Web: http://www.gamian.org/
Works for empowerment of consumers to seek
appropriate healthcare for mental illness without fear of
social stigma. Promotes awareness of mental illness.

**Independent Living Research Utilization
Program at TIRR (ILRU)**
2323 S. Shepherd, Suite 1000
Houston, TX 77019
Ph: (713) 520-0232
TDD: (713) 520-5136
Fax: (713) 520-5785
Web: http://www.bcm.tmc.edu/ilru/
Information, training, research, and technical assistance
in independent living.

Institute on Community Integration
University of Minnesota
102 Pattee Hall
150 Pillsbury Dr. SE
Minneapolis, MN 55455
Ph: (612) 624-6300
Fax: (612) 624-9344
E-mail: info@icimail.coled.umn.edu
Web: http://www.ici.coled.umn.edu/ici/
Works to improve community services and social
supports available to individuals with disabilities and
their families. Research, professional training,
technical assistance, publishing.

**Institutes for the Achievement of Human
Potential**
8801 Stenton Ave.
Philadelphia PA 19038
Ph: (215) 233-2050
Fax: (215) 233-9312
E-mail: institutes@iahp.org
Web: http://www.iahp.org/
Education on child brain development.

Institute for Health and Disability
University of Minnesota
420 Delaware St. SE, Box 721
Minneapolis, MN 55455-0374
Ph/TTY: (612) 626-3939
Fax: (612) 626-2134
E-mail: instihd@tc.umn.edu
Web:
http://www.peds.umn.edu/Centers/ihd/institute.html
Promotes well-being of children with disabilities and
their families.

**International Association of Psychosocial
Rehabilitation Services (IAPSRS)**
10025 Governor Warfield Pkwy., Suite 301
Columbia, MD 21044
Ph: (410) 730-7190
TTY: (410) 730-1723
Fax: (410) 730-5965
E-mail: general@iapsrs.org
Web: http://www.iapsrs.org/
Works to help advance the services for community
readjustment of people with psychiatric disabilities.

Kids on the Block, Inc.
9385-C Gerwig Lane
Columbia, MD 21046-1583
Ph: (800) 368-5437
         (410) 290-9095
Fax: (410) 290-9358
E-mail: kob@kotb.ocm
Web: http://www.kotb.com/
Puppet programs on disabilities, social concerns.

Kids Together, Inc.
P.O. Box 574
Quakertown, PA 18954
E-mail: staff@kidstogether.org
Web: http://www.kidstogether.org
Information and support on inclusion.

Mobility International USA
P.O. Box 10767
Eugene, OR 97440
Ph/TTY: (541) 343-1284
Fax: (541) 343-6812
E-mail: info@miusa.org
Web: http://www.miusa.org
Empowers people with disabilities through
international exchange.

Mothers United for Moral Support (MUMS)
150 Custer Court
Green Bay, WI 54301-1243
Ph: (920) 336-5333
       (877) 336-5333
Fax: (920) 339-0995
E-mail: mums@netnet.net
Web: http://www.netnet.net/mums
Matches parents of children with disorders with the
goal of mutual support.

The National Academy for Child Development
P.O. Box 380
Huntsville, UT 84317
Ph: (801) 621-8606
Ph: (801) 621-8389 (fax)
E-mail: nacdinfo@nacd.org
Web: http://www.nacd.org/
Designs home neurodevelopmental programs for children and adults.

National Adoption Center
1500 Walnut St., Suite 701
Philadelphia, PA 19102
Ph: (215) 735-9988
E-mail: nac@adopt.org
Web: http://adopt.org/adopt/nac/nac.html
Adoption opportunities for children with special needs.

National Alliance for the Mentally Ill (NAMI)
Colonial Place Three
2107 Wilson Blvd., Suite 300
Arlington, VA 22201-3042
Ph: (800) 950-6264
     (703) 524-7600
TDD:(703) 516-7227
Fax: (703) 524-9094
Web: http://www.nami.org/
Selp-help, support, organization of consumers, friends, families of people with severe mental illnesses.

National Artists for Mental Health
369 Main St.
Catskill, NY 12414
Ph: (518) 943-2450
Fax: (518) 943-3825
Web: http://www.namh.org/
Uses art to promote self-help, recovery, independence for recipients of mental health services.

National Arts and Disability Center
UCLA University Affiliated Program
300 UCLA Medical Plaza Suite #3310
Los Angeles, CA 90095-6967
Ph: (310) 794-1141
TTY: (310) 267-2356
Fax: (310) 794-1143
E-mail: oraynor@mednet.ucla.edu
Web: http://nadc.ucla.edu
Promotes inclusion of those with disabilities into the arts communities.

National Association of Developmental Disabilities Council
1234 Massachusetts Ave. NW, Suite 103
Washington, DC 20005
Ph: (202) 347-1234
Fax: (202) 347-4023
Web: http://www.igc.org/NADDC/
Promotes national policy for those with developmental disabilities to be able to make choices regarding the quality of their lives, inclusion.

National Center on Accessibility
Indiana University
2805 East 10th St, Suite 190
Bloomington, IN 47408-2698
Ph: (812) 856-4422
TTY: (812) 856-4421
Fax: (812) 856-4480
E-mail: nca@indiana.edu
Web: http://www.ncaonline.org
Promotes participation in parks, recreation, tourism by people with disabilities.

National Clearinghouse of Rehabilitation Training Materials (NCHRTM)
Oklahoma State University
5202 Richmond Hill Dr.
Stillwater, OK 74078-4080
Ph: (800) 223-5219
     (405) 624-7650
Fax: (405) 624-0695
E-mail: wsharri@www.nchrtm.okstate.edu
Web: http://www.nchrtm.okstate.edu
Training materials for persons with disabilities and for those who work with them.

National Early Childhood Technical Assistance System (NECTAS)
137 East Franklin Street, Suite 500
Chapel Hill, NC 27514-3628
Ph: (919) 962-2001
TDD: (877) 574-3194
Fax: (919) 966-7463
E-mail: nectas@unc.edu
Web: http://www.nectas.unc.edu/
Technical assistance consortium working to support states, jurisdictions, others to improve services for young children with disabilities and their families.

National Family Caregivers Association
10400 Connecticut Ave., #500
Kensington, MD 20895-3944
Ph: (800) 896-3650
Fax: (301) 942-2302
E-mail: info@nfcacares.org
Web: http://www.nfcacares.org/
Educates, supports those who care for chronically ill, aged or disabled loved ones.

The National Father's Network
16120 NE 8th St.
Bellevue, WA 98008-3937
Ph: (425) 747-4004, ext. 218
E-mail: jmay@fathersnetwork.org
Web: http://www.fathersnetwork.org
Supports fathers and families raising children with special health care needs and developmental disabilities.

National Information Center for Children and Youth with Disabilities (NICHY)
P.O. Box 1492
Washington, DC 20013-1492
Ph./TTY: (800) 695-0285
            (202) 884-8200
Fax: (202) 884-8441
E-mail: nichcy@aed.org
Web: http://www.nichcy.org/
Information and referrals on disabilities for families, educators, professionals.

National Institute of Mental Health (NIMH)
Alcohol, Drug Abuse, and Mental Health Administration
6001 Executive Blvd., Room 8184, MSC 9663
Bethesda, MD 20892-9663
Ph: (301) 443-4513
Fax: (301) 443-4279
E-mail: nimhinfo@nih.gov.
Web: http://www.nimh.nih.gov/
Provides information intended to help people better understand mental health and mental disorders.

National Lekotek Center
2100 Ridge Ave.
Evanston, IL 60201
Ph: (847) 328-0001
Fax: (847) 328-5514
E-mail: lekotek@lekotek.org
Web: http://www.lekotek.org/
Toy lending libraries.

National Library Services for the Blind and Physically Handicapped
The Library of Congress
1291 Taylor St. N.W.
Washington, DC 20542
Ph: (202) 707-5100
Fax: (202) 707-0712
TDD:(202) 707-0744
E-mail: nls@loc.gov
Web: http://www.loc.gov/nls/
Library program of braille, recorded materials.

National Mental Health Association
1021 Prince St.
Alexandria, VA 22314-2971
Ph: (800) 969-NMHA
        (703) 684-7722
TTY:(800) 433-5959
Fax: (703) 684-5968
Web: http://www.nmha.org
Advocacy, education, research, services regarding all aspects of mental health and mental illness.

National Mental Health Consumers Self-Help Clearinghouse
1211 Chestnut St., Suite 1207
Philadelphia, PA 19107
Ph: (800) 553-4539
    (215) 751-1810
Fax: (215) 636-6312
E-mail: info@mhselfhelp.org.
Web: http://www.mhselfhelp.org/
Connects mental health consumers to self-help and advocacy resources.

National Organization on Disability
910 16th St. NW, Suite 600
Washington, DC 20006
Ph: (202) 293-5960
TDD: (202) 293-5968
Fax: (202) 293-7999
E-mail: ability@nod.org
Web: http://www.nod.org
Promotes the full inclusion of those with disabilities.

National Organization for Rare Disorders
P.O. Box 8923
New Fairfield, CT 06812-8923
Ph: (800) 999-6673
    (203) 746-6518
Fax: (203) 746-6481
Web: http://www.pcnet.com/~orphan/
Voluntary health organizations serving people with rare disorders. Databases of information on Internet.

National Parent Network on Disabilities
1130 – 17th St., NW, Suite 400
Washington, DC 20036
Ph: (202) 463-2299
Fax: (202) 463-9405
E-mail: NPND@cs.net
Web: http://www.npnd.org/
Information, advocacy on government activities that impact those with disabilities.

National Rehabilitation Information Center
1010 Wayne Ave., Suite 800
Silver Spring, MD 20910
Ph: (800) 346-2742
    (301) 562-2400
TT: (301) 495-5626
Fax: (301) 562-2401
Web: http://www.naric.com
Disseminates results of federal research projects.

National Sports Center for the Disabled
P.O. Box 1290
Winter Park, CO 80482
Ph: (970) 726-1540
    (303) 316-1540
Fax: (970) 726-4112
E-mail: info@nscd.org
Web: http://www.nscd.org
Recreation opportunities for those with disabilities.

National Transition Alliance for Youth with Disabilities
Transition Research Institute, University of Illinois
117 Children's Research Center
51 Gerty Dr.
Champaign, IL 61820
Ph: (217) 333-2325
E-mail: nta@aed.org
Web: http://www.dssc.org/nta/
Promotes transition of disabled youth to secondary, post secondary school/training, independent living, employment.

Office of Special Education and Rehabilitative Services
Web: http://www.ed.gov/offices/OSERS/index.html
Supports programs that assist in educating children with special needs, provides for the rehabilitation of youth and adults with disabilities, and supports research.

Parents Helping Parents
3041 Olcott St.
Santa Clara, CA 95054
Ph: (408) 727-5775
Fax: (408) 727-0182
Web: http://www.php.com/
Supports parents of developmentally disabled children through parent-to-parent matches, special education guidance, information sharing.

President's Committee on Employment of People with Disabilities
1331 F St., N.W., Suite 300
Washington, DC 20004
Ph: (202) 376-6200
Fax: (202) 376-6219
TDD: (202) 376-6205
E-mail: info@pcepd.gov
Web: http://www.pcepd.gov/
Communicates, coordinates public and private efforts to enhance the employment of the disabled.

S.M.A.R.T. Recovery Self-Help Network
7537 Mentor Ave., Suite 306
Mentor, Ohio 44060
Ph: (440) 951-5357
Fax: (440) 951-5358
E-mail: srmail1@aol.com
Web: http://www.smartrecovery.org
Self-management and recovery training. Self-help for people having problems with drinking and using.

Social Security Administration
Office of Public Inquiries
6401 Security Blvd.
Room 4-C-5 Annex
Baltimore, MD 21235-6401
Ph: (800) 772-1213
TTY: (800) 325-0778
Web: http://www.ssa.gov/
Information on disability and supplemental security income program.

Substance Abuse and Mental Health Services Administration
5600 Fishers Lane
Rockville, MD 20857
E-mail: info@samhsa.gov
Web: http://www.samhsa.gov
Prevention, treatment, rehabilitative services designed to reduce illness, death, disability, resulting from substance abuse and mental illnesses.

TASH
29 W. Susquehanna Ave., Suite 210
Baltimore, MD 21204
Ph: (410) 828-8274
Fax: (410) 828-6706
Web: http://www.tash.org/
International association of people with disabilities, family, advocates, professionals working for inclusion.

Toughlove
P.O. Box 1069
Doylestown, PA 18901
Ph: (215) 348-7090
Fax: (215) 348-9874
Web: http://www.toughlove.org
Education, support to families, empowering parents and young people to accept responsibility for their actions.

Transition Research Institute
College of Education
University of Illinois at Urbana-Champaign
113 Children's Research Center
51 Gerty Dr.
Champaign, IL 61820
Ph: (217) 333-2325
Fax: (217) 244-0851
Web: http://www.ed.uiuc.edu/SPED/tri/institute.html
Intervention, evaluation, assistance in transitioning youth with disabilities from school to adult life.

UCLA / School Mental Health Project
Center for Mental Health in Schools, Dept. of
Psychology
P.O. Box 951563
Los Angeles, CA 90095-1563
Ph: (310) 825-3634
Fax: (310) 206-8716
E-mail: smhp@ucla.edu
Web: http://smhp.psych.ucla.edu/
Research, practice, training on mental health,
psychosocial concerns for school interventions.

The Unicorn Children's Foundation
7344 North Western Ave.
Chicago, Illinois 60645
Ph: (888) 782-8321
        (773)761-1003
Fax: (773)761-5011
E-mail: HelpDesk@eunicorn.com
Web: http://www.saveachild.com/
Supports parents, professionals in helping children with
communication, learning disorders.

U.S. Dept. of Health and Human Services
200 Independence Ave., SW
Washington, D.C. 20201
Ph: (877) 696-6775
        (202) 619-0257
E-mail: hhsmail@os.dhhs.gov
Web: http://www.dhhs.gov/
Human services, research, education, prevention,
correction programs.

U.S. National Library of Medicine
National Institutes of Health
8600 Rockville Pike
Bethesda, MD 20894
Ph: (888) 346-3656
        (301) 594-5983
E-mail: custserv@nlm.nih.gov
Web: http://www.nlm.nih.gov
Library of health-related information, some on Internet.

World Federation for Mental Health
1021 Prince St
Alexandria VA 22314-2971
Ph: (703) 519-7648
Fax: (703) 519-7648
E-mail: wfmh@erols.com
Web: http://www.wfmh.com/index.html
Advances the prevention of mental disorders, proper
treatment and care.

World Health Organization
Office at the United Nations
2, United Nations Plaza
DC-2 Bldg.
Rooms 0956 to 0976
New York, NY 10017
Ph: (212) 963-4388
Fax: (212) 223-2920
Web: http://www.who.ch
Coordinates international work, technical cooperation,
research on mental health initiatives.

Wheelchair Sports U.S.A.
3595 E. Fountain Blvd., Suite L-1
Colorado Springs, Colorado 80910
Ph: (719) 574-1150
Fax: (719) 574-9840
E-mail: adminstrator@wsusa.org
Web: http://wsusa.org/
Wheelchaired athletic competitions.

World Institute on Disability
510-16th St., Suite #100
Oakland, CA 94612
Ph: (510) 763-4100
TTY: (510) 208-9496
Fax: (510) 763-4109
Web: http://www.wid.org
Researches disability issues, works to overcome
obstacles to independent living.

---- Teaching Resources

The resources noted below are designed for teachers, homeschoolers, and school personnel. They can help in establishing services, providing information and materials, and understanding and working effectively with challenged children and their families.

Who to Contact
Also refer to "Who Else to Contact." Organizations listed below target their work specifically toward teachers and schools.

ACT Test Administration
P.O. Box 168
2201 North Dodge St.
Iowa City, IA 52243-0168
Ph: (319) 337-1000
Fax: (319) 339-3021
Web: http://www.act.org/
Testing accomodations for special needs students are available.

Admissions Testing Program
College Board Services for Students with Disabilities
P.O. Box 6626
Princeton, NJ 08541-6626
Ph: (609) 771-7137
TTY: (609) 882-4118
Fax: (609) 771-7944
E-mail: ssd@info.collegeboard.org
Web: http://cbweb1.collegeboard.org/ap
Advanced placement testing accomodation services.

American Federation of Teachers
555 New Jersey Ave., N.W.
Washington, DC 20001
Ph: (202) 879-4400
E-mail: online@aft.org
Web: http://www.aft.org
News about special education.

Association for Childhood Education Intl.
17904 Georgia Ave., Suite 215
Olney, MD 20832
Ph: (800) 423-3563
         (301) 570-2111
Fax: (301) 570-2212
E-mail: aceihq@aol.com
Web: http://www.udel.edu/bateman/acei/
Supports teacher development.

Center for Adult Learning Educational Credentials (GED Testing Service)
One DuPont Circle NW, Suite 250
Washington, DC 20036
Ph: (202) 939-9475
E-mail: ged@ace.nche.edu
Web: http://www.gedtest.org/
Accommodations for special-needs test takers.

Center for Effective Collaboration and Practice
1000 Thomas Jefferson St. NW, Suite 400
Washington, DC 20007
Ph: (888) 457-1551
       (202) 944-5300
Fax: (202) 944-5454
E-mail: center@air-dc.org
Web: http://www.air-dc.org/cecp/index.htm
Supports development of emotionally disturbed children.

The Council of Administrators of Special Education (CASE)
615 16th St. N.W.
Albuquerque, NM 87104
Ph: (505) 247-4822
Web: http://members.aol.com/casecec/index.htm
Shapes educational policies/practices.

Educational Equity Concepts, EEC
114 East 32nd St.
New York, NY 10016
Ph/TTY: (212) 725-1803
Fax: (212) 725-0947
E-mail: information@edequity.org
Web: http://www.edequity.org/
Resources to build bias-free learning environments.

Educational Testing Service (ETSS)
Rosedale Road
Princeton, NJ 08541
Ph: (609) 921-9000
Fax: (609) 734-5410
E-mail: etsinfo@ets.org
Web: http://www.ets.org/
Accommodations for those taking the SAT, GRE, other exams.

HEATH Resource Center (Higher Education and Adult Training for People with Handicaps)
One Dupont Circle NW
Washington, DC 20036
Ph/TTY: (800) 544-3284
E-mail: heath@ace.nche.edu
Web:
http://www.acenet.edu/about/programs/Access&Equity/HEATH/
National clearinghouse on post-secondary education for individuals with disabilities.

Indiana Institute on Disability and Community
2853 E. Tenth St.
Bloomington, IN 47408-2696
Ph: (812) 855-6508
Ph: (800) 437-7924
TTY: (812) 855-9396
Fax: (812) 855-9630
E-mail: foshaj@indiana.edu
Web: http://www.iidc.indiana.edu/
Publications on adapting curriculum, using technology in teaching special needs students.

Law School Admission Council, Inc.
Newton, PA 18940
Ph: (215) 968-1001
TDD: (215) 968-1128
Fax: (215) 504-1420
E-mail: Accom@LSAC.org
Web: http://www.lsat.org/
Accommodations for disabled takers of the LSAT.

National Association of Private Schools for Exceptional Children

1522 K St. NW, Suite 1032
Washington, DC 20005
Ph: (202) 408-3338
Fax: (202) 408-3340
E-mail: napsec@aol.com
Web: http://www.napsec.com/
The association consists of private special education schools for individuals with disabilities.

National Association of School Psychologists

4340 East West Highway, Suite 402
Bethesda, MD 20814
Ph: (301) 657-0270
Fax: (301) 657-0275
TDD:(301) 657-4155
E-mail: nasp@naspweb.org
Web: http://www.naspweb.org/
Programs to enhance independence, promote learning.

National Association of State Directors of Special Education (NASDSE)

1800 Diagonal Road, Suite 320
Alexandria, VA 22314
Ph: (703) 519-3800
TDD:(703) 519-7008
Fax: (703) 519-3808
Web: http://www.nasdse.org
Serves state agencies in their efforts to maximize educational outcomes for individuals with disabilities.

National Center on Educational Outcomes

College of Education & Human Develop., U of MN
350 Elliott Hall , 75 East River Road
Minneapolis, MN 55455
Ph: (612) 626-1530
E-mail: nceo@umn.edu
Web: http://www.coled.umn.edu/NCEO
Provides national leadership in the participation of students with disabilities in national/state assessments, standards-setting graduation requirements.

National Center for Family Literacy

325 West Main St., Suite 200
Louisville, KY 40202-4251
Ph: (502) 584-1133
Fax: (502)584-0172
Info. Hotline: (877) FAMLIT-1
E-mail: ncfl@famlit.org
Web: http://www.famlit.org/
Supports family literacy services through programming, training, research, advocacy.

National Center to Improve the Tools of Educators

805 Lincoln St.
Eugene, OR 97401
E-mail: ncite@darkwing.uoregon.edu
Web: http://idea.uoregon.edu/~ncite/
Works to advance the effectiveness of technology, media, and materials for individuals with disabilities.

National Coalition for Parent Involvement in Education (NCPIE)

3929 Old Lee Highway, Suite 91-A
Fairfax, VA 22030-2401
Ph: (703) 359-8973
Fax: (703) 359-0972
E-mail: ferguson@ncea.com
Web: http://www.ncpie.org/
Advocates family involvement in education.

National Institute for Literacy

1775 I St., NW; Suite 730
Washington, DC 20006-2401
Ph: (202) 233-2025
Fax: (202) 233-2050
Web: http://www.nifl.gov
Supports programs and services designed to improve the quality of literacy programs nationwide.

National Library of Education
400 Maryland Ave. SW
Washington, DC 20202
Ph: (800) 424-1616
TTY: (202) 205-7561
Fax: (202) 401-0552
E-mail: library@ed.gov
Web: http://www.ed.gov/NLE/
Wide range of information for teachers.

Office of Special Education and Rehabilitative Services (OSERS)
U.S. Department of Education
400 Maryland Ave., SW
Washington, DC 20202
Web: http://www.ed.gov/offices/OSERS/index.html
Supports programs to educate children with special needs, provides rehabilitation of youth and adults with disabilities, supports research.

Parents Instructing Challenged Children (PICC)
615 Utica St
Fulton, NY 13069-1954
Ph/fax: (315) 592-7257
E-mail: picc@twcny.rr.com
Web: http://www.oswego.edu/~mulvey/picc.html
Network of home schoolers of special needs children. Lending library of books, tapes, videos. Legal information, advocacy.

Reading is Fundamental, Inc.
1825 Connecticut Ave., N.W., Suite 400
Washington, DC 20009
Ph: (877) RIF-READ
        (202) 287-3220
Web: http://www.rif.org/
Develops literacy programs to prepare young children for reading.

U.S. Department of Education
400 Maryland Ave. SW
Washington, D.C. 20202-0498
Ph: (800) 872-5327
E-mail: National_Library_of_Education@ed.gov
Web: http://www.ed.gov/
Ensures equal access to education, promotes educational excellence for all Americans.

Very Special Arts (VSA)
1300 Connecticut Ave. NW, Suite 700
Washington, D.C. 20036
Ph: (800) 933-8721
        (202) 628-8200
TDD: (202) 737-0645
Fax: (202) 737-0725
E-mail: info@vsarts.org
Web: http://www.vsarts.org
Creates learning opportunities through the arts for people with disabilities.

Recommended Reading

Access to Learning for Pupils with Disabilities
John Cornwall
Taylor & Francis, 1997

Adapting Early Childhood Curricula for Children in Inclusive Settings, 4th ed.
Ruth Cook, Annette Tessier, M. Diane Klein
Macmillan Publishing Company, Inc., 1995

Adapting Instruction to Accommodate Students in Inclusive Settings, 3rd ed.
Judy Wood
Prentice Hall, 1997

Adaptive Education Strategies: Building on Diversity
Margaret Wang, Ph.D., et al.
Paul H. Brookes, 1994

Art-Centered Education and Therapy for Children with Disabilities
Frances Anderson
Charles C. Thomas Publisher Ltd., 1994

Assessing Special Needs Students
Libby Cohen, Loraine Spenciner
Addison-Wesley, 1997

At the Crossroads: Special Education Needs and Teacher Education
John Davies, Philip Garner
Taylor & Francis, 1997

Beyond Gentle Teaching: A Nonaversive Approach to Helping Those in Need
John McGee, Frank Menolascino
Plenum Press, 1991

Bold Tracks: Teaching Adaptive Skiing, 3rd. ed.
Hal O'Leary
Johnson Books, 1995

Breaking Ground: Ten Families Building Opportunities Through Integration
C. Beth Schaffner, Barbara Buswell
PEAK Parent Center, Inc., 1989

Career Development & Transition Education for Adolescents with Disabilities, 2nd ed.
Gary Clark, Oliver Kolstoe
Allyn and Bacon, 1994

Case Studies for Teaching Special Needs and At-Risk Students
Judith Buzzell, Robert Piazza
Delmar Publishers, 1994

Characteristics of the Mildly Handicapped: Assisting Teachers, Counselors, Psychologists, and Families to Prepare for Their Roles in Meeting the Needs of the Mildly Handicapped in a Changing Society
Harold Love
Charles C. Thomas Publisher, Ltd., 1996

Characteristics of and Strategies for Teaching Students with Mild Disabilities, 2nd Ed.
Martin Henley, Robert Algozzine, Roberta Ramsey
Allyn and Bacon, 1996

Children with Exceptional Needs in Regular Classrooms
Libby Cohen (Ed.)
NEA, 1992

Collaborative Teams for Students with Severe Disabilities: Integrating Therapy and Educational Services, 2nd ed.
Beverly Rainforth, Ph.D., PT, Jennifer York-Barr, Ph.D., PT
Paul H. Brookes, 1997

College Guide for Students with Disabilities, 13th ed.
Laurel Publications, 1998

Common and Uncommon School Problems: A Parent's Guide
David Gross, M.D., Irl Extein, M.D.
Berkley Books, 1990

Commonsense Methods for Children with Special Needs: Strategies for the Regular Classroom, 3rd ed.
Peter Westwood
Routledge, 1997

Controversial Issues Confronting Special Education: Divergent Perspectives, 2nd ed.
Susan Bray Stainback, William Stainback
Allyn and Bacon, 1995

Controversial Issues in Special Education
Garry Hornby, Mary Atkinson
Taylor & Francis, 1997

Cooperative Learning and Strategies for Inclusion: Celebrating Diversity in the Classroom, 2nd. Ed.
JoAnne Putman, Ph.D.
Paul H. Brookes, 1998

Creating Schools for All Our Students: What 12 Schools Have to Say
Council for Exceptional Children, 1994

Creativity and Collaborative Learning: A Practical Guide to Empowering Students and Teachers
Ann Nevin, Ph.D.
Paul H. Brookes, 1994

Curriculum Content for Students with Moderate & Severe Disabilities in Inclusive Settings
Diane Ryndak, Sandra Alper
Allyn and Bacon, 1995

Designing Interventions for Preschool Learning and Behavior Problems
David Barnett, Karen Carey
Jossey-Bass Publishers, 1992

Developmental -- Adapted Physical Education: Making Ability Count, 3rd ed.
Carl Eichstaedt, Leonard Kalakian
Prentice Hall, 1993

Differentiated Science Teaching: Responding to Individual Differences & to Special Education Needs
Keith Postlethwaite
Taylor & Francis, Inc., 1993

Directory of College Facilities and Services for the Disabled, 4th ed.
William Burgess
Oryx Press, 1995

Directory for Exceptional Children, 13th ed.
Porter Sargent Publications, Inc., 1994

Drama for People with Special Needs
Ann Cattanach
Drama Publishers, 1997

Early Childhood Special Education: Birth to Three, 2nd ed.
June Jordan, James Gallagher, Patricia Hutinger, Merle Karnes
Council for Exceptional Children and its Division for Early Childhood, 1990

Educating Children with Multiple Disabilities: A Transdisciplinary Approach, 3rd ed.
Fred Orelove, Ph.D., Dick Sobsey, R. N., Ed.D.
Paul H. Brookes, 1996

Educating One & All: Students with Disabilities & Standard-Based Reform
Lorraine McDonnell
National Academy of Social Insurance, 1997

Educating Special Learners, 4th ed.
G. Cartwright, Marjorie Ward
Wadsworth, 1995

Education Student & Behavioral Disorder, 2nd ed.
Michael Rosenberg, Rich Wilson
Allyn and Bacon, 1996

Educational Rights of Children with Disabilities: A Primer for Advocates
Eileen Ordover, Kathleen Boundy
Center for Law and Education, Inc., 1991

Exceptional Children: An Introduction to Special Education, 5th ed.
William Heward
Macmillan Publishing Company, Inc., 1995

Exceptional Children and Youth:
An Introduction to Special Education, 2nd ed.
Nancy Hunt, Kathleen Marshall
Houghton Mifflin Co., 1999

Exceptional Individuals in Focus
James Patton, Joseph Blackbourn, Kathleen Fad
Macmillan Publishing Company, Inc., 1996

Exceptional Individuals: An Introduction
Bill Gearheart, Carol Gearheart, Robert Mullen
Brooks/Cole, 1993

Exceptional Lives: Special Education in
Today's Schools, 2nd ed.
Ann Turnbull, Rutherford Turnbull, Marilyn Shank,
Dorothy Leal
Prentice-Hall, Inc., 1998

Experiencing Special Education:
What Children with Special Needs Can Tell Us
Barrie Wade, Maggie Moore
Taylor & Francis, Inc., 1993

A Guide for Educating Mainstreamed
Students, 4th ed.
Philip Mann, Rose Marie McClung, Patricia Suiter
Allyn and Bacon, 1992

Guide to Summer Camps and Summer Schools
Porter Sargent Publications, 1995

Handbook for the Care of Infants, Toddlers,
and Young Children with Disabilities and
Chronic Conditions
Marilyn Krajicek, Geraldine Steinke, Dalice Hertzberg,
Nicholas Anastasiow (Eds.)
PRO-ED, 1997

A Handbook for the K-12 Reading Resource
Specialist
Marguerite Radencich, Jeanne Shay Schumm
Allyn and Bacon, 1993

Handbook of Private Schools: An Annual
Descriptive Survey of Independent Education
Serial
Porter Sargent Publications, 1999

The Handbook of School Art Therapy:
Introducing Art Therapy Into a School System
Janet Bush
Charles C. Thomas Publisher, 1997

A Handbook for Special Needs Assistants
Glenys Fox
Taylor & Francis, Inc., 1993

Helping Children with Reading and Spelling:
A Special Needs Manual, 2nd ed.
Rea Reason, Rene Boote
Routledge, 1994

Home School Relations
Mary Fuller, Glenn Olsen
Allyn and Bacon, 1997

Home Schooling Children with Special Needs
Sharon Hensley
Christian Life Workshop, 1995

The Illusion of Full Inclusion:
A Comprehensive Critique of a Current
Special Education Bandwagon
James Kauffman
PRO-ED, 1994

I'm Somebody, Too - Teacher Handbook
Jeanne Gehret
Verbal Images Press, 1996

**The Impossible Child in School, at Home:
A Guide for Caring Teachers and Parents, 2nd
ed.**
Doris Rapp
Practical Allergy Research Foundation, 1995

**Including Students with Severe and Multiple
Disabilities in Typical Classrooms: Practical
Strategies for Teachers**
June Downing
Paul H.Brookes, 1996

**Including Students with Special Needs:
A Practical Guide for Classroom Teachers, 2nd
ed.**
Marilyn Friend, William Bursuck
Allyn and Bacon, 1998

**Inclusion: 450 Strategies for Success:
A Practical Guide for All Educators Who
Teach Students with Disabilities**
Peggy Hammeken
Peytral Publications, 1995

Inclusion: A Guide for Educators
Susan Stainback, Ed. D., William Stainback, Ed. D.
(Eds.)
Paul H. Brookes, 1996

**Inclusion and School Reform: Transforming
America's Classrooms**
Dorothy Kerzner Lipsky, Ph.D., Alan Gartner, Ph.D.
Paul H. Brookes, 1997

**Inclusion Strategies for Students with Learning
and Behavior Problems: Perspectives,
Experiences, and Best Practices**
Paul Zionts
PRO-ED, 1997

**Inclusion: Strategies for Working with Young
Children: A Resource Guide for Teachers,
Childcare Providers, and Parents**
Lorraine Moore
Peytral Publications, 1997

**Inclusions: An Essential Guide for the
Paraprofessional: A Practical Reference Tool
for All Professionals Working in Inclusionary
Settings**
Peggy Hammeken
Peytral Publications, 1996

**The Integrated Classroom: The Assessment-
Curriculum Link in Early Childhood
Education**
Sue Wortham
Prentice Hall, 1996

**Integrating Pupils with Disabilities in
Mainstream Schools: Making It Happen**
Helen Kenward
Taylor and Francis, 1997

Jumping the Queue
Mark Kelman, Gillian Lester
Harvard University Press, 1997

**Kids with Special Needs: Information and
Activities to Promote Awareness and
Understanding**
Veronica Getskow, Dee Konczal
The Learning Works, Inc., 1995

**Leadership in Educational Reform:
An Administrator's Guide to Changes in
Special Education**
Daniel Sage, Ed.D., Leonard Burrello, Ed.D.
Paul H. Brookes, 1994

**Learning Styles: Food for Thoughts and 130
Practical Tips for Teachers K-4**
Priscilla Vail
Modern Learning Press, 1992

**Learning Through Play: Curriculum and
Activities for the Inclusive Classroom**
Kathleen Dolinar, Candace Boser, Eleanor Holm
Delmar Publications, 1994

**Lovejoy's College Guide for the Learning
Disabled**
Charles Straughn, Marvelle Colby
Monarch, 1988

**Mainstreaming Exceptional Students:
A Guide for Classroom Teachers, 4th ed.**
Jane Schulz, C. Dale Carpenter
Allyn and Bacon, 1995

**Making Drama Special: Developing Drama
Practice for Special Educational Needs**
Melanie Peter
Taylor & Francis, 1995

**Making School Inclusion Work: A Guide to
Everyday Practices**
Katie Blenk, Doris Landau Fine
Brookline Books, 1994

**Meeting Special Needs in Mainstream Schools:
A Practical Guide for Teachers**
Richard Stakes, Garry Hornby
Taylor & Francis, Inc., 1996

**Music for All: Developing Music in the
Curriculum with Pupils with Special
Educational Needs**
Peter Wills, Melanie Peter
Taylor & Francis, Inc., 1995

**Negotiating the Special Education Maze:
A Guide for Parents and Teachers, 3rd ed.**
Winifred Anderson
Woodbine House, 1997

**The New Language of Toys: Teaching
Communication Skills to Special Needs
Children, 2nd ed.**
Sue Schwartz, Joan Heller Miller
Woodbine House, 1996

**Parents' Complete Special-Education Guide:
Tips, Techniques, and Materials for Helping
Your Child Succeed in School and Life**
Roger Pierangelo, Robert Jacoby
Center for Applied Research in Education, 1996

**The Power of the Arts: Creative Strategies for
Teaching Exceptional Learners**
Sally Smith
Paul H. Brooks Publishing, 2000

**A Practical Guide for Teaching Science to
Students with Special Needs in Inclusive Settings**
Margo Mastropieri, Thomas Scruggs
PRO-ED, 1993

**Principal's Guide to Attention Deficit
Hyperactivity Disorder**
Elaine McEwan
Corwin Press, Inc., 1997

**Quick Guides to Inclusion: Ideas for Educating
Students with Disabilities**
Michael Giangreco, Ph.D. (Ed.)
Paul H. Brookes, 1997

Quick Guides to Inclusion 2: Ideas for Educating Students with Disabilities
Michael Giangreco, Ph.D. (Ed.)
Paul H. Brookes, 1998

The Special Education Sourcebook: A Teacher's Guide to Programs, Materials, and Information Sources
Michael Rosenberg, Ph.D., Irene Edmond-Rosenberg, M.P.A.
Woodbine House, 1994

Reading Improvement
Project Innovation of Mobile
Box 8508, Spring Hill
Mobile, AL 36608

The Special Education Teacher's Book of Lists
Roger Pierangelo, Ph.D.
Center for Applied Research in Education, 1997

Ready-To-Use Self Esteem Activities for Secondary Students With Special Needs
Darlene Mannix
Prentice Hall Trade, 1996

Strategies for Teaching Learners with Special Needs, 6th ed.
Edward Polloway, James Patton
Prentice Hall, 1996

Restructuring for Caring and Effective Education: An Administrative Guide to Creating Heterogeneous Schools
Richard Villa, Jacqueline Thousand, William Stainback, Susan Stainback (Eds.)
Paul H. Brookes, 1992

The Student with a Genetic Disorder: Educational Implications for Special Education Teachers and for Physical Therapists, Occupational Therapists, and Speech Pathologist
Diane Plumridge, Robin Bennett, Nihad Dinno, Cynthia Branson
Charles C. Thomas Publisher, 1993

Schooling and Disability
Douglas Biklen, Philip Ferguson, Alison Ford
NSSE, distributed by Paul H. Brookes, 1988

Successful Inclusive Teaching, 2nd rev.
Joyce Choate
Prentice Hall, 1996

Secondary Programs for Students with Developmental Disabilities
John McDonnell, Barbara Wilcox, Michael Hardman
Allyn and Bacon, 1991

Successful Mainstreaming: Proven Ways to Detect and Correct Special Needs
Joyce Choate (Ed.)
Allyn and Bacon, 1992

Smart Kids with School Problems: Things to Know and Ways to Help
Pricilla Vail
New American Library, 1988

Support Networks for Inclusive Schooling: Interdependent Integrated Education
William Stainback, Ed.D., Susan Stainback, Ed.D. (Eds.)
Paul H. Brookes, 1990

Survival Guide for the First-Year Special Education Teacher, Revised
Mary Kemper Cohen, Maureen Gale, Joyce Meyer
Council for Exceptional Children, 1994

A Survival Kit for the Special Education Teacher
Roger Pierangelo, Ph.D.
Ctr. Appl. R., 1996

A Teacher's Guide to Including Students with Disabilities in Regular Physical Education
Martin Block, Ph.D.
Paul H. Brookes, 1994

Teaching Low Achieving and Disadvantaged Students, 2nd ed.
Harles Hargis
Charles C. Thomas Publisher, 1997

Teaching Students with Mild Disabilities
Edward Sabornie, Laurie Debettencourt
Prentice Hall, 1996

Teaching Students with Moderate to Severe Disabilities
Mark Wolery, Melinda Jones Ault, Patricia Munson Doyle
Longman Publishing Group, 1992

Teaching Students with Moderate/Severe Disabilities, Including Autism, 2nd ed.
Elva Duran
Charles C. Thomas Publisher, 1996

Textbooks and the Students Who Can't Read Them: A Guide to Teaching Content
Jean Ciborowski
Brookline, 1995

**When Your Child Needs Testing:
What Parents, Teachers, and Other Helpers Need to Know About Psychological Counseling**
Milton Shore, Patrick Brice, Barbara Love
Cross Timbers, 1996

Videos

Video tapes can be very useful, but may a challenge to find, especially if they aren't new to the market. Try contacting the producers noted even if the tape isn't listed on their web site, book stores and your library.

Collaborating for Change: Creating an Inclusive School   (set of 2)
Produced by the San Francisco Unified School District
Paul H. Brookes, 1997
P.O. Box 10624
Baltimore, MD 21285-0624
Ph: (800) 638-3775
Fax: (410) 337-8539
E-mail: custserv@brookespublishing.com.
Web: http://www.brookespublishing.com/

Kids Belong Together
Expectations Unlimited, Inc., 1989
6613 Cheyenne Court
Longmont, CO 80503
Ph: (303) 652-2727
Integrating special needs children into the regular classroom.

Understanding and Managing the Aggressive and Acting-Out Child in the Public School Setting
Hastings Clinical Associates
P. O. Box 884
Gorham, ME 04038-0660
Ph: (207) 839-6535
E-mail: info@hastingsclinic.com
Web: http://www.hastingsclinic.com

Periodicals / Newsletters

Closing the Gap
P.O. Box 68
526 Main St.
Henderson, MN 56044
Ph: (507) 248-3294
Fax: (507) 248-3810
E-mail: info@closingthegap.ocm
Web: www.closingthegap.com
Use of technology in special education, rehabilitation.

Journal of Adolescent & Adult Literacy
International Reading Assoc., Inc.
800 Barksdale Road
Box 8139
Newark, DE 19714-8139
Ph: (302) 731-1600
Fax: (302) 731-1057
E-mail: membership@reading.org
Web: http://www.reading.org/
For teachers of middle, high school,adult students.

The Journal of Special Education
PRO-ED
8700 Shoal Creek Blvd.
Austin, TX 78757-6897
Ph: (800) 897-3202
Fax: (800) 397-7633
Web: http://www.proedinc.com/
Articles in all subspecialties of special education for individuals with disabilities.

The Reading Teacher
International Reading Assoc., Inc.
800 Barksdale Road
Box 8139
Newark, DE 19714-8139
Ph: (302) 731-1600
Fax: (302) 731-1057
E-mail: membership@reading.org
Web: http://www.reading.org/
Practices in reading and literacy education. For preschool and elementary teachers.

Web Sites

Also see "General Web Sites". Many have sections on schools and disabilities, but they are not listed separately below.

ERIC Clearinghouse on Disabilities and Gift Education

The Council for Exceptional Children (CEC)
1110 North Glebe Road, Suite 300
Arlington, VA 22201-5704
Ph/TTY: (800) 328-0272
E-mail: ericec@cec.sped.org
Web: http://ericec.org/
Information, resources on the education, development of those with disabilities and/or giftedness.

FinAid

Web: http://www.finaid.org
Has a section on financial aid for college-bound students with disabilities.

School Psychology Resources Online

Web:
http://www.bcpl.net/~sandyste/school_psych.html
Information on a variety of disorders for psychologists, parents and educators.

Special Education Resources on the Internet

Web: http://www.hood.edu/seri/serihome.htm
Information resources for those involved in fields related to special education.

Vendors

Academic Therapy Publications

High Noon Books
20 Commercial Blvd.
Novato, CA 94949
Ph: (800) 422-7249
Fax: (415) 883-3720
Email: atpub@aol.com
Web: http://www.atpub.com/
Publishers of materials and curriculum for special education and learning disabilities.

Bright Eye Technology

2 Westwood Place
Asheville, NC 28806
Ph: (828) 253-6658
Fax: (828) 258-2727
E-mail: bw@uptime-csi.com
Web: http://www.brighteye.com/
Scan and listen learning system.

ECL Publications

11121 W. Michigan Ave., Suite A
P.O. Box 26
Youngtown, AZ 85263
Ph: (877) 974-4560
  (623) 974-4560
Fax: (877) 974-6057
  (623) 974-6057
Web: http://www.eclpublications.com/
Speech and language materials for clinic, classroom and home use.

Exceptional Teaching Aids

20102 Woodbine Ave.
Castro Valley, CA 94546
Ph: (800) 549-6999
  (510) 582-4859
Fax: (510) 582-5911
E-mail: ExTeaching@aol.com
Web: http://store.yahoo.com/exceptional/index.html

Franklin Electronic Publishers
One Franklin Plaza
Burlington, NJ 08016-4907
Ph: (800) 266-5626
       (609) 239-5948
Email: service@franklin.com
Web: http://www.franklin.com/
Electronic spell checkers, dictionaries, learning tools.

Freedom Scientific LSG
NASA Ames Moffett Complex
Bldg. 23
P.O. Box 215
Moffett Field, CA 94035-0215
Ph: (888) 223-3344
       (650) 603-8877
Fax: (650) 603-8871
E-mail: WYNN@arkenstone.org
Web: http://www.arkenstone.org/
Scan and listen software.

HumanWare
6245 King Road
Loomis, CA 95650
Ph: (800) 722-3393
E-mail: webmaster@humanware.com
Web: http://www.humanware.com
Electronic assistive technology for students with visual
and learning difficulties.

Kaplan School Supply
1310 Lewisville-Clemmons Road
P.O. Box 609
Lewisville, NC 27023-0609
Ph: (800) 334-2014
Fax: (800) 452-7526
E-mail: info@Kaplanco.com
Web: http://www.kaplanco.com/
Catalog for exceptional children to evaluate and build
skills, assistive equipment.

LRP Publications
Ph: (800) 341-7874
Fax: (215) 784-9639
E-mail: custserve@LRP.com
Web: http://www.lrp.com/ed/
Publications on special education and disability issues.

Maxi-Aids
42 Executive Blvd.
Farmingdale, NY 11735
Ph: (631) 752-0521
Fax: (631) 752-0689
E-mail: sales@maxiaids.com
Web: www.maxiaids.com
Independent living products for those with visual
impairments.

Remedia Publications
10135 East Via Linda, Suite #D-124
Scottsdale, AZ 85258
Ph: (800) 826-4740
Fax: (877) 661-9901
E-mail: remedia@rempub.com
Web: http://www.rempub.com/
Educational materials to build skills for students
significantly below grade level.

The Riggs Institute
4185 SW 102nd Ave.
Beaverton, OR 97005
Ph: (503) 646-9459
Fax: (503) 644-5191
E-mail: riggs@riggsinst.org
Web: http://www.riggsinst.org
Non-profit publisher of educational materials for
special education to advanced students.

Super Duper Publications
P.O. Box 24997
Greenville, SC 29616
Ph: (864) 288-3426
Fax: (864) 288-3380
E-mail: custserv@superduperinc.com
Web: http://www.superduperinc.com/
Materials for speech-language pathologists, special
educators, teachers, parents, and caregivers.

---- Paying Attention to Siblings

Siblings of challenged children have support needs, too. The resources listed below can help parents and other caregivers to understand siblings' situations and provide needed assistance. Some references for siblings are also included in individual sections.

Who to Contact
Also refer to "Who Else to Contact." Organizations listed below target their work specifically toward siblings.

The Sibling Support Project
Children's Hospital and Medical Center
P.O. Box 5371, CL-09
Seattle, WA 98105
Ph: (206) 527-5712
Fax: (206) 527-5705
E-mail: dmeyer@chmc.org
Web: http://www.seattlechildrens.org/sibsupp/
For siblings of people with special health and developmental needs.

Recommended Reading

Anguished Voices: Siblings and Adult Children of Persons with Psychiatric Disabilities
Rex Dickens, Diane Marsh (Eds.)
Center for Psychiatric Rehabilitation, Sargent College of Allied Health Professions, Boston, 1994

Brothers, Sisters, and Special Needs: Information and Activities for Helping Young Siblings of Children with Chronic Illnesses and Developmental Disabilities
Debra Lobato
Paul Brookes, 1990

Brothers and Sisters: A Special Part of Exceptional Families, 2nd ed.
Thomas Powell, Peggy Arenhold Ogle
Paul H. Brookes, 1993

The Four of Us
Farrar, Straus, Giroux
E. Swados, 1991

How to Cope with Mental Illness in Your Family: A Guide for Siblings and Offspring
Diane March, Rex Dickens
Putnam Publishing, 1998

Sibshops: Implementing Workshops for Brothers and Sisters of Children with Special Health and Developmental Needs
Donald Meyer, Patricia Vadasy
Paul H. Brookes, 1995

It Isn't Fair! Siblings of Children With Disabilities
Stanley Klein, Stanley Schleifer (Eds.)
Greenwood Publishing, 1993

Troubled Journey: Coming to Terms with the Mental Illness of a Sibling or Parent
Diane Marsh
J.P. Tarcher/Putnam, 1997

Living with a Brother or Sister with Special Needs, 2nd ed.
Donald Meyer
University of Washington Press, 1996

What About Me? Growing Up With a Developmentally Disabled Sibling
Bryna Siegel, Stuart Silverstein
Plenum Publishing Corp., 1994

Mad House: Growing Up in the Company of Mentally Ill Siblings
Clea Simon
Viking Penguin, 1998

When Madness Comes Home: Help and Hope for the Children, Siblings and Partners of the Mentally Ill
Victoria Secunda
Hyperion, 1998

The Sibling: A Handbook for Understanding the Sibling of a Child with a Handicap
Barbara Azrialy
Azrialy Publishing, 1992

Books for Youth

Brothers, Sisters, and Disability
Lydia Gans
Fairview Press, 1997

My Brother Matthew
Mary Thompson
Woodbine House, 1992

Coping With a Physically Challenged Brother or Sister
Linda Lee Ratto
Rosen Publishing Group, 1992

Princess Pooh
Kathleen Muldoon
Albert Whiteman & Co., 1991

Finding a Way: Living with Exceptional Brothers and Sisters
Maxine Rosenberg
Lothrop, Lee & Shepard, 1988

Tru Confessions
Janet Tashjian
Henry Holt & Co., 1997

Periodicals / Newsletters

Sib to Sib
Little Red School House
P.O. Box 992
Lynnwood, WA 98046
Web: http://www.seattlechildrens.org/sibsupp/
For siblings of special needs children.

---- *Additional Recommended Reading*

These books provide information on a range of topics related to children's health. For sites related to specific disorders, such as ADD, see sections on individual disorders.

9 Highland Road: Sane Living for the Mentally Ill
Michael Winerip
Random House, 1995

Abnormalities of Personality: Within and Beyond the Realm of Treatment
Michael Stone
W.W. Norton, 1992

Active Learning for Children with Disabilities
Pam Bailey
Addison-Wesley, 1996
For day care providers.

An Activity-Based Approach to Early Intervention, 2nd ed.
Diane Bricker, Natalya McComas, Kristie Pretti-Frontczak
Paul H. Brookes, 1998

Adapting PCs for Disabilities
Joseph Lazzaro
Addison-Wesley, 1995

Adaptive Technology for Special Human Needs
Arlene Brett, Eugene Provenzo
State U. NY, 1995

Adolescents at Risk: Prevalence and Prevention
Joy Dryfoos
Oxford University Press, 1991

Adopting and Advocating for the Special Needs Child: A Guide for Parents and Professionals
L. Anne Babb, Rita Laws
Greenwood Publishing Group, 1997

Advocacy, Self-Advocacy and Special Needs
Philip Garner, Sarah Sandow (Eds.)
Taylor & Francis, Inc., 1995

Anatomy of a Psychiatric Illness: Healing the Mind and the Brain
Keith Ablow, M.D.
American Psychiatric Press, 1993

Assistive Technology: A Resource for School, Work, and Community
Karen Flippo, M.R.A., Katherine Inge, Ph.D., O.T.R., Michael Barcus, M.Ed. (Eds.)
Paul H. Brookes, 1995

Augmentative and Alternative Communication: Management of Severe Communication Disorders in Children and Adults, 2nd ed.
David Beukelman, Ph.D., Pat Mirenda, Ph.D.
Paul H. Brookes, 1998

Backyards and Butterflies: Ways to Include Children with Disabilities in Outdoor Activities
Doreen Greenstein
Brookline Books, 1995

Barrier-Free Friendships: Bridging the Distance Between You and Disabled Friends, rev. ed.
Steve Jensen, Joni Eareckson Tada
Zondervan Pub. House, 1997

Birth to Five: Early Childhood Special Education
Frank Bowe, Ph.D.
Delmar Publications, 1995

Bold Tracks: Teaching Adaptive Skiing, 3rd ed.
Hal O'Leary
Johnson Books, 1994

Breaking the Silence: Spiritual Help When Someone You Love Is Mentally Ill
Cecil Murphey
Westminster-Knox Press, 1989

Bridging the Gap: A National Directory of Services for Women and Girls with Disabilities
Ellen Rubin, Merle Froschl
Educational Equity Concepts, 1990

Building Supportive Communities for At-Risk Adolescents: It Takes More Than Services
Martha Burt, Gary Resnick, Emily Novick
American Psychological Association, 1998

Career Counseling for People with Disabilities: A Practical Guide to Finding Employment
Karen Wolffe
PRO-ED, 1997

Caregiver's Reprieve: Guide to Emotional Survival When You're Caring for Someone You Love
Avrene Brandt, Ph.D.
Impact Publications, 1997

Caregiving: The Spiritual Journey of Love, Loss and Renewal
Beth Witrogen McLeod
John Wiley and Sons, 1999

Caring for the Mind: The Comprehensive Guide to Mental Health
Dianne Hales, Robert Hales, M.D.
Bantam Books, 1996

Case Studies of Exceptional Students: Handicapped and Gifted
Carroll Jones
Charles C. Thomas, 1993

Child Sexual Abuse Curriculum for the Developmentally Disabled
Sol Rappaport, Sandra Burkhardt, Anthony Rotatori
Charles C. Thomas Publisher, Ltd., 1997

Children and Adolescents with Mental Illness: A Parents Guide
Evelyn McElroy (Ed.)
Woodbine House, 1988

Children with Disabilities: A Medical Primer, 3rd ed.
Mark Batshaw, M.D., Yvonne Perret, MA., M.S.W., L.C.S.W.
Paul H. Brookes, 1992

Children's Understanding of Disability
Ann Lewis
Routledge, 1995

Choosing Options and Accommodations for Children (COACH): A Guide to Planning Inclusive Education, 2nd ed.
Michael Giangreco, Ph.D., Chigee Cloninger, Ph.D., Virginia Iverson, M.Ed.
Paul H. Brookes, 1998

Christian Healing: A Practical and Comprehensive Guide, 2nd ed.
Mark Pearson
Chosen Books, 1995

Chronic Mental Illness in Children and Adolescents
John Looney, M.D. (Ed.)
American Psychiatric Press, 1988

Circles of Friends: People with Disabilities and Their Friends Enrich the Lives of One Another
Robert Perske
Abingdon Press, 1988

A Community Approach to an Integrated Service System for Children with Special Needs
Robin Hazel, M.A., Patricia Barber, et. al.
Paul H. Brookes, 1988

Community-Based Curriculum: Instructional Strategies for Students with Severe Handicaps, 2nd. Ed.
Mary Falvey, Ph.D.
Paul H. Brookes, 1989

Community Mental Health: A Practical Guide
Loren Mosher, Lorenzo Burti
W. W. Norton, 1993

Community Recreation and Persons with Disabilities: Strategies for Integration, 2nd ed.
Stuart Schleien, Ph.D., CTRS, CLP, M. Tipton Ray, M.Ed., CTRS
Paul H. Brookes, 1997

The Complete IEP Guide: How to Advocate for Your Special Education Child
Lawrence Siegel
Nolo Press, 1997

Computer Resources for People with Disabilities: A Guide to Exploring Today's Assistive Technology, 2nd ed.
Alliance for Technology Access
Hunter House Publishing, 1996

A Consumer's Guide to Psychiatric Diagnosis
Mark Gould, M.D.
PIA Press, 1998

The Consumer's Guide to Psychotherapy
Jack Engler
Simon and Schuster, 1992

Contagious Emotions: Staying Well When Your Loved One is Depressed
Ronald Podell, Porter Shimmer
Pocket Books, 1992

Coping With Caregiver Worries
James Sherman, Ph.D.
Pathway Books, 1998

Coping with Emotional Disorders
Carolyn Simpson
Rosen Publishing Group, 1991

Creative Caregiving
James R. Sherman, Ph.D.
Pathway Books, 1997

Creative Play Activities for Children with Disabilities: A Resource Book for Teachers and Parents, 2nd ed.
Lisa Rappaport Morris, Linda Schulz
Human Kinetics Publishers, 1990

The Developmentally Appropriate Inclusive Classroom in Early Education
Regina Miller, Ph.D.
Delmar Publications, 1995

Dictionary of Developmental Disabilities Terminology
Pasquale Accardo, Barbara Whitman
Paul H. Brookes, 1996

Disabled, Female, and Proud! 2nd ed.
Harilyn Rousso, Susan Gushie O'Malley, Mary Severance
Greenwood Publishing, 1993

Directory of Grants for Organizations Serving People with Disabilities
Research Grant Guides
P.O. Box 1214
Loxahatchee, FL 33470

Directory of Travel Agencies for the Disabled, 6th ed.
Helen Hecker
Twin Peaks Press, 1996

Disability and the Family: A Guide to Decisions for Adulthood
H. Rutherford Turnbull (Ed.)
Paul H. Brookes, 1989

Disability and the Family
Judy Berry, Michael Hardman
Allyn and Bacon, 1997

Disruptive Behavior Disorders in Children: Treatment-Focused Assessment
Michael Breen, Ph.D., Thomas Altepeter
Guilford Publications, 1990

Disturbed Children: Assessment Through Team Process
Menninger Clinic Children's Division
Jason Aronson, 1996

Do They Grow Out of It? Long-Term Outcomes of Childhood Disorders
Lily Hechtman, M.D., FRCPC
American Psychiatric Press, 1996

Does My Child Need a Therapist?
Colleen Alexander-Roberts, Mark Snyder, M.D.
Taylor Publishing, 1997

Dual Diagnosis: Evaluation, Treatment, Training, and Program Development
Joel Solomon, Edward Shollar, Sheldon Zimberg (Eds.)
Plenum Press, 1993

The Early Intervention Dictionary: A Multidisciplinary Guide to Terminology
Jeanine Coleman
Woodbine House, 1996

Early Intervention/Early Childhood Special Education: Recommended Practices
Samuel Odom, Mary McLean
PRO-ED, 1996

Early Intervention: Implementing Child and Family Services for Infants and Toddlers Who are at Risk or Disabled, 2nd ed.
Marci Hanson, Eleanor Lynch
PRO-ED, 1995

Early Services for Children with Special Needs: Transactions for Family Support, 2nd. ed.
Alfred Healy, M.D., Patricia Keesee, M.S., CCC-SP, Barbara Smith, M.S.
Paul H. Brookes, 1989

The Effectiveness of Early Intervention
Michael Guralnick, Ph.D. (Ed.)
Paul H. Brookes, 1997

Electroconvulsive Therapy, 3rd ed.
Richard Abrams
Oxford University Press, 1997

Emotional Behavioral Disorders: Theory & Practice, 3rd ed.
Margaret Cecil Coleman
Allyn and Bacon, 1996

Emotional Disorders
M. Nikki Goldman
Marshall Cavendish Corp., 1994

The Empty Core: An Object Relations Approach to Psychotherapy of the Schizoid Personality
Jeffrey Seinfeld
Jason Aronson, Inc., 1993

Encyclopedia of Associations: Regional, State, and Local Organizations of the US, 8th ed.
Gale Research, 1998

Encyclopedia of Associations: Volume 1 National Organizations of the U.S.: 34th ed.
Gale Research, Inc., 1998

Encyclopedia of Mental and Physical Handicaps
David Tver, Betty Tver
PRO-ED, 1991

Enhance Self-Concepts and Achievement of Mildly Handicapped Students: Learning Disabled, Mildly Mentally Retarded, and Behavior Disordered
Carroll Jones
Charles C. Thomas, Publisher, 1992

Essential Psychopathology and Its Treatment Second Edition, 2nd ed.
Jerrold Maxmen, Nicholas Ward
W.W. Norton and Co., 1994

Everybody's Different: Understanding and Changing Our Reactions to Disabilities
Nancy Miller, Catherine Sammons
Paul H. Brookes, 1999

Everyday Social Interaction: A Program for People with Disabilities, 2nd ed.
Vivienne Riches
Paul H. Brookes, 1997

Family Education in Mental Illness
Agnes Hatfield
Guilford Publications, 1990

The Exceptional Child: Inclusion In Early Childhood Education, 3rd ed.
K. Eileen Allen
Delmar Publishers, 1995

The Family Guide to Mental Health
Benjamin Wolman (Ed.)
Prentice Hall, 1991

The Explosive Child: A New Approach for Understanding and Parenting Easily Frustrated "Chronically Inflexible" Children
Ross Greene, Ph.D.
Harper Collins, 1998

The Family Mental Health Encyclopedia
Frank Bruno
John Wiley and Sons, 1889

Families as Allies in Treatment of the Mentally Ill: New Directions for Mental Health Professionals
Harriet Lefley, Ph.D., Dale Johnson, Ph.D. (Eds.)
American Psychiatric Press, 1990

Feeding the Brain: How Foods Affect Children
Keith Connors
Plenum Press, 1989

Families, Illness, and Disability: An Integrative Treatment Model
John Roland
Basic Books, 1994

Finding Help: A Reference Guide for Personal Concerns
Nan Giblin, Barbara Bales
Charles C. Thomas Publisher, 1995

Families, Professionals and Exceptionality: A Special Partnership, 3rd ed.
Ann Turnbull, H. Rutherford Turnbull
Prentice Hall Publishers, 1997

The First Whole Rehab Catalog: A Comprehensive Guide to Products and Services for the Physically Disadvantaged
A. Jay Abrams, Margaret Ann Abrams
Betterway Publications, 1990

Families of Students with Disabilities: Consultation & Advocacy
Sandra Alper, Cynthia Schloss
Allyn and Bacon, 1993

From the Heart: On Being the Mother of a Child With Special Needs
Patricia Bowman, et. al.
Woodbine House, 1995

Family Caregiving in Mental Illness
Harriet Lefley, Ph.D.
Sage Publications, 1996

From Ritual to Repertoire: A Cognitive-Developmental Systems with Behavior-Disordered Children
Arnold Miller, Eileen Eller-Miller
John Wiley and Sons, Inc., 1989

Functional Analysis of Problem Behavior: From Effective Assessment to Effective Support
Alan Repp, Robert Horner
Wadsworth Publishing, 1999

Genetics and Mental Illness: Evolving Issues for Research and Society
Laura Lee Hall (Ed.)
Plenum Press, 1996

Get Help: Solving the Problems in Your Life
Sara Gilbert
Morrow Junior Books, 1989

Getting Help: A Consumer's Guide to Therapy
Christine Ammer
Paragon House, 1991

Getting Unstuck: Help for People Bogged Down in Recovery
Robert McGee, Pat Springle
Rapha Publishing, 1992

Girl, Interrupted
Susanna Kaysen
Random House, 1994

God Plays Piano, Too: The Spiritual Lives of Disabled Children
Brett Webb-Mitchell
Crossroad/Herder & Herder, 1993

Grieving Mental Illness: A Guide for Patients and Their Caregivers
Virginia LaFond
University of Toronto Free Press, 1994

Growing Up Proud: A Parent's Guide to the Psychological Care of Children with Disabilities
James Lindemann, Ph.D., Sally Lindemann, M.S.
Warner Books, 1988

A Guide to Psychotherapy
Gerald Amada, Ph.D.
Ballantine Books, 1995

The Handbook of Assistive Technology
Gregory Church, M.S., M.S.A., Sharon Glennen, Ph.D.
Singular Publishing Company, 1991

The Handbook of Infant, Child, and Adolescent Psychotherapy: A Guide to Diagnosis and Treatment
Bonnie Mark, James Incorvaia (Eds.)
Jason Aronson Publishers, 1997

Health Resources Online: A Guide for Mental Health and Addiction Specialists, 2nd ed.
Laurie Sheerer, Colette Kimball, Brian Zevnik (Eds.)
Integrated Publishing, 1999

Help Yourself: Problem Solving for the Disabled
Douglas Bucy
MacMillan General Reference, 1996

Helping Families Cope with Mental Illness
Harriet Lefley, Mona Wasow
Gordon & Breach Science, 1994

Helping Parents Cope with Children's Adjustment Problems: An Advice-Giving Guide for Professionals
Gary Crow, Letha Crow
Charles C. Thomas Publisher, 1997

Helping Someone With Mental Illness
Rosalyn Carter
Times Books, 1999

**Helping Your Special Needs Child:
A Practical & Reassuring Resource Guide**
Sandy Tovray, Sandra Selegman
Prima Publishing, 1995

**Heredity and Ability: How Genetics Affects
Your Child and What You Can Do About It**
Charles Strom
Insight Books, 1990

**Hidden Victims -- Hidden Healers: An Eight-
Stage Healing Process for Families and Friends
of the Mentally Ill, 2nd ed.**
Julie Johnson
PEMA Publications, Inc., 1994

**How to Find Help for a Troubled Kid:
A Parent's Guide to Program and Services for
Adolescents**
John Reaves, James Austin
Henry Holt & Company, Inc., 1990

**How to Live with a Mentally Ill Person:
A Handbook of Strategies**
Christine Adamec
John Wiley and Sons, 1996

**How Therapists Diagnose: Seeing Through the
Psychiatric Eye**
Bruce Hamstra, M.D.
St. Martins Press, 1995

**Improving the Social Skills of Children and
Youth with Emotional/Behavioral Disorders**
Lyndal Bullock, Robert Gable, Robert Rutherford, Jr.
(Eds.)
Council for Exceptional Children, 1996

**In Time and with Love: Caring for the Special
Needs Baby**
Marilyn Segal, Ph.D.
Newmarket Press, 1992

**Inclusion: An Essential Guide for the
Paraprofessional**
Peggy Hammeken
Peytral Publications, 1996

**The Insider's Guide to Mental Health
Resources Online**
John Grohol, Psy.D.
Guilford Publications, 1997

**Instruction of Persons with Severe Disabilities,
4th ed.**
Martha Snell
Prentice Hall, 1993

The Invulnerable Child
E. James Anthony, Bertram Cohler (Eds.)
Guilford Publications, 1987

**Is it "Just a Phase?" How to Tell Common
Childhood Phases from More Serious
Problems**
Susan Swedo, M.D., Henrietta Leonard, M.D.
Golden Books, 1998

**Is This Your Child? Discovering and Treating
Unrecognized Allergies**
Doris Rapp
William Morrow & Co., 1992

**It's Nobody's Fault: New Hope and Help for
Difficult Children**
Harold Koplewicz, M.D.
Times Books / Random House, 1996

Job-Hunting Tips for the So-Called Handicapped or People Who Have Disabilities: A Supplement to What Color Is Your Parachute?
Richard Nelson Bolles
Ten Speed Press, 1992

Job Strategies for People with Disabilities: Enable Yourself for Today's Job Market
Melanie Astaire Witt, Joyce Lain Kennedy
Peterson's Guides, 1992

Just Another Kid
Torey Hayden
Avon, 1989

Kids With Special Needs: Information and Activities to Promote Awareness and Understanding
Veronica Getskow, Dee Konczal
Learning Works, 1995

Language Development in Children with Special Needs: Performative Communication
Irene Johansson, Eva Thomas (Translator)
Taylor & Francis, Inc., 1994

Late-Talking Children
Thomas Sowell
Basic Books, 1997

Laying Community Foundations for Your Child with a Disability -- How to Establish Relationships That Will Support Your Child After You're Gone
Linda Stengle, M.A.
Woodbine House, 1996

Life Beyond the Classroom: Transition Strategies for Young People with Disabilities, 2nd ed.
Paul Wehman, Ph.D.
Paul H. Brookes, 1996

Life on a Roller Coaster: Coping with the Ups and Downs of Mood Disorders
Ekkehard Othmer, M.D, Ph.D., Sieglinde Othmer, Ph.D.
Berkeley Books, 1991

Life Skills Activities for Special Children
Darlene Mannix
Center for Applied Research in Education, 1991

Little Children, Big Needs: Parents Discuss Raising Children With Exceptional Needs
Don Weinhouse, Marilyn Weinhouse
University Press of Colorado, 1994

Living on the Border of Disorder: How to Cope With an Addictive Person
Cherry Boone O'Neill, Dan O'Neill
Bethany House, 1992

Living in the State of Stuck: How Technology Affects Persons With Disabilities, 2nd ed.
Marcia Scherer
Brookline Books, 1996

Living Well: A Twelve-Step Response to Chronic Illness and Disability
Martha Cleveland
Ballantine Books, 1993

The Magic of Humor in Caregiving
James Sherman, Ph.D.
Pathway Books, 1995

Making Changes: Family Voices on Living With Disabilities
Jan Spiegle, Richard van den Pol
Brookline Books, 1993

Managing Special Needs in the Primary School
Joan Dean
Routledge, 1996

The Neurotic Child and Adolescent
M. Hossein Etezady, M.D. (Ed.)
Jason Aronson, 1990

Mending Minds: A Guide to the New Psychiatry of Depression, Anxiety and Other Serious Mental Disorders
Leonard Heston, M.D.
W. H. Freeman 1991

The New Psychiatry: The Essential Guide to State-of-the-Art Therapy, Medication, and Emotional Health
Jack Gorman, M.D.
St. Martin's Press, 1996

Mental Illness Heal Yourself
Mary Harris
BBCS, 1994

New Voices: Self-Advocacy by People With Disabilities
Gunnar Dybwad, Hank Bersani
Brookline Books, 1996

Mental Wellness for Women
Rita Baron-Faust
William Morrow & Co., 1998

Nobody's Child
Marie Balter, Richard Katz
Addison-Wesley Publishing Co., 1992

Mentally Ill Child Grows Up: Transitions to the World of Work
Bertram Black
Brunner/Mazel, 1994

Nobody's Perfect: Living and Growing With Children Who Have Special Needs
Nancy Miller, Ph.D., M.S.W., Susie Burmester, Diane Callahan, Janet Dieterle, Stephanie Niedermeyer
Paul H. Brookes, 1994

'My Child Needs Special Services': Parents Talk About What Helps...and What Doesn't
Nancy Wilson
Mills & Sanderson Pub., 1994

Normal Children Have Problems, Too: How Parents can Understand and Help
Stanley Turecki, M.D., Sara Wernick, Ph.D.
Bantam Books, 1995

National Directory of Children, Youth and Family Services, 1998-99
National Directory of Child and Youth Safety, 1998

Oppenheim Toy Portfolio: The Best Toys, Books, & Videos and Software for Kids, 2001
Joanne Oppenheim, Stephanie Oppenheim
Oppenheim Toy Portfolio, Inc., 2001

Negotiating the Disability Maze: Critical Knowledge for Parents, Professionals, and Other Caring Persons, 2nd ed.
Les Sternberg, Ronald Taylor, Steven Russell
Charles C. Thomas Publisher, Ltd., 1996

Nothing About Us Without Us
Karen Stone
Volcano Press, 1997

Ordinary Families, Special Children:
A Systems Approach to Childhood Disability,
2nd ed.
Milton Seligman, Rosalyn Benjamin Darling
Guilford Publications, 1996

Out of the Shadows: Confronting America's
Mental Illness Crisis
E. Fuller Torrey
John Wiley and Sons, 1998

The Parent's Guide to Coaching Physically
Challenged Children
Richard Zulewski
F&W Publications, 1994

The Parental Voice: Problems Faced by
Parents of the Deaf-Blind, Severely and
Profoundly Handicapped Child
Robert Holzberg, Sara Walsh-Burton
Charles C. Thomas Publisher Ltd., 1995

Physical Education for Exceptional Students:
Theory to Practice
Douglas Wiseman
Delmar Publications, 1994

Planning for the Future: Providing a
Meaningful Life for a Child with a Disability
After Your Death
L. Mark Russell (Ed.)
American Publishing Co., 1993

Positive Caregiver Attitudes
James Sherman, Ph.D.
Pathway Books, 1996

The Power of the Powerless, 2nd ed.
Christopher de Vinck
Zondervan Publishing House, 1995

The Pre-Referral Intervention Manual:
The Most Common Learning & Behavior
Problems Encountered in the Educational
Environment, rev. ed.
Stephen McCarney, Kathy Wunderlich
Hawthorne Educational Services, 1993

Preventing Caregiver Burnout
James Sherman, Ph.D.
Pathway Books, 1997

Preventing Mental Health Disturbances in
Childhood
Stephen Goldston, Ed.D., MSPH, Joel Yager, M.D.,
Christoph Heinicke, Ph.D., Robert Pynoos, M.D., MPH
(Eds.)
American Psychiatric Press, 1990

The Price of Greatness: Resolving the Creativity
and Madness Controversy
Arnold Ludwig
Guilford Publications, 1995

Principles of Child Psychotherapy:
From Initial Assessment to Termination
Donald Carek
Jason Aronson Publishers, 1996

Psychiatric and Developmental Disorders in
Children With Communication Disorder
Dennis Cantwell, M.D., Lorian Baker, Ph.D.
American Psychiatric Press, 1994

Psychiatric Dictionary, 7th ed.
Robert Campbell
Oxford University Press, 1996

Psychiatric Disabilities, Employment, and the
Americans with Disabilities Act
Office of Technology Assessment, 1994

**Psychiatric Disorders in America:
The Epidemiologic Catchment Area Study**
Lee Robins, Darrel Regier (Eds.)
Free Press, 1990

**Psychiatric Hospitalization of School-Age
Children**
Richard Dalton, M.D., Marc A. Forman, M.D.
American Psychiatric Press, 1992

**Psychiatric Skeletons: Tracing the Legacy of
Mental Illness in the Family**
Steven Targum, M.D.
PIA Press, 1989

**Psychological Consultation in Educational
Settings: Casebook for Working with
Administrators, Teachers, Students, and
Community**
Judith Alpert and Assoc.
Jason Aronson Publishers, 1996

**Psychoses and Pervasive Developmental
Disorders in Childhood and Adolescence**
Fred Volkmar, M.D. (Ed.)
American Psychiatric Press, 1996

Psychotherapy with Children
Richard Gardner
Jason Aronson Publishers, 1995

**Quality of Life I: Conceptualization and
Measurement**
Robert Schalock, Gary Siperstein (Eds.)
American Association on Mental Retardation, 1996

**Quest for Answers: A Primer of
Understanding and Treating Severe
Personality Disorders**
Salman Akhtar
Jason Aronson Publishers, 1995

Raising a Child Who Has a Physical Disability
Donna Albrecht
John Wiley and Sons, 1995

**Reach for Joy: How to Find the Right
Therapist and Therapy for You**
Lynne Finney
Crossing Press, 1995

**A Reader's Guide for Parents of Children with
Mental Physical, or Emotional Disabilities, 3rd
ed.**
Cory Moore
Woodbine House, 1990

**The Relevance of the Family to Psychoanalytic
Theory**
Theodore Lidz
International Universities Press, Inc., 1992

**Religion and Prevention in Mental Health:
Research, Vision, and Action**
Kenneth Pargament, Ph.D., Kenneth Mato, Ph.D.,
Robert Hess, Ph.D. (Eds.)
Haworth Press, 1992

**Residential Treatment: A Cooperative,
Competency-Based Approach to Therapy and
Program Design**
Michael Durrant
W. W. Norton & Co., 1993

**Residential Treatment: A Tapestry of Many
Therapies**
Vera Fahlberg, M.D. (Ed.)
Perspectives Press, 1990

**The Resourceful Caregiver: Helping Family
Caregivers Help Themselves**
National Family Caregivers Association
Mosby Year Book, 1996

School and Family Partnerships: Case Studies for Regular and Special Education
Judith Buzzell
Delmar Publications, 1995

The Search for the Real Self: Unmasking the Personality Disorders of Our Age
James Masterson
Free Press, 1990

Secrets of Serotonin: The Natural Hormone that Curbs Food and Alcohol Cravings, Elevates Your Mood, Reduces Pain, and Boosts Energy, Vol. 1
Carol Hart
St. Martins Press, 1996

Sexuality and People with Intellectual Disability, 2nd ed.
Lydia Fegan, Anne Rauch
Paul H. Brookes, 1997

Shadow Syndromes: Recognizing and Coping with the Hidden Psychological Disorders That Can Influence Your Behavior and Silently Determine the Course of Your Life
John Ratey, M.D., Catherine Johnson, Ph.D.
Pantheon, 1997

Skills Training for Children with Behavior Disorders-A Parent and Therapist Guidebook
Michael Bloomquist
Guilford Publications, 1996

The Skipping Stone: Ripple Effects of Mental Illness on the Family
Mona Wasnow
Science and Behavior, 1996

Something's Wrong with My Child!
Harriet Rose
Charles C. Thomas, 1998

Souls Are Made of Endurance: Surviving Mental Illness in the Family
Stewart Govig
Westminister John Knox Press, 1994

The Special Child: A Source Book for Parents of Children With Developmental Disabilities, 2nd ed.
Siegfried Pueschel, M.D., Ph.D., M.P.H., Patricia Scola, M.D., M.P.H., Leslie Weidenman, Ph.D., James Bernier, A.C.S.W.
Paul H. Brookes, 1995

Special Children, Challenged Parents: The Struggles and Rewards of Raising a Child With a Disability
Robert Naseef, Ph.D.
Carol Publishing Group, 1996

Special Education Technology: Classroom Applications
Rena Lewis
Brooks/Cole, 1993

Special Parent, Special Child: Parents of Children with Disabilities Share Their Trials, Triumphs, and Hard-Won Wisdom
Tom Sullivan
Putnam Publishing Group, 1996

Speechless: Facilitating Communication for People Without Voices
Rosemary Crossley
NAL/Dutton, 1997

Sports Everyone! Recreation and Sports for the Physically Challenged of All Ages
Conway Greene, John Nesbitt, Jean Driscoll
Conway Greene Pub. Co., 1995

Sports and Recreation for the Disabled, 2nd ed.
Michael Paciorek, Jeffery Jones
Cooper Publishing, 1994

Steps to Independence: Teaching Everyday Skills to Children with Special Needs, 3rd ed.
Bruce Baker, Ph.D., Alan Brightman, Ph.D., with Jan. Blacher, Ph.D., Louis Heifetz, Ph.D., Stephen Hinshaw, Ph.D., Diane Murphy, R.N.
Paul H. Brookes, 1997

Stranger Than Fiction: When Our Minds Betray Us
Marc Feldman, M.D., Jacqueline Feldman, M.D., Roxenne Smith, M.A.
American Psychiatric Press, 1998

Strategies for Working With Families of Young Children With Disabilities
Paula Beckman, Ph.D., (Ed.)
Paul H. Brookes, 1996

Successful Job Search Strategies for the Disabled: Understanding the ADA
Jeffrey Allen
John Wiley and Sons, 1994

Supported Employment: A Community Implementation Guide
G. Thomas Bellamy, Ph.D., Larry Rhodes, Ph.D., David Mank, Ph.D., Joyce Albin, M.Ed.
Paul H. Brookes, 1987

Technology for Inclusion, 3rd ed.
Mary Male
Allyn and Bacon, 1996

That's My Child: Strategies for Parents of Children With Disabilities
Lizanne Capper
Child Welfare League of America, 1996

Therapeutic Recreation for Exceptional Children: Let Me In, I Want to Play, 2nd ed.
Aubrey Fine, Nya Fine
Charles C. Thomas Publisher, 1996

Transition from School to Work: New Challenges for Youth with Severe Disabilities
Paul Wehman, Ph.D., M. Sherril Moon, Ed.D., Jane Everson, M.S., Wendy Wood, M.S., J. Michael Barcus, M.S.
Paul H. Brookes, 1987

Uncommon Fathers: Reflections on Raising a Child with a Disability
Donald Meyer (Ed.)
Woodbine House, 1995

Uncommon Voyage: Parenting a Special Needs Child in the World of Alternative Medicine
Laura Shapiro Kramer
Faber and Faber, 1997

Understanding Disability
Peggy Quinn
Sage Publications, 1997

Unexpected Guests at God's Banquet: Welcoming People with Disabilities into the Church
Brett Webb-Mitchell
Crossroad Publications Co., 1994

Universal Design: Creative Solutions for ADA Compliance
Roberta L. Null Ph. D., Kenneth Cherry
Professional Publications, 1996

Waist-High in the World: A Life Among the Nondisabled
Nancy Mairs
G.K. Hall & Co., 1997

We Have a Problem: A Parent's Sourcebook
Jane Marks
American Psychiatric Press, 1993

Welcome to My Country
Lauren Slater
Random House, 1996

When Acting Out Isn't Acting: Understanding Child and Adolescent Temper, Anger, and Behavior
Lynne Weisberg
PIA Press, 1988

When Growing Up Hurts Too Much: A Parent's Guide to Knowing When and How to Choose a Therapist for Your Teenager
Scott Harris, Ph.D., Edward Reynolds, Ph.D.
Lexington Books, 1990

When Someone You Love Has a Mental Illness: A Handbook for Family, Friends, and Caregivers
Rebecca Woolis, M.F.C.C.
Putnam Publishing Group, 1992

When You Worry About the Child You Love: Emotional and Learning Problems in Children
Edward Hallowell
Fireside, 1997

Where Can We Turn?
Jacki Allred
The Jefferson Resource Institute, Inc., 1995

Why Can't My Child Behave? Why Can't She Cope? Why Can't He Learn?
Jane Hersey, Robert Lawlor
Pear Tree Press, 1996

Wings to Fly: Bringing Theatre Arts to Students With Special Needs
Sally Bailey
Woodbine House, 1993

Women Who Hurt Themselves: A Book of Hope and Understanding
Dusty Miller
Basic Books, 1995

Work and Disability: Issues and Strategies in Career Development and Job Placement
Edna Szymanski, Randall Parker
PRO-ED, 1996

Working Together: Workplace Culture, Supported Employment, and Persons with Disabilities
David Hagner, Dale Dileo
Brookline Books, 1995

A World of Options: Guide to International Exchange, Community Service, and Travel for Persons with Disabilities, 3rd ed.
Christa Bucks
Mobility International, 1997

You Are Not Your Illness: Seven Principles for Meeting the Challenge
Linda Noble Topf, Hal Zina Bennett
Simon and Schuster Trade, 1995

Young Children with Special Needs, 3rd. ed.
Warren Umansky, Stephen Hooper
Prentice Hall, 1997

Books for Youth

The Berenstain Bears and the Wheelchair Commando
Stan Berenstain, Jan Berenstain
Random House, 1993

A Child's First Book About Play Therapy
Marc Nemiroff, Jane Annunziata
American Psychological Association, 1991

Emotional Illness in Your Family: Helping Your Relative, Helping Yourself
Harvey Greenberg, M.D.
Macmillan Publishing, 1989

Extraordinary People with Disabilities
Deborah Kent, Kathryn Quinlan
Children's Press, 1997

The Face at the Window
Regina Hanson
Houghton Mifflin Co., 1997

The Facts About Mental and Emotional Disabilities
Jean Dick
Crestwood House, 1988

Friends at School
Rochelle Bunnett
Star Bright, 1996

Ignatius Finds Help: A Story About Psychotherapy for Children
Matthew Galvin, M.D.
Magination Press, 1987

Just Kids: Visiting a Class for Children with Special Needs
Ellen Senisi
Dutton Books, 1998

Keith Edward's Different Day
Karin Schwier
Impact, 1992

Kids Explore the Gifts of Children With Special Needs
Westridge Young Writers Workshop
John Muir Publications, 1994

Know About Mental Illness
Margaret Hyde
Walker and Company, 1996

Living With Physical Handicap
John Shenkman
Franklin Watts, 1990

Mental Disturbances
Patrick Young
Chelsea House Publishers, 1990

My Brother Is Different
Nancy Paris
Winston-Derek Publishers, Inc., 1993

Nothing to Be Ashamed Of: Growing Up with Mental Illness in Your Family
Sherry Dinner
William Morrow and Co., 1991

Solving Your Problems Together: Family Therapy for the Whole Family
Jane Annunziata, Phyllis Jacobson-Kram
American Psychological Association, 1994

Someone Special, Just Like You
Tricia Brown
Henry Holt, 1995

Taking Charge: Teenagers Talk About Life and Physical Disabilities
Kay Harris Kriegsman, Elinor Zaslow, Jennifer D'Zmura-Rechsteiner
Woodbine House, 1993

Understanding Mental Illness: For Teens who Care About Someone with Mental Illness
Julie Johnson
Lerner Publications, 1989

Tanya and the Tobo Man: A Story for Children Entering Therapy
Lesley Koplow
Magination Press, 1991

A Very Special Critter
Mercer Mayer
Golden Books, 1993

Videos

Video tapes can be very useful, but may a challenge to find, especially if they aren't new to the market. Try contacting the producers noted even if the tape isn't listed on their web site, book stores and your library.

Equal Partners: African American Fathers and Systems of Health Care
National Fathers Network
Kindering Center
16120 N.E. 8th Street
Bellevue, WA 98008-3937
Ph: (425) 747-4004, ext. 218
Web: http://www.fathersnetwork.org/
What African American fathers experience when a child has a disabling condition or chronic illness. How health care professionals can support him.

Parenting Children with Special Needs
AGC United Learning
1560 Sherman Ave., Suite 100
Evanston, Il 60201
Ph: (800) 323-9084
        (847) 328-6700
Fax: (847) 328-6706
E-mail: info@agcunited.com
Web: http://www.agcunitedlearning.com
Parenting children with mental or physical disabilities. Birth and diagnosis, impact on the family, stages that parents experience, intervention programs, laws.

On This Journey Together: A Series
Child Developmental Media
5632 Van Nuys Blvd., Suite 286
Van Nuys, CA 91401
Ph: (800) 405-8942
Fax: (818) 994-6549
E-mail: info@childdevelopmentmedia.com
Web: http://www.childdevmedia.com/
Raising a child with developmental disabilities.

Parents' Views of Living with a Child with Disabilities
AGC United Learning
1560 Sherman Ave., Suite 100
Evanston, Il 60201
Ph: (800) 323-9084
        (847) 328-6700
Fax: (847) 328-6706
E-mail: info@agcunited.com
Web: http://www.agcunitedlearning.com
Interviews with parents of children with disabilities.

Perilous Passage: Fathers Talk About Their Children with Disabilities
Child Development Media
5632 Van Nuys Blvd., Suite 286
Van Nuys, CA 91401
Ph: (800) 405-8942
Fax: (818) 994-6549
E-mail: info@childdevelopmentmedia.com
Web: http://www.childdevmedia.com/
Fathers' experiences of caring, advocating for special needs children.

Special Kids, Special Dads: Fathers of Children with Disabilities
National Fathers Network
Kindering Center
16120 N.E. 8th Street
Bellevue, WA 98008-3937
Ph: (425) 747-4004, ext. 218
Email: jmay@fathersnetwork.org
Web: http://www.fathersnetwork.org/
Fosters understanding for assisting fathers in parenting their children with special health needs.

This Child is Not Alone
J.F.K. Center for Developmental Disabilities
University of Colorado
Avail. Through: Child Developmental Media
5632 Van Nuys Blvd., Suite 286
Van Nuys, CA 91401
Ph: (800) 405-8942
Fax: (818) 994-0153
Web: http://www.childdevmedia.com/
Explores the thoughts and feelings of family members after the birth of a child with special needs.

-- Additional Web Sites

These web sites provide information on a range of topics related to children's health. For sites related to specific disorders, such as ADD, see sections on individual disorders.

The Able Informer
Web: http://www.sasquatch.com/ableinfo/index.html
Resource newsletter for people with disabilities.

Adolescent Services International
Web: http://adolescentservices.com/info-aa.html
Directory of specialty services for youth in crisis.

Family Village
Web: http://www.familyvillage.wisc.edu
Large collection of disability resources.

Hattie B. Munroe Barkley Memorial Augmentative and Alternative Communication Centers
Web: http://aac.unl.edu/
Augmentative communication, hardware and software.

Health-Center.com
Web: http://www.health-center.com
Reference site on a variety of disorders.

Healthier You
Web: http://www.healthieryou.com/
Health reference site.

Internet Mental Health
Web: http://www.mentalhealth.com
Reference site on a variety of disorders.

Internet Special Education Resources (ISER)
Web: http://www.iser.com/
National directory of professionals who serve the learning disabilities and special education communities.

Kid Source Online
Web: http://www.kidsource.com/
Health care and disability articles.

KidsHealth.Org
Web: http://www.kidshealth.org/
Variety of health information articles, including articles for children.

Knowledge Exchange Network
Web: http://www.mentalhealth.org
Reference site on a variety of disorders.

Mental Health Infosource
Web: http://www.mhsource.com
Articles on a variety of disorders.

Post Adoptive Resource
Web:
http://www.geocities.com/Heartland/Prairie/4786
Information and support for parents who are caring for
an adopted child with challenging behaviors.

Psych. Central: Dr. Grohol's Mental Health Page
Web: http://psychcentral.com/
Reference site on a variety of disorders.

For Youth

Band-Aides & Blackboards
Web: http://funrsc.fairfield.edu/~jfleitas/teenstor.html
Stories by kids for kids with medical challenges.

---- *Periodicals / Newsletters*

Below is a listing of periodicals that relate to mental health and disability issues in general. More challenged-focused periodicals may be found in the chapter for each specific challenge.

Ability Magazine
1001 W. 17th Street
Costa Mesa, CA 92627
Ph: (949) 854-8700
Fax: (949) 548-5966
Web: http://www.abilitymagazine.com
Technologies, ADA, leisure, human interest stories, resource centers.

Accent on Living Magazine
Cheever Publishing
P.O. Box 700
Bloomington, IL 61702-0700
Ph: (309) 378-2961
Fax: (309) 378-4420
E-mail: cheeverpub@aol.com
Web: http://www.accentonliving.com/
Products, organizations, medical information for those with physical handicaps.

Career Development for Exceptional Individuals
Council for Exceptional Children
1110 North Glebe Road, Suite 300
Arlington, VA 22201-5704
Ph: (888) 232-7733
         (703) 620-3660
TTY: (703) 264-9446
Fax: (703) 264-9494
E-mail: service@cec.sped.org
Web: http://www.cec.sped.org

Careers and the disABLED
Equal Opportunity Publications
1160 E Jericho Turnpike, Suite 200
Huntington, NY 11743
Ph: (631) 421-9421
Fax: (631) 421-0359
E-mail: info@eop.com
Web: http://www.eop.com
Career-guidance, recruitment for those with disabilities.

Communication Outlook
Artificial Language Laboratory, Michigan State Univ.
405 Computer Center
East Lansing, MI 48824-1042
Ph: (517) 353-0870
Fax: (517) 353-4766
E-mail: artlang@pilot.msu.edu
Web: http://allmac3.cps.msu.edu/ALLStaff.html
Developments in augmentative communication.

Disability Resources Monthly
Disability Resources, Inc.
Four Glatter Lane
Centereach, NY 11720-1032
Ph/Fax: (631) 585-0290
E-mail: info@disabilityresources.org
Web: http://www.disabilityresources.org/
Resources for independent living.

The Exceptional Parent
555 Kinderkamack Road
Oradell, NJ 07649-1517
Ph: (201) 634-6550
Fax: (201) 634-5699
Web: http://www.exceptionalparent.com/
Information, support, ideas, encouragement and
outreach for parents and families of children with
disabilities and professionals.

Inclusion Times
National Professional Resources
25 South Regent St.
Port Chester, NY 10573
Ph: (800) 453-7461
     (914) 937-8879
Fax: (914) 937-9327
E-mail: info@nprinc.com
Web: http://www.nprinc.com/
Helps parents and professionals to work effectively
with children with disabilities.

Journal of Emotional and Behavioral Disorders
PRO-ED Journals
8700 Shoal Creek Blvd
Austin, TX 78757
Ph: (800) 897-3202
Fax: (800) 397-7633
Web: http://www.proedinc.com/
Research, practice, theory on emotional and
behavioral disorders.

Latitudes
Association for Comprehensive NeuroTherapy
P. O. Box 210848
Royal Palm Beach, FL 33421-0848
Ph: (561) 798-0472
Fax: (561) 798-9820
E-mail: acn@latitudes.org
Web: www.latitudes.org
Updates on research, reviews of publications, new
products. Articles on autism, Tourette's syndrome,
attention disorders, learning problems.

The Mental and Physical Disability Law Reporter
American Bar Association
Commission on Mental/Physical Disability Law
740 15th St. NW
Washington, DC 20005
Ph: (202) 662-1581
     (202) 662-1570
Fax: (202) 662-1032
Web: http://www.abanet.org/disability/reporter/home.html
Case law, legislation, regulatory developments.

Palaestra
Challenge Publications, Ltd.
P.O. Box 508
Macomb, IL 61455
Ph/Fax: (309) 833-1902
E-mail: challpub@macomb.com
Web: http://www.palaestra.com/
Sports, physical education, recreation for those with
disabilities.

Reclaiming Children and Youth: Journal of Strength-Based Interventions
PRO-ED
8700 Shoal Creek Blvd.
Austin, TX 78757
Ph: (888) 888-2201
     (602) 224-0500, ext. 19
Fax: (602) 224-0507
E-mail: sizu@pnnews.com
Web: http://www.proedinc.com
Research-validated strategies for use with young people in
conflict with school, family, community. Reframes
problems as opportunities for teaching proper social
behavior and values.

Sports 'n Spokes
2111 East Highland Ave., Suite 180
Phoenix, AZ 85016
Ph: (888) 888-2201
     (602) 224-0500 ext. 319
Fax: (602) 224-0507
E-mail: pnsns@extremezone.com
Web: http://www.sns-magazine.com/sns/default.htm
Wheelchair sports, recreational activities.

TASH Newsletter
29 W. Susquehana Ave., Suite 210
Baltimore, MD 21264
Ph: (410) 828-8274
Fax: (410) 828-6706
Web: http://www.tash.org
Latest developments in the disability field. Best
practices, family concerns, events, opportunities.

Today's Caregiver
6365 Taft St., Suite 3006
Hollywood, FL 33024
Ph: (954) 893-0550
Fax: (954) 893-1779
E-mail: info@caregiver.com
Web: http://www.caregiver.com/
Information, support and guidance for family and
professional caregivers.

---- Additional Vendors

These vendors provide products and services related to children's health. Also see the vendor sections within chapters for individual disorders.

Abilitations
One Sportime Way
Atlanta, GA 30340
Ph: (800) 850-8603
Web: http://www2.abilitations.com/
Special equipment for physical, mental development.

Ablenet
1081 Tenth Ave. SE.
Minneapolis, MN 55414
Ph: (800) 322-0956
       (612) 379-0956
Fax: (612) 379-9143
E-mail: CustomerService@ablenetinc.com
Web: http://www.ablenetinc.com/
Assistive teaching products, books, toys.

Ability Research
P.O. Box 1721
Minnetonka, MN 55345-0721
Ph: (952) 939-0121
Fax: (612) 890-8393
E-mail: ability@skypoint.com
Web: http://www.skypoint.com/~ability/
Communication aids, switches.

Adaptivation, Inc.
2225 W. 50th St., Suite 100
Sioux Falls, SD 57105
Ph: (800) 723-2783
       (605) 335-4445
Fax: (605) 335-4446
E-mail: info@adaptivation.com
Web: http://www.adaptivation.com/
Communication boxes and switches.

Achievement Products for Children
P.O. Box 9033
1621 Warner Road SE
Canton, OH 44707
Ph: (800) 373-4699
       (330) 453-2122
Fax: (330) 453-0222
E-mail: achievepro@aol.com
Living aids.

Attainment Company, Inc.
P.O. Box 930160
Verona, WI 53593-0160
Ph: (800) 327-4269
E-mail: info@attainmentcompany.com
Web: http://www.attainmentcompany.com
Communication devices, software, videos, materials.

Augmentative Communication Consultants, Inc.
280 B Moon Clinton Road
Moon Township, PA 15108
Ph: (800) 982-2248
       (412) 264-6121
Fax: (412) 269-0923
E-mail: acci@!usaor_net
Web: http://www.ACCIinc.com
Assistive communication devices and related consulting.

Child Development Media
5632 Van Nuys Blvd., Suite 286
Van Nuys, CA 91401
Ph: (800) 405-8942
Fax: (818) 994-0153
E-mail: info@childdevelopmentmedia.com
Web: http://www.childdevmedia.com/
Videos on child development, challenged kids.

Childswork/Childsplay
135 Dupont St.
P.O. Box 760
Plainview, NY 11803-0760
Ph: (516) 349-5520
Ph: (800) 962-1141
E-mail: info@Childswork.com
Web: http://www.childswork.com/
Materials, games on child development, feelings.

Chime Time
P.O. Box 369
Landisville, PA 17538
Ph: (800) 677-5075
Fax: (800) 219-5253
E-mail: service@e-c-direct.com
Web: http://www.chimetime.com
Movement products for young children.

Crestwood Company
6625 N. Sidney Place
Milwaukee, WI 53209-3259
Ph: (414) 352-5678
Fax: (414) 352-5679
E-mail: crestcomm@aol.com
Web: http://www.communicationaids.com
Communication aids for children and adults.

DEKRO Software Co.
2758 Margaret Mitchell Dr.
Atlanta, GA 30327
Ph/Fax: (404) 351-1103
Web: http://www.mindspring.com/~dekro/home.htm
Software for cognitively challenged individuals.

DU-IT Control Systems Group, Inc.
236 North Main St.
Shreve, OH 44676
Ph: (330) 567-2001
Environmental control systems.

DynaVox Systems
2100 Wharton St., Suite 4
Pittsburgh, PA 15203
Ph: (888) 697-7332
Fax: (412) 381-5241
E-mail: sales@dynavoxsys.com
Web: http://www.sentient-sys.com/
Augmentative communication devices.

Evan Kemp & Assoc. Health, Mobility Systems
9151 Hampton Overlook
Capitol Heights, MD 20743
Ph/TTY: (301) 324-0118
Fax: (301) 324-0121
E-mail: solutions@eka.com
Web: http://www.eka.com
Health, mobility, communication, living aids.

Fanlight Productions
4196 Washington St., Suite 2
Boston, MA 02131
Ph: (800) 937-4113
       (617) 469-4999
Fax: (617) 469-3379
E-mail: info@fanlight.com
Web: http://www.fanlight.com
Videos on health care, mental health, disabilities, more.

Flaghouse, Inc.
601 Flaghouse Dr.
Hasbrouck Heights, NJ 07604-3116
Ph: (800) 793-7900
     (201) 288-7600
Fax: (201) 288-7887
     (800) 793-7922
E-mail: sales@flaghouse.com
Web: http://www.flaghouse.com
Physical education, furniture, rehabilitation products.

Frame Technology
W681 Pearl St.
Oneida, WI 54155
Ph: (920) 869-2979
Fax: (920) 869-2881
E-mail: cframe@netnet.net
Web: http://www.frame-tech.com
Communication aids for non-speaking persons.

Funtastic Learning
206 Woodland Road
Hampton, NH 03824
Ph: (800) 722-7375
     (603) 926-0071
Fax: (603) 926-5905
E-mail: sales@funtasticlearning.com
Web: http://www.funtasticlearning.com
Toys, games, tools for children with skill-development needs.

Hatch Associates
P.O. Box 11927
Winston-Salem, NC 27106
Ph: (336) 744-7280
     (800) 624-7968
Fax: (800) 410-7282
Web: http://www.hatchstuff.com
Integrates technology solutions into early childhood environments.

Hope Press
P.O. Box 188
Duarte, CA 91009-0188
Ph: (800) 321-4039
Fax: (626) 358-3520
E-mail: dcomings@mail.earthlink.net
Web: http://www.hopepress.com
Publishes books on psychological, behavioral problems.

Imaginart
307 Arizona St.
Bisbee, AZ 85603
Ph: (800) 828-1376
     (520) 432-5741
Fax: (800) 737-1376
     (520) 432-5134
Web: http://www.imaginartonline.com
Educational and functional materials for OT, special education, speech.

Independent Living Products
6227 N. 22nd Dr.
Phoenix, AZ 85015-1955
Ph: (800) 377-8033
     (602) 249-0455
Fax: (602) 335-0577
E-mail: info@ilp-online.com
Web: http://www.ilp-online.com
Assistive devices for daily living.

Indiana Institute on Disability and Community
2853 E. Tenth St.
Bloomington, IN 47408-2696
Ph: (812) 855-6508
Ph: (800) 437-7924
TTY: (812) 855-9396
Fax: (812) 855-9630
E-mail: foshaj@indiana.edu
Web: http://www.iidc.indiana.edu/
Assortment of resources.

Inspiration Software
7412 SW Beaverton Hillsdale Hwy., Suite 102
Portland, OR 97225-2167
Ph: (800) 877-4292
       (503) 297-3004
Fax: (503) 297-4676
E-mail: sales@inspiration.com
Web: http://www.inspiration.com
Software to help students in visual thinking, learning.

Judy Lynn Software
P.O. Box 373
East Brunswick, NJ 08816
Ph/Fax: (732) 390-8845
E-mail: judylynn@castle.net
Web: http://www.castle.net/~judylynn
Software for children with developmental and motor delays.

Kapable Kids, Inc.
P.O. Box 250
Bohemia, NY 11716
Ph: (866) KAPABLE
Fax: (631) 563-7179
Web: http://www.kapablekids.com/
Educational toys, living aids for special needs children.

Kay Elemetrics Corp.
2 Bridgewater Lane
Lincoln Park, NJ 07035
Ph: (973) 628-620
Fax: (973) 628-6363
E-mail: info@kayelemetrics.com
Web: http://www.kayelemetrics.com
Speech, voice, swallowing instrumentation.

Luminaud, Inc.
8688 Tyler Blvd.
Mentor, OH 44060
Ph: (800) 255-3408
       (440) 255-9082
Fax: (440) 255-2250
E-mail: info@luminaud.com
Web: http://www.luminaud.com
Electronic speech equipment products.

Magination Press
750 First St., NE
Washington, DC 20002-4242
Ph: (800) 374-2721
Fax: (202) 336-5502
E-mail: magination@apa.org
Web: http://www.maginationpress.com
Publishes books for children on various problems.

Mayer-Johnson Co.
P.O. Box 1579
Solana Beach, CA 92075
Ph: (800) 588-4548
       (858) 550-0084
Fax: (858) 550-0449
E-mail: mayerj@mayer-johnson.com
Web: http://www.mayer-johnson.com
Augmentative communication products.

Micro Video
P.O. Box 7357
Ann Arbor, MI 48107
Ph: (800) 537-2182
       (734) 996-0626
Fax: (734) 996-3838
E-mail: mv@videovoice.com
Web: http://www.videovoice.com
Computer-based speech therapy aids.

Oppenheim Toy Portfolio
40 E. 9th St., Suite 14M
New York, NY 10003
Ph: (212) 598-0502
Web: http://www.toyportfolio.com/
Guide to toys, books, software, adapted toys.

Parrot Software
P.O. Box 250755
West Bloomfield, MI 48325
Ph: (800) 727-7681
       (248) 788-3223
Fax: (248) 788-3224
E-mail: catalog@parrotsoftware.com
Web: http://www.parrotsoftware.com
Software for those with communication disorders.

Pathways to Promise
5400 Arsenal St.
St. Louis, MO 63139
Fax: (314) 644-8834
E-mail: pathways@inklink.com
Web: http://www.pathways2promise.org/index.htm
An interfaith technical assistance and resource center offering liturgical and educational materials for ministering to people with mental illness and their families.

People of Every Stripe
Box 12
Portland, OR 97212
Ph: (800) 282-0612
     (503) 282-0612
Fax: (503) 282-0615
Web: http://www.teleport.com/~people
Makes dolls with disabilities.

Real Life Storybooks
8370 Kentland Ave.
Canoga Park, CA 91304
Ph: (818) 887-6431
E-mail: webmaster@reallifestories.com
Web: http://www.reallifestories.com/
Storybooks on disabilities, illness from child's view.

S&S Worldwide
P.O. Box 513
75 Mill St.
Colchester, CT 06415
Ph: (860) 537-3451
Fax: (800) 566-6678
E-mail: service@snswwide.com
Web: http://www.snswwide.com/
Recreation, education, physical education, therapy and rehabilitation products.

Slater Software, Inc.
351 Badger Lane
Guffey, CO 80820
Ph: (877) 306-6968
     (719) 479-2255
Fax: (719) 479-2254
Web: http://www.slatersoftware.com
Literacy and communication products for special needs.

Toys for Special Children & Enabling Devices
385 Warburton Ave.
Hastings-on-Hudson, NY 10706
Ph: (800) 832-8697
     (914) 478-0960
Fax: (914) 478-7030
E-mail: info@enablingdevices.com
Web: http://www.enablingdevices.com/
Toys, computer interfaces, switches for disabled.

Agnosia	A disorder in which a person can't recognize objects or events with his or her senses. With auditory agnosia, one doesn't recognize nonverbal sounds such as the ring of a telephone. With auditory verbal agnosia, one doesn't understand spoken words. With tactile agnosia, one doesn't recognize objects through touch. With visual or optic agnosia one doesn't recognize people, places, or objects by sight. There are also some very specific kinds of visual agnosia, such as the inability to recognize faces.
Agraphia	The inability to write due to poor motor and/or perception skills.
Akathisia	Inability to be still, such as when sitting. Can be a side effect of neuroleptic medication.
Akinesia	Muscle fatigue and weakness, slowing movement, making it seem "zombie" like. Can be a side effect of strong antipsychotic medication.
Alexia	The loss of ability to recognize words or letters. Can be caused by an injury or nervous system disorder.
Alexithymia	The inability to recognize or describe what one feels. Common in post-traumatic stress disorder and psychosomatic disorders.
Alpha-fetoprotein (AFP)	Fetal protein found in amniotic fluid of pregnant women. Used to test for Down syndrome.
Ambivalent use of hands	Situation in which a child doesn't have a dominant hand (right or left).
Amenorrhea	Situation in which menstruation has stopped for more than 3 months. May occur in the presence of eating disorders.
Amusica	Inability to produce or recognize musical sounds.
Anaclitic depression	Depression in an infant's first 18 months of life. Primary cause is separation from a parent, usually the mother. Aggravated if the child has little social stimulation. More common in institutions than in a home setting.
Angelman syndrome	Neurological disorder associated with mental and developmental delay, protruding tongue and jaw, frequent smiling, excessive laughing, seizures, sleep disturbances, hyperactive behavior, jerky movements.

Anhedonia	Inability to feel a normal range of emotional responses. Common with some types of schizophrenia and depression.
Aniseikonia	Inability to focus one's eyes. May cause reading problems such as mixing letters in words, reversing letters and words, losing one's place when reading, reading slowly.
Anomia	Inability to remember the names of things, people, and places. Often seen with long term auditory memory problems.
Anomie	Condition in which a person feels that the norms and laws of society aren't irrelevant to themselves.
Anosmia	Loss of the sense of smell.
Anoxia	Lack of oxygen causing cell death or damage.
Anticholinergic	Type of side effects caused by many psychiatric and antidepressant drugs. Includes dry mouth, constipation, difficulty urinating, blurry vision.
Anticipatory anxiety	Worry that occurs between panic attacks concerning when the next one will occur.
Antidepressants	Medication to treat depression.
Antipsychotics	Medications that reduce agitation, hallucinations, and destructive behavior. May also aid with other thought disorders. Side effects include speech and movement changes, other reactions affecting the blood, skin, liver and eyes.
Aphasia	Inability to produce meaningful speech.
Aphonia	Inability to speak with normal volume.
Apraxia	A speech disorder in which one cannot correctly pronounce words because of an inability to position the face, tongue, lips, or jaw properly.
Articulation disorder	Speech disorder in one can't master speech sounds.
Asperger's syndrome	Pervasive developmental disorder in which language is present, but social development is deficient.
Assistive technologies	Technology and equipment that aids in academic, social, and other life functioning.
Ataxia	Difficulty with muscle movements, moving arms and legs in a jerky way, low muscle tone.
Attending	Paying attention.
Atypical depression	Depression in which one displays vegetative behavior, e.g., over eating, oversleeping, anxiety, low energy, little interest in anything, sensitivity to rejection.
Auditory closure disorder	Inability to discern each word a speaker is saying and fill in gaps at the same time.

Auditory discrimination	The ability to differentiate speech sounds.
Auditory dyslexia	Language communication disorder in which one has difficulty linking sounds to their printed versions.
Auditory perceptual disorder	Language communication disorder in which one has difficulty identifying, organizing, and interpreting sounds.
Auditory processing	Understanding what one hears, and distinguishing between sounds.
Augmented communication	Methods of communication that are based on symbols or gestures.
Automaticity	Ability to quickly recall a fact or skill.
Autonomic	Reaction in post-traumatic stress syndrome in which one perceives a life-threatening situation, but doesn't think through how to handle it logically. Trauma survivors may experience autonomic arousal when remembering traumatic events.
Avolition	An inability to initiate and complete goal-oriented activities. May become pervasive enough that it prevents one from working and caring for oneself.
Behavior modification	A method for changing a child's behavior by rewarding desirable behavior and ignoring undesirable behavior.
Behavior therapy	A form of therapy that focuses on modifying undesirable behavior by manipulating the environment. Examples include anxiety management training, assertiveness training, aversion therapy, biofeedback, and desensitization.
Blending	The blending of letter sounds and syllables to make a word.
Body mass index	A measure used to determine if one is of normal weight, underweight, or obese.
Brief reactive psychosis	A stress- or trauma-triggered disorder that lasts from a few hours to one month. It is preceded by a major stressor. Also referred to as brief psychotic disorder.
Broca's aphasia	Condition in which one omits small words and suffixes in speech.
Broca's area	Area of the brain that processes speech.
Bruxism	Repeated grinding of teeth.
Butyrophenones	Medications which are used to control Tourette syndrome, psychosis, and self-injurious behavior.
Cataplexy	Episodes in which one loses muscle tone and collapses. Often happens as a result of intense emotions, e.g., anger, fear, surprise, laughter.
Catatonic behavior	Physical immobility, certain types of excessive motor activity, refusal to move or talk. Stereotyped movements.
Catatonic depression	Extreme withdrawal making one appear to be in a stupor.

Chunking	Method for reading in which one organizes small units (e.g., letters) into larger units (e.g., words) until the result is meaningful.
Cluttering disorder	Speech disorder in which one alternates between rapid and slow speech, speaking in a"singsong" tone.
Cognitive disorder	Disorders of the brain that affect one's ability to learn, to reason, make judgments, develop ideas, perceive information.
Chorea	Abrupt, jerky movements of the head, neck, arms, or legs.
Chronic	Refers to any condition that typically develops slowly and continues for a long time.
Chronic anxiety	Continual state of general anxiety.
Clinical depression	Depression that is severe and long lasting enough to require treatment.
Cognitive behavior therapy	Therapy aimed at changing ineffective thinking so that a behavior change occurs.
Cognitive therapy	Therapy that uses mental imagery, perceptions, attitudes, beliefs, and personal affirmations to positively influence coping mechanisms.
Commitment	Involuntary hospitalization. Outcome from legal proceedings which show that one either is a danger to oneself or isn't capable of self care.
Co-morbidity	Two or more disorders co-existing. One is said to be "co-morbid" with the other.
Computerized axial tomography (CAT)	X-ray process that gives a detailed image of the structure of an internal organ such as the brain. Image produced is called a CAT scan or CT scan.
Congenital	Existing before birth or occurring at birth.
Coprolalia	Compulsive use of foul language and/or obscene gestures.
Copycat suicide	A suicide that occurs in response to someone else's recent suicide.
Cretinism	Mental retardation caused by hypothyroidism.
Decoding	Understanding written or spoken symbols by analyzing and sounding out individual letters, then blending them to recognize individual words.
Delay	When a child is learning appropriate skills, but more slowly than others.
Delusion	Belief that has no basis in reality, such as believing oneself is famous.
Dementia	Mental disorders in which there is a loss of intellectual abilities, (e.g., memory, judgment, abstract thinking.)
Depersonalization disorder	Disorder in which one feels she is watching herself from outside her own body.
Derealization	Feeling of detachment from the world.

Developmental articulation disorder	Disorder in which a child's ability to talk is delayed. He may prefer baby talk or omit or substitute words or letters.
Developmental disability, delay, disorder	A problem in physical or mental development that appears before age 18. One is unable to adequate perform physically and/or mentally against age-appropriate developmental guidelines. May be categorized as pervasive or specific. Pervasive developmental problems affect all aspects of child's functioning: cognition, perception, social skills, self-help skills, motor skills. Autistic disorder is the principal pervasive developmental disorder. Causes are typically biological, genetically induced, and can be complicated by mental retardation.
Developmental expressive disorder	Delay in oral or written communications development even though other areas of development are normal. In oral delays, one's vocabulary is small, which is compensated for this through the use of substituted words, generalizations, omissions. In some cases, one may not speak at all. Writing delays may affect composition, grammar, spelling, punctuation abilities.
Developmental reading disorder	Delay in reading skills in which one mixes up, skips, or substitutes words.
Developmental receptive disorder	Delay in one's ability to understand someone else's speech.
Diagnostic overshadowing	Tendency to attribute all problems to an existing diagnosis, possibly leaving other co-existing problems undiagnosed.
Directionality	Inability to perceive and name directions (e.g., left/right, up/down, in/out, front back.)
Discrimination	The ability to distinguish one thing from another through one's senses. Discrimination disorder is a condition in which one has difficulty differentiating these sensory inputs, such as various sounds.
Disequilibrium	Unsteadiness, imbalance. Frequently a result of spatial disorientation, the sensation of not knowing where one's body is relative to the ground and vertical planes.
Disinhibition	Situation in which one becomes more hostile and impulsive. Can be caused by certain antianxiety medications.
Disordered reading	A learning disorder in which one randomly adds, removes, and substitutes words and parts of words while reading, resulting in great confusion.
Dominance	Preference for using one side of the body when using hands, feet, eyes, ears, etc.
Dopamine	Brain neurotransmitter that affects the perception of reality.
Dual diagnosis	Co-existence of two disorders or illnesses. Also called co-morbodity.
Dyscalculia	Inability to do basic math functions or to apply these functions. Also called "developmental arithmetic disorder."
Dyseidetic	Type of dyslexia in which one cannot apply patterns to letter groupings. Words are read and spelled based on sound.

Dysgraphia	A writing-related learning disorder caused by challenges with small motor and visual perception skills. One may omit or reverse words or letters, spell words incorrectly, cross i's and dot t's, randomly mix upper and lower case letters, not follow line and margin guides.
Dyslalia	Disorder in which one's articulation is delayed.
Dyslexia	A learning disorder in which one has difficulty remembering and recognizing written letters, numbers, and words. The result may be backwards reading, writing, poor handwriting, reversing letters such as b's and d's, failure to learn to read at peer level regardless of intelligence or exposure to reading.
Dysmorphophobia	Anxiety caused by one's perception of having an ugly body. Also called body dysmorphic disorder.
Dysnomia	Inability to remember and name objects, substituting other words, such as "thing."
Dysorthographia	Condition in which one's handwriting is so poor that it's considered a disorder.
Dysphasia	Speech disorder in which one does not arrange words in the proper order. Affects understanding, speaking and/or writing.
Dysphonetic	Form of dyslexia in which one can't use phonics to sound out words, and so makes unusual spelling errors that are unrelated to the sound of the word.
Dysphonia	Impaired voice quality.
Dyspraxia	Confusion in coordinating one's voluntary muscles.
Dysprosodia	Situation in which one can't recognize the melodic quality and tone of voices.
Dysthymia	Mild chronic form of depression which lasts at least one year in which one experiences low self esteem, hopelessness, poor concentration, low energy, and changes in school performance, sleep patterns, and appetite.
Dystonia	Condition in which one experiences severe muscle spasms of the tongue, jaw, eyes, neck, and even the entire body. Can be caused by some psychoactive medications.
Echolalia	Persistent, rapid repetition of words or phrases, either one's own or another's.
Echopraxia	Disorder in which one automatically and inappropriately imitates others' movements.
Electroconvulsive therapy	Form of psychiatric therapy in which low-voltage electric current is sent to the brain to induce a convulsion or seizure. Generally used only for severe psychotic depression or mania and only after exhausting medication options. Shock therapy.
Electroencephalogram (EEG)	A test which measures the output of one's brain.
Electromygraphy	Test which gathers information about muscle function by recording the electrical signals produced during movement.
Emotional lability	Condition in which one's emotions are not stable, frequently change, quickly turn to anger.

Encephalopathy	Acute disturbance of brain function. Caused by encephalitis.
Encoding	The ability to identify symbols as meaningful pieces of communication.
Endogenous	Depression that supposedly comes out of the blue, with no obvious cause.
Endogenous anxiety	Anxiety that's caused by genetics (heredity.)
Etiology	Causes of a condition.
Euthymic bipolarity	Normal mood, neither depressed nor manic. (A term used in relation to bipolar disorder.)
Exacerbation	Increase in the severity of a symptoms or condition.
Exogenous anxiety	Defensive anxiety that's a reaction to an understandable source.
Explosive (rage) disorder	Rare impulsive control disorder characterized by sudden aggressive behavior that may result in others being physically hurt or threatened, and property damaged. May be the result of brain tumors, epilepsy, minimal brain dysfunction. But psychological cause is more common. One may appear to be passive but be suppressing anger which reaches an "overflow" point and explosive behavior results. Also referred to as snapping, rage disorder, intermittent explosive disorder.
Exposure therapy	Therapy in which one is exposed to fearful situations gradually.
Expressive language disorder	Difficulty expressing oneself through verbal language (speech, writing, tone of voice) as well as nonverbal language (gestures, body language).
External locus of control	Personality characteristic in which one believes his or her personal success or failure is controlled by other people or factors.
Family therapy	Therapy form in which one's family members are included.
Figure-ground discrimination or perception	The ability to identify and fix on important information (referred to as foreground) from its surrounding environment (background.) There is auditory figure-ground discrimination (e.g., hearing one voice over others) and visual figure-ground (e.g., finding something on a grocery store shelf.)
Fine motor dyspraxia	Condition in which one can't make the proper muscles respond to complete a task.
Fine motor problems	Situation in which one has difficulty using his or her hands to perform tasks such as writing or manipulating things.
Finger agnosia	A disorder in which one is unsure of where his or her fingers are without looking at them. May be unable to identify which fingers have been touched.
Flashbacks	A type of spontaneous reaction common to victims of acute trauma in the form of dreams or nightmares from which one awakens but stays affected by the dream and has hard time "coming back" to reality; conscious flashbacks, in which one may or may not lose contact with reality and which may include multisensory hallucinations; or unconscious flashbacks, in which a person "relives" a traumatic event. Later one may be unaware of the connection between the flashback and the past trauma.

Flooding	A therapy technique in which a person with an anxiety disorder or avoidant behavior is heavily exposed to anxiety-triggering stimuli and then not permitted to leave the situation to reduce anxiety.
Fluent aphasia	Language disorder in which one is articulate and uses normal speech rhythm, but the speech includes long phrases of nonsense words or sounds.
Frontal lobes	Parts of the brain that control judgment, attention, behavior, some emotions.
Global aphasia	Loss of all language function.
Gross motor function	A standardized observational instrument that measures changes in gross motor function in those with cerebral palsy.
Gross motor problems	A disorder in the use of large muscles that are used to run, jump, hop, etc.
Hallucination	False sensory perception in which one sees, hears, feels, or smells things that aren't there.
Hard signs	Evidence that can be seen with medical technology, i.e., MRIs.
Hemiplegia	Altered muscle tone or paralysis of half the body (right or left).
Hydrocephalus	Abnormally large head and potential mental retardation caused by excessive amounts of fluid in the brain. May be present at birth or develop later with an infection.
Hyperobesity	Great obesity. One criterion used is ideal weight plus 100 pounds.
Hyperkinesis	Restless behavior.
Hyperamnesia	The experience of heightened memory (vivid recall) which is a symptom of post traumatic stress disorder. The opposite of amnesia.
Hypersomnia	Situation in which one sleeps excessively.
Hyperventilation	Very rapid breathing associated with panic disorder. May lead to fainting.
Hypervigilance	A symptom of post traumatic stress disorder in which one is overly sensitive to sounds and sights, always watching for danger and feeling on edge. One may also have a high startle response as well as problems with memory and concentration.
Hypoactivity	The opposite of hyperactivity in that one is notably inattentive, inactive, sluggish, quiet, nonresponsive. One may appear to be shy or fatigued.
Hypomania	Bipolar disorder form in which the person displays mild manic behavior, sometimes for years and then falls into depression. Usually affects very gifted individuals.
Hypotonia	Situation in which one's muscle tone is usually poor or "floppy". Normally one's entire body is affected.
Inclusion	The practice of including children with special needs in the classroom full time. Also referred to as "full inclusion."

Information processing disorder	Inability to organize, make sense of, and store information.
Intelligence quotient	A rating of the amount of learning ability one has. The number expresses the ratio:

Chronological age
-------------------- X 100
  mental years

Mental years are measured by an intelligence test. Though regularly used at elementary levels, this score often doesn't stabilize until after puberty. Average IQ is 100.

Internal locus of control	Personality characteristic in which one believes he or she controls his or her own personal success or failure.
Interpersonal psychotherapy	Therapy in which the patient and therapist pre-define the nature, difficulty, and time needed for therapy to clarify and resolve issues such as disputes and loneliness.
Kinesthetic perception	Perception of movement that comes through one's sensations of muscular activity.
Kinetics	Refers to the forces that cause motion such as joint movements. Kinematics refers to the measurement of motion (geometry), disregarding the causes of motion.
Labile	Unstable emotional state.
Lalling	A speech problem in which one misuses the letters r, l, t, or d.
Language disorder	A disorder in which one has difficulty using symbols to communicate.
Laterality	Ability to discriminate between right and left. Lateralization is a preference to do certain tasks more on one side than the other.
Least restrictive environment	Learning environment in which special needs students participate as much as possible with other students.
Left to right orientation disorder	A disorder in which one confuses left from right.
Magical thinking	Belief that one's thoughts or actions will result in a certain outcome.
Mainstreaming	The inclusion of special needs children in regular classes.
Major depression	Severe depression that may last for months and recur if not treated.
Maladaptive behavior	Behavior that does not enhance or ensure one's survival.
Maturation lag	Delay in character development and mental capacity.
Medial	Toward the midline of one's body (vertical midline that runs head to foot.)
Medicaid	Joint state and federal program that offers medical assistance to people who are entitled to receive Supplementary Security Income.

Medicare	Federal program that pays for medical care for those receiving Social Security payments.
Melancholia	Situation in which one withdraws from others, doesn't find pleasure in most activities.
Microcenephaly	Disorder in which one's head is smaller than normal; retardation frequently results.
Midline difficulty	Avoiding movement of any one part of the body across the body's vertical midline, e.g., touching a left shoulder with a right hand.
Mood normalizers	Medications that are used to help stabilize wide mood swings found in manic and manic-depressive conditions.
Motor cortex	The part of the brain that controls muscle movement.
Motor plan	Ability to think of and execute a sequence of unfamiliar tasks.
MRI	Magnetic resonance imaging scans. A machine/technology that produces detailed pictures of the body using magnetic fields and radio waves.
Nervous breakdown	An outdated term that refers to one or more mental health disorders in an acute phase.
Norm-referenced test	A test that has been given to a large number of people with published procedures for administration and scoring. Also called "standardized tests."
Neuroleptics	Medications which produce symptoms which resemble nervous system disorders.
Neurosis	An anxiety disorder of which one is unaware. Neuroses are characterized by problematic interpersonal relationships and chronic psychological discomfort.
Neurotic disorder	Milder mental condition characterized by anxiety, fear, obsessive thoughts, compulsive acts, dissociation, and depression. Tendency to attribute all other problems to that diagnosis. An obsolete term.
Neurotransmitters	Brain chemicals that send electrical signals from one nerve cell to another. This "signaling" causes neural interactions that affect our behaviors and thoughts.
Nominal recall	The ability to remember and then recall names of people, places, or things.
Norepinephrine	A neurotransmitter that affects attention and concentration.
Nuclear magnetic resonance (NMR)	A procedure that's used to help diagnose and evaluate neurological and psychiatric disorders by producing and assembling images of the brain and other soft tissue.
Occipital lobes	Part of the brain that interprets and uses visual information.
Oral dyspraxia	Disorder in which one has difficulty speaking because he or she is uncertain about which mouth, tongue, and jaw muscles to move and in what order. Result is mispronounced words, hesitation.

Overanxiety	A disorder associated with either childhood or adolescence in which one experiences frequent anxiety over such things as real or imagined mistakes, personal ability, upcoming events. One may experience tension, headaches, upset stomach. If the disorder continues past the age of 18, it often develops into an anxiety disorder.
Palilalia	Rapid and driven repetition of words.
Parietal lobes	Parts of the brain that interpret sensations, feelings from skin, muscles, joints, etc.
Passive-aggressive personality disorder	A personality disorder in which one is hostile but expresses it subtlety. Symptoms include postponing important tasks, being sloppy, not cooperating, inattention. One typically has low self esteem and feels helpless in the presence of authority.
Perceptual disorder	Difficulty in receiving, processing, and/or interpreting information from senses.
Perceptual-motor impairment	Difficulty in coordinating visual or auditory stimulus with a motor act.
Perseveration	Condition in which one has difficulty stopping a task or thought and moving to another. May be a habit in which one relentlessly pursues a topic.
Pervasive developmental disorder (PDD)	See developmental disability.
Phobia	Involuntary fear that's not appropriate to the situation. The result is that one either intensively avoids the situation or endures extreme discomfort while experiencing it.
Phoneme	The smallest unit of sound in speech.
Pica	Eating unusual substances with no nutritional value, e.g., clay, chalk, ashes, dirt, paper, peeling paint, tiny rocks, dried animal feces. Children with pica usually also enjoy ordinary food. In most cases, children spontaneously outgrow the behavior.
Playlalia	Situation in which a child sets up and/or plays a game exactly the same way each time.
Premorbid	The period right before the point that an illness becomes apparent.
Pre-suicide syndrome	Group of symptoms that people experience who are on the verge of suicide. Symptoms include hopelessness, helplessness, and deep depression.
Primary depression	Depression that is not accompanied by another illness.
Prodrome	An early sign or symptom of a disorder.
Proprioceptive	Pertaining to sensory information that muscles and tendons give regarding body position and movement.
Prosody	The ability to perceive meaning in the melodic tone of voices (receptive prosody) and the ability to give meaning through one's own melodic voice tone (expressive prosody).

Pseudodementia	Form of depression in which memory appears to fade, and complex thinking and concentration become difficult.
Psychopharmacology	Branch of medicine that specializes in the use of medication to correct psychiatric illness.
Psychotic depression	Depression characterized by a sad mood, delusions, and hallucinations. Fifteen percent of people with major depression develop psychotic depression and are at major risk for suicide.
Psychiatrist	Mental health professional (physician) who can prescribe medication.
Psychogenic	Refers to behavior something that's caused by motivation or psychological causes, not organic causes.
Psychogenic amnesia	Inability to recall important personal information that's too extensive to be caused by forgetfulness and has no apparent biological cause. Also referred to as "functional amnesia."
Psychologist	A mental health professional with a master's or doctorate degree who administers psychological and educational tests, does evaluations and therapy.
Psychometrics	Standardized psychological tests of intelligence, perception, personality, etc.
Psychosis	Confused thinking, hallucinations, delusions, agitation or stupor.
Psychotherapy	Therapy that has a goal of healing troubled thoughts, relieving strong or hurt feelings, and changing ineffective behavior.
Psychotic	Broad term that refers to conditions in which one has delusions or hallucinations with no insight into the biological nature of the problem. Can appear to be a loss of reality or ego boundaries.
Rapid cycling	Form of bipolar disorder in which the one has four or more recurrences of depression or mania annually. Some may cycle between depression and mania monthly and even daily.
Reactive depression	Depression that is caused by a traumatic life event, e.g., loss of a loved one or job termination.
Receptive language	The ability to understand ideas conveyed through words and sentences.
Regressive behavior	Behavior that was characteristic of an earlier stage in one's life, such is infancy.
Repetition	Re-enactment of earlier traumatic experiences in an attempt to psychologically gain control over it.
Repression	An unconscious defense mechanism in which unacceptable ideas are kept out of awareness.
Respite	Situation in which trained health care workers fill in for caregivers of people with special needs, giving the caregiver a temporary break.

Revictimization	Describes the experience of a trauma survivor being victimized or traumatized again after the original trauma. This may occur as the victim works with authorities on his or her case or during therapy in reliving the experience.
Scatter performance	Situation in which one's developmental is uneven. Some abilities are very strong, other very poor.
Schizoid	Condition in which one is emotionally aloof, indifferent to praise and criticism, and is socially isolated.
Schizophasia	A severe form of thought disorder.
Screen memory	A partially true memory that one subconsciously creates if the real memory is intolerable, e.g., blaming abuse on a distant relative rather than on a parent.
Secondary depression	Depression that occurs as a result of another illness, e.g., alcoholism, drug dependency, or another medical illness.
Selective mutism	An anxiety disorder in which one is unable to speak in social situations.
Sensory defensiveness	Condition in which one is hypersensitive to input from his or her senses (i.e., touch, sound, smell, movement).
Separation anxiety	Excessive worry about separation from important people, such as a parent.
Sequencing disorder	Tendency to reverse the order of words and numbers.
Serotonin	Neurotransmitter related to anxiety, depression, and aggression.
Simple phobia	Condition in which one dreads and may avoid certain objects or situations, e.g., snakes, highway driving.
Social phobia	Condition in which one feels anxiety and panic in social situations, often fearing being noticed and judged by others and thus embarrassed. These feelings may manifest themselves in situations such as public speaking, eating in public, dating.
Soft signs	Neurological signs that suggest an immature or disordered central nervous system, e.g., inability to balance on one foot.
Spontaneous anxiety attacks or panic	Surges of anxious feelings that appear suddenly for no apparent reason.
S.S.D.I	Social Security Disability Insurance.
S.S.I.	Supplemental Security Income.
State dependent memory	Memory of a traumatic event that's induced when one is under the same level of fear as during the original event. Also referred to as context dependent memory.

Stereotyped movements	Nonfunctional, repetitive motor behavior that appears to be "driven" (e.g., hand waving, body rocking, head banging, mouthing objects, self-biting, picking at body.)
Substitution	A speech problem in which one replaces one letter with another.
Suicide cluster	A situation in which several suicides occur in the same area within a short time.
Suicide pact	An agreement between two or more people to commit suicide together.
Supportive therapy	Therapy that focuses on managing resolving current difficulties and using one's strengths and available resources.
Syndrome	A group of symptoms that produce a recognizable physical or mental condition.
Synthesia	Pattern of brain neurons that blends one's perceptions in unusual ways, e.g., giving words color.
Systematic desensitization	A method of desensitizing one to anxiety-producing situations by exposure to the situation at an easy level and then working gradually toward the most anxiety-producing situation. Coping mechanisms are developed at each level.
Tactile defensiveness	Sensory dysfunction in which even light touch can cause excessive negative reactions.
Tardive dyskinesia	A syndrome involving purposeless, sudden jerky movement as a result of long-term use of neuroleptic medications. May appear from three months to several years after initial use of these medications. Withdrawal often worsens the symptoms. Common movements include facial tics, grimacing, eye blinking, lip smacking, tongue thrusting, moving one's head back or to the side, foot tapping, ankle movements, shuffled gait, and head nodding. Tardive dyskinesia may also lead to respiratory problems, inability to eat, mouth sores, and difficulty standing and walking.
Temporal lobes	The part of the brain that interprets language.
Teratogenic	Descriptive word for medications that can cause birth defects.
Thalamus	The part of the brain which routes sensations to other parts of the brain for interpretation and use.
Tics	Frequent involuntary muscle spasms. The most noticeable ones involve facial muscles, but tics may also be vocal, involving sudden, uncontrollable, loud sounds.
Tracking disorder	Difficulty following an object visually. Can prevent one from staying on the same line when reading.
Tranquilizers	Medications that help calm agitation and anxiety.
Transient situational disorders	Emotional disturbances caused by an event, e.g., the death of a loved one.
Trichotillomania	Continuously pulling hair out of head, eyebrows, eyelashes, other parts of the body.

Trigger   Something such as an event, object, or person which reminds a person of some aspect of a past traumatic event.

Visual closure   A disorder in which one has difficulty visually "finishing" an incomplete image, e.g., a stop sign with a missing letter.

Visual foreground disorder   A disorder in which one has difficulty focusing on one thing on a printed page because of the distraction of other images on the page (e.g., numbers, pictures.)

Visual perceptual disorder   Inability to identify, organize, and interpret visual images.

---- *Index*